Annals of Theoretical Psychology

Volume 20

The Annals of Theoretical Psychology is devoted to understanding theoretical developments and advances in psychological theory. This series is designed to further the dialogue on theoretical issues in the field of psychology and to unify the discipline through a theoretical synthesis of ideas on key issues of debate. Core themes of the Annals vary from one volume to another, moving beyond a focus on one particular aspect or approach to theory. Each book consists of invited and submitted papers and commentaries that explore a facet of innovative theory in psychology. Of particular interest is moving the discussion and exploration of theory into application for use in research, practice and teaching, taking into account the globalized nature of contemporary psychology. The enduring objective of the Annals of Theoretical Psychology is the exploration of key concepts that require further inquiry, dialogue, and theoretical integration within psychology and related fields.

Sven Hroar Klempe • Anna Madill
Editors

French Psychoanalysis Revisited

Springer

Editors
Sven Hroar Klempe
Department of Psychology
Norwegian University of Science and Technology (NTNU)
Trondheim, Norway

Anna Madill
School of Psychology
University of Leeds
Leeds, UK

ISSN 0747-5241 ISSN 2512-2207 (electronic)
Annals of Theoretical Psychology
ISBN 978-3-031-68533-0 ISBN 978-3-031-68534-7 (eBook)
https://doi.org/10.1007/978-3-031-68534-7

This Springer imprint is published by the registered company Springer Nature Switzerland AG
The registered company address is: Gewerbestrasse 11, 6330 Cham, Switzerland

Preface

The title of this book, *French Psychoanalysis Revisited*, can be understood in many ways. One could be to reawake a specified historical epoch. Another could be about psychoanalysis in a certain nation. A third could be to present an authoritative understanding of Lacanianism, for example. However, none of these is the actual aim of this book. Rather, the book's aim is to explore how French psychoanalysis still inspires an abundance of scholars all over the world even though its probable heyday in the 1970s is a passed epoch. Thus, this compilation of chapters offers just a taste of the ways in which French psychoanalytic thought is being utilized and developed today across many countries. Notably, this compilation does not take an historical stance but has attempted to present a wide variety of perspectives and topics.

Consequently, this volume of *Annals of Theoretical Psychology* is an invitation to dialogues on different levels. One relevant inspiration is the way in which Jacques Lacan's seminars represents an intense dialogue with Sigmund Freud's writings, returning to, but also rethinking in many ways key psychoanalytic concepts. Similarly, aspects of Lacan's work were developed through dialoguing with that of Ferdinand de Saussure and French structuralism in general. Moreover, during the 1980s, French philosophy, structuralism, and semiology benefited from being placed in dialogue with American pragmatism. In line with this, we hope that the philosophical, conceptual, and methodological dialogues inherent to each chapter and the implicit dialogues between the chapters in this volume provoke reflection, insights, and inspiration to continue to draw fruitfully on French psychoanalysis in the future.

Another important aspect to this compilation that we would like to highlight is that of criticism: a scholarly activity with a long historical tradition and characteristic of Western modernity in general. As a fundamental approach, criticism can be traced back to Immanuel Kant. Having considered preceding attempts to develop a metaphysics, Kant acknowledged two crucial factors required for a valid metaphysical system: the importance of ontology and that one can never be completely certain of its borders. Hence, criticism is not an aspect of ontology but a method for deciding an entity's ontological status through a search for the criteria defining its borders. Kant operationalized this in terms of a model for cognition, from which logical reasoning and inferences may lead to proper fundamentals in ontology. Although psychoanalysis in general, and poststructuralism especially, operates with a different model of human cognition to that of Kant, criticism is still an important method for exploring and investigating the relationship between psychology and ontology. This likely explains to some extent why many psychoanalysts refer to Kant, but also to why Michel Foucault allegedly referred to himself a "Kantian". The activity of scholarly criticism unites all the chapters in this volume of *Annals of Theoretical Psychology*.

We invite the reader to join us on the exciting journey through French psychoanalysis as it has inspired each author who has contributed to this volume!

Trondheim, Norway Sven Hroar Klempe
Leeds, UK Anna Madill

Contents

Chapter 1
Introduction: French Psychoanalysis Revisited

Sven Hroar Klempe and Anna Madill

At the beginning of January 1979, a 23-year-old Norwegian philosophy student arrived in Paris. He had completed the journey from Oslo by train, which had been particularly complicated due to a rare cold spell across Europe. The train itinerary was changed constantly to various local trains and so lasted much longer than the scheduled 30 hours. But all these problems did not affect the student much since he had a very specific goal for the trip. The purpose was to gain more insight into the intellectual wave for which Paris had become famous, even in Northern Europe where few had a strong grasp on what was happening. The student had made a quick decision and all he had managed to arrange in advance was a room at the Maison de Norvège at the Cité Internationale Universitaire de Paris. He had no registration at any university, nor monetary resources other than his own savings—and the length of his stay would only last as long as these savings.

The student's background and motive for going to Paris were complex. One reason was his philosophical interest in exploring the relationship between rationality and irrationality. He was also an amateur musician, and the importance of the topic of rationality was reinforced by his interest in music. Based on this, he formulated the following question: "Why on Earth sing when one can talk?" Hence, the decisive reason he looked toward Paris was to attend a class specifically on French structuralism given a recent experience in which he had gained a completely new way of understanding communication and rationality.

S. H. Klempe (✉)
Department of Psychology, Norwegian University of Science and Technology (NTNU), Trondheim, Norway
e-mail: hroar.klempe@ntnu.no

A. Madill
School of Psychology, University of Leeds, Leeds, UK
e-mail: a.l.madill@leeds.ac.uk

S. H. Klempe, A. Madill (eds.), *French Psychoanalysis Revisited*, Annals of Theoretical Psychology 20, https://doi.org/10.1007/978-3-031-68534-7_1

The student had had the good fortune of attending a class by a young graduate student who had just returned from Paris having studied under Jacques Derrida at the École Normale Supérieure. This class represented an exception in Norwegian academia at that time. Some Norwegian students were certainly familiar with Michel Foucault, but few understood the major applicable context. The critical approach at Norwegian universities was dominated by the neo-Marxism of the Frankfurt School. There was little room for other approaches to critical thinking. The student became aware of this when his plans to travel to Paris were mentioned accidentally to one of the most prominent philosophers in Norway at the time. "Why go to Paris? No, I'll stick to the German stalwart Protestants," the philosopher commented. Five years later, the same philosopher toured Norway with lectures on "postmodernism."

The other residents of the Maison de Norvège were not particularly interested in French structuralism either. Most studied literature and languages, while some focused on music or other subjects. But after some research, the student found that the intellectuals he was looking for were primarily located at the Collège de France—an easy Métro ride away from the Cité. Fortunately, the Collège de France is an honorary university where specially selected researchers are required to hold public lectures. There he found notices that announced Roland Barthes would start his lecture series on haiku poetry on January 6th (Barthes, 2011), in just a few days. In addition, Michel Foucault would begin his lectures on the birth of biopolitics on January 10th (Foucault, 2008). Both these lecture series were followed up with seminars where students presented their work and received comments from the lecturers. Moreover, it was possible to attend presentations by several other famous academics at the college such as Claude Lévi-Strauss, Pierre Bourdieu, and Pierre Boulez. The student decided to attend Barthes' and Foucault's courses.

There were several interesting intellectuals still active in Paris that spring semester. For example, Jacques Lacan still held his seminars at Place du Panthéon—not far from Collège de France. The young student had admittedly read a bit of Lacan, but even though he had a good insight into Freud and a few years' experience with musical therapy for severely affected psychiatric patients, he had given up trying to make sense of Lacan's writings. Hence, he did not attend Lacan's seminar that spring, but nevertheless obtained a copy of *Écrits* (Lacan, 1966) just in case. He also read the small book *Comprendre Jacques Lacan* (Fages, 1971), hoping that he might be able eventually to crack the Lacanian code.

Instead, the student sought out Université Paris 8 Vincennes, which that spring was still located in the Vincennes Park a few kilometers outside the center of Paris. There he found, among others, Jean-François Lyotard and Gilles Deleuze, both still active lecturers at that time. He attended a couple of their lectures and also mustered the courage to have conversations with both of them. This led to some interesting meetings, particularly his conversation with Lyotard. Lyotard was very responsive and friendly and was more than willing to discuss one of his articles on Freud and music (Lyotard, 1972).

Deleuze was not as easy to get to know, so when meeting him, the interesting aspect was Deleuze's appearance. Deleuze had a slightly slouched sitting position in the middle of a somewhat shabby classroom. Students were sitting everywhere, including on chairs, on benches, and even on the window sills. The classroom atmosphere had the feeling of being an afterthought of the revolutionary movements behind the student uprising of 1968, but also the powerful scandals that had characterized this newly established university in its early years. This impression was reinforced by Deleuze's wearing an old, black, and perhaps too big overcoat. He lectured without a script, had a beer bottle in one hand, and a lit cigarette in the other. Most particular, however, were his untrimmed fingernails, which were so long that the young student could hardly believe his eyes. Deleuze lectured with great empathy despite, reportedly, having a punctured lung and seeming capable of collapsing at any moment. Nevertheless, it would turn out that he still had many productive years ahead of him.

At this university, the young student also connected well with Nicolas Ruwet who had introduced Noam Chomsky's linguistic theories to French audience and was particularly interested in music. With Deleuze on one side of the spectrum and Ruwet on the other, this university reflected the tension that has characterized French thought and culture for several hundred years. There have been, and still are, deep disagreements, but people nevertheless live side by side, confront each other, and engage in enthusiastic discussions.

Collège de France stood in stark contrast to Vincennes University. While the latter had various access restrictions, there was in reality no control. So in practice students could come and go as they pleased, regardless of their affiliation. At Collège de France, however, openness was, and still is, a basic principle. Nevertheless, there were many guards there, who (among other things) made sure that the number of people in each hall did not exceed the number of chairs. The biggest contrast between Collège de France versus Deleuze and Vincennes' universities was probably represented by Claude Lévi-Strauss. Just before his lecture was to begin, one of the guards entered with his lecture notes. They were solemnly and almost ritually placed on the lectern. The then 70-year-old Lévi-Strauss immediately followed with a straight and an uptight posture. He had an introverted gaze, which gave the impression that he neither registered, nor cared about, those in the room. He sketched some genealogical and settlement patterns on the board, commented on them, and then discussed them without looking at the manuscript or the audience. Once the last word of his lecture had been uttered, he disappeared out via the staff entrance.

The most popular lecturers at Collège de France that spring were undoubtedly Roland Barthes and Michel Foucault. If one wanted to hear them, one had to arrive early. The two were, however, very different. Roland Barthes had a distinguished appearance, with calmness and presence that seemed inviting and confidence-building. His appearance stood in contrast to the radical perspective on language and poetry that he drew from his analyses of haiku poetry. The young Norwegian student also happened to meet him again later at a cello concert one evening. Barthes sat in the back row, a few seats to his right. Barthes was not alone. He was accompanied by three or four boys in their 20s. The young Norwegian student looked at him at first, but then felt how Barthes' gaze fixed on the back of his neck. He did not look much more in the direction of Barthes at that concert, but certainly continued to follow his lectures and seminars.

Michel Foucault did not show the same composure as Barthes. When Foucault lectured, he rarely sat still. He wandered around restlessly, rarely fixing his gaze on the people in front of him. On the contrary, he seemed to look wide-eyed right through them or into the air as a torrent of words poured out of his mouth. In addition, it became impossible to overlook his shiny cranium, which made his pointed ears very visible. His appearance was almost demonic. It could also seem as if Foucault himself did not have complete control over his own flow of words. He never got to the topic that had been announced, namely the birth of biopolitics. However, this was that spring that Foucault developed and presented—or perhaps it was in the opposite order—his theories on neoliberalism. In any case, the effect was powerful, and the young Norwegian philosophy student was not the only one who left deeply impressed. In that room sat a number of professors from different parts of the world who spent their sabbatical right there in the Latin Quarter in Paris that very spring.

With all these experiences, the young Norwegian philosophy student reached his goal. He had not experienced just a *small* piece of the intellectual wave that had crashed into Paris the preceding decades. He felt he had submerged his entire self in its strong after-currents. The famous intellectuals were not only still active, but also widely available to anyone who wanted to seek their expertise. He did not just meet them at the universities either. Their writings filled the shelves of bookshops, and one could find writings both from and about them in some of the colored magazines sold in the kiosks on the street. But in the bookstores, there was also another impression that became etched into the young student's memory. One particular shelf section was often found in the most central part of the stores. It did not contain books by French writers, but instead included writings by three famous German-language authors: Freud, Nietzsche, and Marx. Although French thinking was very avant-garde, these three were nevertheless seen as the intellectual father figures who could not be overlooked, even in Paris at that time.

In retrospect, it turned out that 1979 represented a period in which the 20-year reign of French structuralism was coming to an end. Lévi-Strauss' lectures were no longer the most popular. Moreover, Barthes and Foucault's discussions subsequently had almost no traces of Saussure. Instead, a critical post-structuralist breakdown of logocentrism began to characterize their lecture series. Moreover, both Barthes and Lacan died in the following years. Concurrently, other French intellectuals became so popular abroad that many of them ended up living outside of France for extended periods of time, not least in the United States. A few decades later, the same Paris bookstores gradually carried fewer and fewer volumes on structuralism. Instead, their shelves were filled with new literature on economics and public management.

This heyday of French thinking that the young Norwegian student—of course, the editor of this volume Sven Hroar Klempe—experienced in 1979 is probably difficult to experience by revisiting Paris. Nevertheless, it should still be possible to reflect on what this extraordinary period in time birthed by inviting some of those who were inspired by what was happening in Paris during the 1970s. In addition, such a revisit should focus on something that the thinking of that time was founded on, namely psychoanalysis. To this end, the coeditor Anna Madill was fortunate to meet Hroar on a staff selection committee and to discover a shared interest in French psychoanalysis. Anna completed her PhD in the mid-1990s in which she explored change process in psychodynamic-interpersonal psychotherapy (Madill, 1996). This topic was inspired by a long-standing interest in Carl Jung and new passion for discourse analysis, which developed into a deep appreciation for Sigmund Freud and, in recent years, for Jacques Lacan. Hence, she jumped at the chance to work with Hroar to bring together this volume. This is the background for this anthology where we hope to be able to find viable remnants of this time through the contributions that followed the French tradition of psychoanalysis: contributions which have been reshaped to suit a new time and a new environment.

We have invited ten scholars, who all have particular interest in French psychoanalysis, and not least in Jacques Lacan. But French psychoanalysis includes several scholars, and not all can be included. However, there is a diverse selection of names that may appear along with Lacan like Vera John-Steiner, André Green, Sophie de Mijolla-Mejor, and René Lew, among others, who demonstrate how both Freudian and Lacanian perspectives are developing. This is a core aspect of psychoanalysis from the very beginning as we see Sigmund Freud developing new perspectives, one of the best known being his changed opinion about the role of hypnosis. Maybe less well known is his rethinking of the relationship between privacy and universals, for example, in dreams. In the *Interpretation of Dreams* (1899/1913), one may easily find traces of the search for universals and standardized symbols, whereas, 6 years later, in *Jokes and Their Relation to the Unconscious* (1905/1976, p. 238), he stated very clearly that a dream is a private phenomenon.

Apparently, Freud may have appeared to be a quite authoritarian and strict person, which is nicely demonstrated in Gordon Allport's report about his meeting with him around 1920 (see, https://www.youtube.com/watch?v=bxtY7YP1cpA). In line with all the conflicts around him, Lacan's personality may have been similar and possibly reflected in his slogan: "Return to Freud." However, Lacan's psychoanalysis introduces a Saussurean understanding of the role of language and its relationship to the unconscious, and his thesis of the arbitrary sign dissolves any unchangeable perspectives on language. According to Saussure, not only the single sign is arbitrary but also the linguistic system itself, because it is continuously changing and developing. The latter forms the condition for suggesting the thesis of the arbitrary sign. That said, there is no reason to pursue or search for the "correct" or "pure" Lacanian psychoanalysis. His psychoanalysis went through several changes, and this revisit to French psychoanalysis aims to trace some of these changes but also how diverse French-inspired psychoanalysts may appear today.

Language is one of the core factors in Lacan's rereading of Freud. However, how to understand the nature of language forms another open question. One of the reasons for why Lacan is so difficult to read is that he built his theories on different theories of language. Nevertheless, he merged them into a complicated, but united, network of theories and used this to explain many aspects of conscious and unconscious functioning. This complexity is the topic "Raffaele De Luca Picione" writing in Chap. 2. In contrast to Freud, Lacan was highly influenced by the Swiss linguist Ferdinand de Saussure, who developed the tenet on the arbitrary sign by highlighting the radical distinction between the signifier and the signified. The arbitrary connection between these two aspects of a sign opens up for slow changes in the development of the uses of languages. This counts for all other types of symbolic sign systems in sounds and figures. The Czech linguist Roman Jakobson also influenced Lacan. The latter criticized Saussure for making a sharp and definite distinction between the actual (*in praesentia*) and latent (*in absentia*) aspects of language. Moreover, Saussure argued that, in language, it is only possible to articulate one sound at the time. Jakobson challenged this by saying also the latent aspects of language must be present in our daily use of language. De Luca Picione argues also for the importance of the tripartition of the sign that the American pragmatist Charles Sanders Peirce introduced. This process may well form all systems of symbols, and De Luca Picione demonstrates how Lacan turns all these aspects of language into an integrated culturally oriented psychoanalytic theory. Furthermore, De Luca Picione's essay helps to clarify how in Lacan's theoretical and clinical thoughts there is not only an exclusive tendency to show the processes of symbolization and signification, but also the recognition of an ever-present drive toward nonsense, to the impossibility of knowledge, namely an area of absolute contingency and impossibility of human experience, which takes the name of register of the *Real*.

In Chap. 3, Anna Madill grapples with the interspace of Lacanian psychoanalysis, discourse analysis, and methodology rigor through an analysis of a carefully transcribed, watched, and listened to piece of TV programming. Demonstrating the reach of Lacanian ideas into the study of popular culture, Madill considers the applicability of Lacanian theory for understanding the reality paranormal genre which has been popular since the early 2000s. This is done by analyzing a sequence from an American television miniseries from 2016 called *Deadly Possessions*. Focusing on the story of supernatural events related to a mirror, Madill explores the relevance of the Lacanian mirror stage for understanding disturbing, yet recognizable, psychic mechanisms functioning in everyday life experiences. She draws on other Lacanian concepts, such as the *objets a* and the staging of fantasy, to explore how the ordinary objects come to haunt us and how these stories are enhanced for an uncanny effect through the use of cameras, sound, lightning, colors, etc. Different layers of oneself and one's relationship to the other are revealed as interdependency between the two, and the Lacanian terminology helps us to understand some of the nuances in this process.

This understanding of Lacanian psychoanalysis as relevant for the way we deal with entertainments in everyday life is followed up by Brendon Nichols in Chap. 4. Instead of TV programming, reading and literature are at stake in Nichols' chapter. By means of the South African author Bessie Head and her novella *The Cardinals*, Nichols brings us into the core of how metaphors may produce an overwhelming pleasure in reading. Specifically, he applies a Lacanian understanding of the Möbius strip to argue that a metaphor is not necessarily applied for making the meaning deeper. Rather, metaphor may be considered through the Möbius topology to bring meaning back to the initial terms for both author and reader. That is, through being captured in the circuit of the single-sided Möbius strip, the reader and the author have an editorial function. The novella *The Cardinals* is an excellent example of this circulation of topologically entrenched signs, because it references cases on which Bessie Head reported as a journalist within its fictional content. On this basis, Nichols challenges the reader's conception of the role of metaphor in literature.

Literature is also a core aspect in Chap. 5, as Marcela Antelo makes an analysis of feminine jouissance by letting the poetry of the British Romantic poet Percy Shelley (1792–1822) form a point of departure. However, the main aim of this chapter is to demonstrate the big difference between Freud's and Lacan's understanding of feminine jouissance. What Shelley and Lacan have in common is, according to Antelo, that they both unveiled some of the mysterious secrets around feminine *jouissance*. Whereas Freud regarded women's sexual needs to be just mysterious, Lacan meant that a study of women's sexual enjoyment is an entrance to understand the core of *jouissance* in general. Thus, feminine jouissance is to be understood as a label for enjoyment for both women and men, existing beyond, and reflecting the borderline between, the symbolic and the real.

Chapter 6 also deals with jouissance. Here Marcelo Veras elaborates on Lacan's statement that "The woman does not exist" and position that "woman" is the Other sex for all speaking beings. Veras argues that no gender can be characterized as coming from Venus: We are all from Mars. This is in fact a following-up to Antela's discussion about the mystical aspect of jouissance in the sense that ultimate sexual jouissance may never appear together with a partner, as some unrelieved drops of drives always will remain. In line with this, drives are canalized in other bodily aspects and not least how it is presented in a public sphere. This is exactly what Veras examines in this chapter, namely how the construction of a body, which may apparently not be incorporated in the Lacanian symbolic field. As many Lacanians will support, Veras underlines the body's symbolic function. By developing a symbolic order, which may include the construction of the body, Veras explains how surgery more or less can be regarded as being "the new sex." The body style as the new sex is illustrated by pointing at Lady Gaga as an example.

From a focus on "enjoyment," in Chap. 7, Tania Zittoun moves us into, what Freud would consider to be, the opposite to the territory of the reality principle: i.e., that of "pleasure." Specifically, Zittoun concentrates on a highly ignored type of pleasure, namely the pleasure of thinking. In fact, Freud was occupied by this aspect of pleasure and tried to develop an explanation from a psychoanalytic perspective. Freud's writings about this from the 1890s form a good starting point for this investigation as he connects thinking and problem-solving to interactions between bound and unbound cathectic energy. Although Lacan does not explore this type of pleasure, two of his younger associates in French psychoanalysis, namely André Green and Sophie de Mijolla-Mejor, provide a substantial contribution on this topic. Zittoun broadens the discussion even more, arguing for five different modalities of the pleasure of thinking using cultural psychology alongside psychoanalytic theory.

One of the most challenging aspects to grasp in Lacan's psychoanalysis is his understanding of the real. This is the main topic taken on by Sergio Salvatore in

Chap. 8. Although the Lacanian conception of the real can be understood as, beyond philosophical understanding, Salvatore argues that there exists a connection here. A traditional metaphysical position posits a clear distinction between what is the result of thinking and the facts that exist in the external world. This perspective is almost unimpededly accepted in psychology as we apply the term "representation" as if ideas in our minds just mirror objects in the world "out there." Salvatore argues that this cannot be accepted as a valid ontology. Even Kant, he suggests, did not accept this metaphysical position. Kant posited time and space to be a product of the transcendental mind, although it is an open question how transcendental, in fact, is the human. Salvatore argues that time and space form examples that, rather than based on substance, existence consists of interchangeable relations. On this basis, Salvatore argues for a processual ontology which implies that existence is not dependent on an entity's substantial quality, but it is a result of how we are dealing with this entity. Salvatore refers to a banknote as an example. As is true for currency in general, the value of a banknote is just a result of how stakeholders relate themselves to it and it is only on this basis that money functions as a holder of value. Similarly, for Lacan, reality is created symbolically through the signifiers of the Other.

What language is, or is not, is also a matter for interrogation. There are of course several angles from which this discussion can be addressed. One of these is by way of logic, and this is the path pursued by the ChileanDanish psychoanalyst Osvaldo Cariola in Chap. 9. Lacan's teachings, searching to give Freud's metapsychology a formal determination, have therefore themselves ended up in the ontologizing Freud's heirs had turned psychoanalysis into. Since the 1980s, the French psychoanalyst René Lew (1946–) has worked to give the doctrine of the signifier the formalization that Lacan called for by deducing the logic of the topological conditions on which psychoanalytic experience is based. This has led, among other things, to a reading of Lacan that is reminiscent of Lacan's own reading of Freud, a clarification of the foundations of psychoanalysis, and a closer examination of the specific conditions that characterize the function of the signifier. All these through a reformulation of the basic problems of psychoanalysis and in a discussion with standard logic (as established by logical positivism), considering the insights of psychoanalysis itself and the latest developments in the "deviant" logics (hypothetical, temporal, modal, derealistic, etc.) to which Goodman, Hintikka, Girard, and others have given us access. The key concept here is *signifiance*, which delineates the peculiarity of the signifier function and whose conceptualization has consequences for all aspects of psychoanalysis (technical, clinical, metapsychological, political, ethical, etc.). Cariola has chosen to concentrate in his text on the epistemic consequences of such considerations, to point out that the rationality of psychoanalysis is not to blame when judged by the parameters of the impredicative sciences.

Although logic is intimately related to the dichotomy "rational/irrational," these terms can be replaced by the terms "predicative/impredicative," i.e., to what extent an outcome is predictable or not. This replacement of terms subverts ontology as a factor in this discussion and opens up instead the aspects of interpretation, and this is what the meta-psychological project is supposed to be about: namely to what extent psychoanalysis does offer the proper tools for achieving prosperous interpretations. That said, Cariola demonstrates how modal logic provides a proper *organon* for psychoanalysis as it may point at different interpretative strategies by means of the square of opposites.

One of the missing factors in most discussions about psychoanalysis is the role of music. Most likely, Freud himself might be the reason for this given that he said openly that he disliked music. Nevertheless, some aspects of music and sound in psychoanalysis are the topics Sven Hroar Klempe pursues in Chap. 10. To make a smooth connection between psychoanalysis and music, Klempe refers to an amateur painting from 1948 which, allegedly, was an outcome of a dream the painter had about a concert with a symphony orchestra. The painting demonstrates very well the Freudian dream processes in terms of condensations and replacements. Furthermore, it demonstrates how sound is embedded in the metaphoric and metonymic features of the painting.

Lacan implicitly argues for the importance of sound in dreams, as he highlights the role of the signifier over that of the signified. Roman Jakobson also underlined the importance of sound in language, as he developed the phonology. Roman Jakobson influenced Lacan, and his phonology emphasizes that the each phoneme in language does not represent just one sound, but several articulated at the same time. The sound of a phoneme is comparable with a chord or musical counterpoint as musical harmony and polyphony mean that different tones are sounding simultaneously. Thus, the idea of language as being linear does not reflect any actual uses of language. Moreover, it may not reflect our thinking either. Klempe argues that this is in line with the position of the Russian psychologist Lev Vygotsky who made a sharp distinction between the use of language and the process of thinking. The former appears as linear, whereas the latter appears as condensed units of complex meanings. To be understood by others, thinking has to be translated into sequential verbal utterances. Although Vygotsky was not a psychoanalyst, the author concludes that there are anyway some connections here.

All the chapters point in several and quite different directions. Nevertheless, they are all united by sharing some important common factors. One of them is of course that Sigmund Freud represents a direct point of departure for all of them. This is natural and even obvious when psychoanalysis is at stake. As mentioned, Freud can easily be experienced as an authoritarian scholar, and very many of his followers have understood him to be so. However, the contributions in this compilation point rather in another direction, namely that Freud's investigations and reflections, represent an inspiring source for free creative thinking in approaching and investigations of the human mind. Already at the beginning of the twentieth century, he inspired not only psychiatrists and psychologists, but also artists who felt that Freud opened new ways to understand the human nature. This had huge consequences for how morality is to be understood as well. In many ways, Freud's psychoanalysis gave flesh to the Nietzschean program saying, *Umweltung alle Werte*—all values turned upside down. This process has continued, and French thinking in the 1960s and the 1970s represent maybe some of the clearest peak points in these types of intellectual efforts.

This is not only the most inspiring aspect of Freud and French poststructuralism in general, but maybe even more by the thinking of Jacques Lacan. The reception history of Jacques Lacan demonstrates very well that the understanding of him has been extremely polarized. He is presented either as a genius or as a charlatan (Matthews, 2020). However, this compilation aims at presenting both him and other scholars in French psychoanalysis as neither. The extreme formulations and thoughts that characterized French poststructuralist thinking from the 1960s and the 1970s can easily be misunderstood if they are taken literally and not least if one is searching for a consistent moral or rationality. On this background, one may quite simply say that not only scholars in the United States but also those in the Protestant Europe may have misunderstood parts of French thinking (Liu, 2010, p. 13). The key to correct this is not only to remind about Nietzsche's analyses of morality, but also to point at Lyotard's analysis of the conditions of postmodernism, namely that the big and consistent narratives in sciences have collapsed (Lyotard, 1979/1984). This was probably what Lacan demonstrated when he scandalized everyone at Massachusetts Institute of Technology (MIT) in 1975 in a meeting with Noam Chomsky by answering the latter's question about thinking with: "We think we think with our brains; personally, I think with my feet" (Matthews, 2020, p. 6). French psychoanalysis may represent boundary-breaking thinking, and it should inspire everyone to do the same, yet not necessarily losing one's mind completely.

References

Barthes, R. (2011). *The preparation of the novel. Lecture courses and seminars at the Collège de France (1978–1979 and 1979–1980)* (K. Briggs, Trans.). Columbia University Press.

Fages, J.-B. (1971). *Comprendre Jacques Lacan*. Privat, éditeur.

Foucault, M. (2008). *The Birth of Biopolitics. Lectures at the Collège de France 1978–1979* (G. Burchell, Trans.). Palgrave Macmillan.

Freud, S. (1899/1913). *The Interpretation of Dreams* (A. A. Brill, Trans.). Macmillan. https://www.gutenberg.org/cache/epub/66048/pg66048-images.html

Freud, S. (1905/1976). *Jokes and their Relation to the Unconscious*. Penguin Books.

Lacan, J. (1966). *Écrits*. Éditions du Seuil.

Liu, L. H. (2010). *The Freudian Robot. Digital media and the future of the unconscious*. The University of Chicago Press.

Lyotard, J.-F. (1972, Novembre). Plusieurs silences. *Musique en jeu. No. 9. Psychoanalyse musique*. Éditions du Seuil. 64–76.

Lyotard, J.-F. (1979/1984). *The postmodern condition: A report on knowledge* (G. Bennington & B. Massumi, Trans.). University of Minnesota Press.

Madill, A. (1996). *Developing a discourse analytic approach to change processes in psychodynamic-interpersonal psychotherapy*. Access at: https://etheses.whiterose.ac.uk/10245/1/364304.pdf

Matthews, P. D. (2020). *Lacan the Charlatan*. Palgrave Macmillan.

Sven Hroar Klempe (Mag.art., Dr.art.) is Professor in Psychology at the Department of Psychology, Norwegian University of Science and Technology (NTNU), Trondheim, Norway. His background includes Professor in Musicology, Assoc. Prof. in Media Studies, teacher and journalist. His research is cross-disciplinary with an emphasis on the history of psychology, culture and psychology, theory of science, communication and music psychology.

Anna Madill specializes in qualitative methods, with particular interest in visual approaches. She is Chair in Qualitative Inquiry and former Interim Head of the School of Psychology, University of Leeds UK. Anna is a Chartered Psychologist, Fellow of the British Psychological Society and Fellow of the Academy of Social Sciences. She Co-Founded and Chaired (2008-11) the British Psychological Society Qualitative Methods in Psychology Section. Some of her research projects can be found at https://projectresilience.co.uk/

Chapter 2
Jacques Lacan's Liminal Subject: Semiotic and Anti-semiotic Thrusts of a Psychoanalytic Theory of the Subjectivity

Raffaele De Luca Picione

Jacques Lacan is considered one of the most influential thinkers and intellectuals of the second half of the last century. He was a French psychoanalyst who offered a new understanding of the human psyche and the unconscious in order to develop new elements at the service of psychoanalytic clinics. His influence goes far beyond the psychoanalytic domain and has touched all areas of culture, philosophy, literature, art, politics, and human sciences.

In the 1950s, Lacan reread Freudian teaching starting from the primacy of the Symbolic register, the field of the *Other*, of language, namely a field that preexists the subject itself and without which the subject is unthinkable. Starting from the texts of structural anthropology by Lévi-Strauss (1949) and those of structuralist linguistics by Ferdinand de Saussure (1916), Lacan initially adopts a full structural point of view. For the psychoanalytic perspective, this paradigm implies the detachment from a genetic evolutionary approach (which considers the individual in the course of their development, diachronically), to place instead the subject in the foreground, in constitutive dependence on a Symbolic structure that preexists them.

One of the major critical attacks aimed at structuralism is that of minimizing (or even nullifying) the incidence of the subject within the anthropological system to which it belongs. However, Lacan does not eliminate the notion of subject starting from the preexistence of the structure, since he considers that the subject *enters the game as dead, but then one will play as alive* (Lacan, 1966). The structure is a constituent of the effects of meaning, i.e., it is the cause of meaning, but with respect to it the subject is not a mere effect, a simple *puppet of the signifier*, but the subject is *both caused and causal*, and he assumes a specific position for which it is always responsible (Lacan, 1966).

R. De Luca Picione (✉)
Giustino Fortunato University, Benevento, Italy
e-mail: r.delucapicione@unifortunato.eu

S. H. Klempe, A. Madill (eds.), *French Psychoanalysis Revisited*, Annals of Theoretical Psychology 20, https://doi.org/10.1007/978-3-031-68534-7_2

In this period, Lacan insists on the opposition between the register of the *Imaginary* and that of the *Symbolic* and its primacy in the constitution of the reality of the subject. This consists in subordinating the imaginary vicissitudes of the ego (i.e., the history of multiple identifications) to the Symbolic order, endowed with its own laws and its own autonomy, irreducible to the specular symmetry of the imaginary register.

However, over the course of three decades, Lacan develops the question further through a progressive theoretical and clinical elaboration of another register, the so-called *Real*. In the following paragraphs, the three registers of experience are presented to offer the basis for our discussion on the *semiotic and anti-semiotic* status of human experience and of subjectivity.

The Three Registers of Human Experience: Imaginary, Symbolic, and Real

The Imaginary

The *Imaginary* is primarily something that should not be confused with the illusory, with fiction. The subject is always captured in the meshes of the imaginary and their very identity; their ego is constituted on the fabric of the imaginary representations that concern them. These representations that constitute the ego are not produced by chance but in the dyadic relationship that the subject maintains with the fundamental figures of their life, with their *others*, from which they draw to constitute their own identity. With respect to this point, Lacan places the fundamental difference between the ego (*moi*) and the subject (*Je*).

The ego has a structurally narcissistic constitution, as it is the unconscious product of the subject's identifications with the signifiers through which the others in his life (primarily their parents) have designated their identity within the family discourse. The constitution of the ego is therefore—from the outset and forever—alienated (Lacan says that "*the ego is another*"). Since the ego offers the subject an image of oneself in which to recognize oneself, it distances them from their desire. For this reason, for Lacan the split of the ego is understood as an irreducible split between the subject of the unconscious (*Je*, the subject of the *enunciation*) and the ego (*moi*, the subject of the *enunciated*). While the ego (*moi*) has an imaginary status, the subject (*Je*) of the unconscious has a Symbolic status. The *Je* manifests itself in the points of contradiction, of vacillation, of the formations of the unconscious (i.e., dreams, slips, and symptoms), and of emptiness inside the statements of the discourse of the patient in analysis (Recalcati, 2012, 2016; Cosenza, 2003).

The Imaginary register is the register centered on the mirror relationship (Lacan, 1966; De Luca Picione et al., 2022). According to Lacan, in the mirror stage, there is the experience of recognition. By a jubilatory way, the child—between 6 and

18 months (therefore still in a phase of dependence, fragmentation, and nonmastery of the body)—makes experience of their own unitary image in front of the mirror. This phase represents a structural crossroads in the psychogenesis of subjectivity. This process hinges on the dual relationship, which finds its evident form in the child's relationship with the maternal desire indistinguishable from their own (namely the subject's desire is indistinguishable from that of the other).

The subject is able to find an anchor point beyond the imaginary—with the emergence of their own singular desire—only through the recognition of a *Third* who exists beyond the dual relationship and who sets a limit and instantiates the Law (*the Symbolic*) that regulates the relationship between the two (De Luca Picione & Freda, 2022). The point at stake is central and leads us to the relevance of the Symbolic register. Jacques Lacan elaborated the notion of the *Third* in an original way. In fact, the Third is the *Other* (with a capital letter), recognizing the preeminence of the Symbolic and structural order that preexists every single individual (see the following paragraph to deepen such an issue). While within dual relationships with the *other* (based on the imaginary effect of identification with the other) clashes and conflicts are possible, instead the relationship with the *Other* (as third) ensures the possibility of stay in relationship with other individuals and share with them the Symbolic system. Let us make an example: two people clash in a discursive dynamic, contrasting their views and opinions (it is a dual relationship); but they do so from (and thanks to the support and mediation of) a superordinate system of language (in the position of a third party) that they both obey and share. This means that although two subjects interact with each other there is always a third party mediating their social relationship.

The Symbolic

The Symbolic register is constituted in the first place by the field of language, within which the subject's speech finds the conditions of its own particular enunciation. This register is made up of the signifying and codified system. Note that the Symbolic order does not coincide only with verbal language, but it includes any signifying system with a predefined code shared among human beings.

On a more clinical level, the Symbolic order is represented by the dimension of the *Third*, which functions as an asymmetrical law for the components of the dual relationship. In the child's dual relationship captured by the mother's desire, the Father acts as a separating function that preserves the child from the "cannibalism" of the mother's desire, allowing the subjectivation of the child.

This perspective allows Lacan to reread ex novo the Oedipus Complex, by introducing new elements to the old debate between psychoanalysis and anthropology (which posed the problem of its real existence in societies where the figure of the father was more peripheral). The Oedipus Complex is reinterpreted by Lacan. Here the *signifier of the Father*—the so-called *Name-of-the-Father*[1]—offers itself at the same time as a *Law*, which deprives the child of the exclusivity of the mother, and provides a Symbolic ideal (ideal of the ego) for becoming an adult. The signifier *Name-of-the-Father* is written in the child through the word of the mother, who testifies to him that in her desire not only the child exists, but also an Other (a man, the father) to whom she has remained linked as woman, which functions for her as *Third* with respect to the child.

It is worthy to note that this signifier can therefore ignore the existence of the biological father—who can also be dead or be distant—and can also concern someone who exercises the function of father even though he is neither biologically nor juridically. Lacan calls this signifier *Name-of-the-Father* and defines its action in the constitution of the subject, as a *paternal metaphor*, namely an operation that allows the child to remove the *Desire-of-the-Mother* in which they risk being totally absorbed. This separation permits the child to constitute themself as a desiring subject. Becoming a desiring subject means having experienced *Symbolic castration*, i.e., the renunciation of a part of one's own satisfaction, recognizing oneself as lacking something that is enigmatic, and which one seeks throughout one's existence (Cosenza, 2003; Di Ciaccia & Recalcati, 2000).

The Symbolic register is the field of the *Other* (with the initial capital letter), in opposition to the lowercase *other* which coincides with the similar specular imaginary relationship. The notion of *Other* designates the historical-linguistic-cultural Symbolic dimension within which the subject is constituted as a result of the signifying action. Through the concept of the Other, Lacan reformulates the Freudian notion of the unconscious by placing its radical historicity at the core of human experience: *the unconscious is the locus of the Other.*

The Real

Alongside the registers of the Imaginary and the Symbolic, for Lacan, there is the register of the *Real*. This register is very enigmatic and difficult. It is mute, definable only in a negative form as a deviation from the axes of the Imaginary and the Symbolic, as it is not of the order of the image, nor of the order of the symbol.

We need to make a distinction: the Real is not the reality! Lacan defines such a difference from the German terms that Freud himself uses: *Wirklichkeit* is used to designate reality in the common meaning of the term, as an objective external reality, and *Realität* is concerning instead the dimension of psychic reality (see the *Seminar IV*—Lacan, 1994). For Lacan, the Real is the Real of the subject, that is, it inheres in everything that is inescapable that distinguishes psychic mode of

[1] One of Lacan's major clinical contributions has been the notion of *foreclosure*. In psychosis, there would be the foreclosure of the signifier of the *Name-of-the-Father*. This lack makes it impossible to access the Symbolic register, preventing the development of subjectivity. This lack impede to share a process of sensemaking of reality which limits the experience of the Real.

functioning and the economy of the satisfaction, beyond any criterion of adaptation of reality.

It is interesting to observe that for Lacan the Real is the *impossible*. It is what one cannot get out of. The *Real* designates the very being of the subject, the node that structures his psychic reality. While the Imaginary and the Symbolic are open to the dimension of the *possible* and the *necessary*, the Real marks the *impossible* of the subject, i.e., the very matrix of his most intimate fabric. Here we meet a paradox: we are trying to define what is not definable: the Real is "out of sense," asemantic, unrepresentable, unpredictable, outside the grasp of the image and the Symbolic. Furthermore, the Real is the real of the drive body; it is the Real of the drive economy of the subject's *jouissance*, the engine of its economy of satisfaction (Miller, 1999; Recalcati, 2012; Pagliardini, 2016; Cosenza, 2003).

It is important to note that the register of the Real since the 1960s has progressively undergone various further elaborations and transformations. In *Seminar VII* (Lacan, 2005a), Lacan defines the Real starting from the loss of *the Thing* (*das Ding*), namely the object of the first mythical experience of satisfaction of the subject. In *Seminar XI* (1964), the Real is defined as the real of the drive object of the erogenous zones. It enters the experience of the human being as a lost object whose drive to find it structures the subject's libidinal economy. In addition to Freud's partial drive objects (the *oral object* and the *anal object*), Lacan adds the *voice-object* and the *gaze-object*. All those objects are deeply linked to the drive experience and linked to the orifices of the body—mouth, anus, ears, and eyes: they are openings/cuts in the body surface on which the influence of the other acts (De Luca Picione, 2023a, b/in press).

These considerations lead Lacan to reformulate the status of the *small object a*, as a lost object of the first mythical satisfaction. Lacan formulates the theory of the *object (a)* as an object that causes desire, an object of repetition, and an object around which the construction of the fundamental subjective fantasy is structured and that regulates the satisfaction economy of the neurotic subject from childhood (De Luca Picione, 2017). Lacan develops the theme of *Real* also defining it as the core of Freud's death drive, as a principle of entropy, of self-destructive satisfaction, taking up the elaboration of *Beyond the Pleasure Principle* (Freud, 1920) as the basis of the functioning of psychic apparatus. Starting from this Freudian contribution, Lacan develops and elaborates the concept of *enjoyment* (*jouissance*). This notion becomes ever more central in the register of the Real and acts as a self-destructive and malignant satisfaction, as an irresistible libidinal drive toward something that causes the subject suffering, which nonetheless makes him enjoy.

Finally, starting in the 1970s, Lacan thinks of the Real as *the Real of sex*. This clinical and theoretical elaboration makes possible to overcome the ideal of genital maturation (as anatomic-physiological development that allows reproduction) and to root human sexuality in the structural experience of the loss of satisfaction, of a partially missed pleasure. The sexual partner assumes the position of substitute for the lost object of the first mythic experience of satisfaction. In this sense, sexual intercourse does not represent an encounter with the other, with another subjectivity. Rather sexual intercourse for the human being is always on the one hand an attempt to find the lost object of the first mythical experience of satisfaction, and on the other hand, it is the frustrating experience of failure of this research with the reproposition of the trauma of loss.

Sexual encounter is always for the human being a partially missed encounter, a satisfaction that is always at a loss. This is where *Real* emerges. It deals with the real of the loss of the object of satisfaction and its traumatic repetition in the sexual experience. Sexuality for human beings is never a natural, an instinctual, a genetically predetermined experience or one that can be exercised through good educational practices. The sexuality always brings with it something unrepresentable, something that can never be completely harnessed by the meshes of the Symbolic, and always fails in the subject's illusion of completing himself through the encounter with the other. Lacan's paradoxical definition—often criticized for its cryptic nature—is that *there is no sexual relationship* (*ne pas rapport sexuelle*), meaning precisely that there will never be the possibility of an encounter with a fully satisfying partner that completes one's constitutive sense of lack.

The Subject as a Lack of Being (*manque à être*)

From the initial formalization of the stage of the mirror—which highlights the role of the *Imaginary* in the constitution of the subject—Lacan highlights the constitutive dimension of the lack of human subjectivity. This lack is initially based on the role of the other; then, it is rooted in the drive nature of *jouissance*. As regards the function of the *Other* in the constitution of subjectivity, the same imaginary experience opens the space for the centrality of the role of the other to emerge, but also of the Symbolic itself. The identification process begins thanks to the presence of the *Other*, the maternal Other: it induces *recognition*; it indicates to the child the image that the mirror sends back to him and above all testifies to the jubilation of the child. In this experience that roots the identity of the subject in terms of imaginary identification, Lacan recognizes a constitutively paranoid movement. Lacan affirms that *the ego of every normal person is paranoid*. The experience of the mirror stage—establishing itself on a dual imaginary relationship—generates a rivalry between the two antagonists. Paranoid traits necessarily accompany the constitution of the ego, without, however, this implying that in fact all people are affected by a paranoid psychosis.

It is precisely the *Symbolic* for Lacan—*the Other*—that allows decentralization with respect to this purely imaginary axis that captures the subject: the preexisting Other is the very condition of the possibility of the existence of the subject. The subject inevitably finds themself subordinated from birth to the Symbolic structure, endowed with precise laws. The Symbolic structure is not a mere cage made up of constraints, prescriptions, obligations, and prohibitions; this would risk focusing on a purely privative and coercive aspect. The Symbolic structure through a process of limitation of pleasure and satisfaction—a Symbolic castration—allows the individual to become a human subject and enter in the field of desire. The Symbolic is the field of language, and human being can access it only if they renounce the full and mythic illusion of total satisfaction.

The subject of the unconscious is not the subject of imaginary identifications nor the biological individual, immersed in their bodily reality, but it is an effect of entering in the field of the *Other* and in the action of Symbolic language. This leads Lacan to elaborate his classic affirmation that the *unconscious is structured like a language* (Lacan, 1966). The unconscious is woven, it is concatenated by the language, and it is a fabric of language. For Lacan, the unconscious is not a container of meanings, it is not the place of depth, but it is like a topological surface (De Luca Picione, 2020a, b) in continuous formation. The unconscious is endowed with a logic that is expressed through the laws of language itself. The unconscious for Lacan is the place of the unfolding of speech.

In an inaugural work of his so-called return to Freud—*The Function and the Field of Speech and Language in Psychoanalysis* of the year 1953 (Lacan, 1966)—Lacan believes that the fundamental law of human language is that every word always calls for a response. A word—i.e., any particular linguistic act—always addresses another, on which the outcome of the word itself depends. The word is always a request for something, and first of all, it is a request for recognition. The word founds the intersubjective dialectic and invariably invests a recipient, whose response—even silence—profoundly affects the meaning of the word uttered by the subject. Lacan used to state that speech is a communication in which the sender receives his message in an inverted form from the receiver (Lacan, 1966). The sense of the formula can be shown through a very simple example: when I say to my wife “"you are my wife,” this act of speech always calls for a response, which will have an inverse form for the sender, i.e., in this case, “I am your husband” (Tarizzo, 2003; Palombi, 2019). According to Lacan, the question of the subject is the question “who am I?” which is always latent in every act of speaking addressed to otherness.[2]

[2] This analysis of the structure of speech is very relevant in the observation of psychotic phenomena. In auditory hallucinations, in fact, what the subject receives as coming from the outside, from the reality, is not his own message in an inverted form, but his own word and his own message. We find here total exclusion of the Other, since words are uttered by the specular and imaginary reflection of the subject itself, without any symbolic mediation. Lacan says that in madness on the one hand we observe the negative freedom of a word that has given up being recognized and on the other hand we observe the singular formation of a delusion which objectifies the subject in a language without dialectic. Lacan states that the stereotypes of discourse in the psychotic individual clearly reveal that the subject is spoken more than they do not speak (Lacan, 1966). The psychotic subject is certainly in the language. Yet their speech instead of being articulated in a discourse that creates a social bond tends to isolate itself and become autonomous, freed from any relationship of recognition. It tends to crystallize in an anti-dialectical stereotype, closed to any sort of ambivalence and opposition, which suggests the drama of psychotic certainty: there is no postponement, there is no sliding, and there is only petrification (Bonifati, 2000).

The Original Lacanian Dialectic Between Structuralist Semiotics and Pragmatistic Semiotics

The Influence of Structuralist Semiotics

Since the mid-1950s, Lacan's attention has shifted ever more decisively from the structure of the word to that of language and its laws. Lacan shows that language is not a property of humankind, nor a psychological faculty; rather language envelops and determines human life. The place of the *Other* (i.e., language) appears as a net that envelops the being of the subject even before its birth. From this point of view, Lacan points out that language is by no means exhausted in a subjective faculty that is evolutionarily acquired through experience and memory.

According to Lacan, it is not the human being who learns to speak, but it is language that speaks human being, in the sense that the human being structurally depends on the horizon of language. Language is not a mere and simple communication tool, but it is a field, a network, and a structure that determines the subject as it preexists human being. From Lévi-Strauss' structuralist anthropology (1949), Lacan incorporates the subordination of the phenomenal elements to the laws of the structure, as demonstrated, for example, by the studies carried out on the laws of kinship, which guide and determine the behavior with respect to the creation of family ties. According to Lévi-Strauss, it is the laws of the structure that condition and regulate individual actions. From the structuralist lesson, Lacan accepts the dependence of the speech on the laws of language.

From Ferdinand de Saussure's structuralist linguistics, Lacan uses the lesson that the subjective function of speech (*parole*) depends on the laws of language (*langue*). De Saussure (1916) places the study of the sign within the language (*langue*) which is considered as a system of signs that form the code of an idiom. The phonemes, words, and other linguistic elements that compose the code have value only in the relations of equivalence and opposition that connect them to each other. De Saussure, opposing the conception of language as a simple nomenclature (i.e., a close correspondence between things and names), proposes the linguistic sign as a totality.

According to Ferdinand de Saussure, the sign consists of two components such as the sensitive acoustic component (the *signifier* or expression) and the *cognitive trace of a concept* (the *signified* or content). *Significant* and *signified* are like two sides of a coin being inseparable and continually referring to each other. This relationship has two properties: (a) *arbitrariness*: There is no constraint or necessity internal to the link itself—there is no natural and given relationship between what is represented and what it represents. This is essentially true for every natural language. (b) *exclusivity*: Once a linguistic system has assumed its structure, a *principle of exclusivity* intervenes, according to which one signified corresponds to one and only one signifier and vice versa.

The association between signified and signifier is not tied to any natural law, as demonstrated by the variety of idioms, even if once established in each language it becomes canonical and can no longer be modified by the individual speaker. Furthermore, the "value" of an element of the language can be identified only in a "differential" way, through the relationship with the other terms of the system that allow its identification by "opposition." This consideration places priority on the study of the system itself rather than on its individual parts. *Langue* has the character of a social convention and is opposed to *parole*, i.e., the individual and unrepeatable linguistic act of those who speak.

The value of any term is determined by its surroundings. This principle sums up the sense of the structuralist paradigm according to which the relationships always precede the elements. The value of an element is always given by the place it occupies in the system of which it belongs; without a system, understood as a network of necessary relationships, no element is possible.

Saussure has considered two particular forms of possible relationships between signs: syntagmatic relationships and associative relationships (only the latter defined as paradigmatic—Hjelmslev, 1963).

The associative/paradigmatic relationships move in search of meaning along a vertical direction that associates the individual words or components of the text with other words or components that are absent, in the specific text, but similar in terms of a semantic criterion. The components of the text are associated *in absentia*, because one associates with another that is not present in the text on the basis of having some aspects in common (e.g., king, monarch, imperator, dux, leader, and so on). Paradigmatic relationships provide for a *principle of substitutability* (De Luca Picione, 2015).

The syntagmatic relationships carry out a process of signification on a horizontal plane: the components of the text take on meaning by virtue of their linking with those that follow and/or precede them. The combinations of words within the sentence are called *syntagmas*, where an element acquires its value only because it complements or opposes those that precede and follow it. Syntagmatic relationships are defined *in praesentia*, i.e., the elements of the relationship must be present in a text or sentence. Here the elements are connected to each other in a relationship that is not one of similarity, but one of completion/opposition (De Luca Picione, 2015).

Lacan leads this argument to its extreme implications: *the condition of possibility of the act of speech is the existence of the universal code of language*. The pivotal thesis of 1957 in *The Instance of the Letter in the Unconscious, or Reason Since Freud* (Lacan, 1966) places language as absolutely transcendent with respect to the somatic and psychic functions which are at the service of the speaking subject. The subject themself appears as a veritable servant of language, caught up in a discourse in which their place is already inscribed at their birth.[3]

[3] The same attribution of the name to the unborn child represents its initial entry and harnessing into the symbolic world of language.

The Influence of Peircean Semiotics and Pragmatism

However, Lacan is not limited to being a faithful spokesman or supporter of the Saussurean lesson, but he rereads the concepts of the structuralist linguistics, making substantial changes to them. Lacan takes up Saussure's concept of the sign and redefines the articulation between the *signifier* and the *signified*, proposing the algorithm S/s (read as "*the Signifier above the signified*") in place of de Saussure's unifying scheme of the sign. By inverting the order given by de Saussure to the two components of the sign, he highlights the supremacy of the signifier to which the subject is subordinated, and he attributes to the bar "/" a function of division, of separation—instead of a unifying function. The bar shows the resistance to the meaning. In Freudian terms, the bar indicates the repression, that is, the discord between the signified and the signifier determined by any censorship of social origin.

In this revolutionary passage, it is possible to find a very close affinity with the pragmatistic and interpretative semiotics of Charles Sanders Peirce. In fact, according to a well-known definition by Peirce, a *sign* or *representamen* is something that stands to someone for something in some respect or capacity and creates in this someone an equivalent, or perhaps more developed sign (CP 2.228, fragment of 1897—Peirce, 1935). The representation function of the sign is not biunique, linear and absolute. The sense-making process is always constituted within a semiotic chain in a contextual dimension that defines its pertinence. Here we find clearly expressed the criticism of the dyadic relationship between sign and object as well. The central idea that moves all of Peirce's vast intellectual production is the *triadicity* of semiosis.[4]

Peirce's model of sign favors the triadic relational aspect of semiosis, a crucial characteristic for ensuring semiotic dynamism and its incessant processuality. Peirce believes that for the realization of any semiosis a triadic relationship must be established. Each sign interprets another sign, and the basic condition of semiosis is precisely this condition of infinite regress (the so-called *unlimited semiosis*). In this perspective, each interpretant of a given sign, being itself a sign, becomes a transitory construction. That is, a chain of interpretants is set up, each of which consists of a different response, mediated by the *sign* that has aroused that *interpretant*. The Sign (representamen) stands for the Object not in every possible aspect, but only

[4] Peirce, in articulating all his thought in triadic processes, comes to define three phenomenological categories defined as *farenoscopic*. They are the notions of *Firstness* (referring to pure qualities and possibilities), *Secondness* (realization, actual existence, and determining relationships), and *Thirdness* (mediation, the sign, thought, and law), which underlie all relational semiotic phenomena.

Something single and isolated can only be a quality or a possibility (or both). An "effective existent" enters into dual relationships, of copresence, or cause–effect. A law always has a mediating function (for example, between those to whom it applies and what it applies to). In this articulation, it is possible to find a further affinity between the notion of firstness, secondness, and thirdness with the three registers of the Real, Imaginary, and Symbolic as they are presented and argued by Lacan in the course of his work.

starting from a determined choice of pertinence. The sign is not perfectly equivalent to its Object, but selects (and develops) some properties, neglecting others.

Lacanian discourse shows interesting affinities with Peirce's triadic vision. In fact, Lacan defines that the signifier is the material of language; it is what is heard in the moment in which one speaks. Every signifier is, as such, a signifier that signifies nothing, being in itself without its own signification.

Meaning, understood as a diachronic set of concretely pronounced discourses, does not coincide at all with objects and with things. A meaning always refers to another meaning. The implication of this discourse is the further observation of the subjective division: the subject is divided as a result of the signifying action, because the meaning can never be grasped as an object but slips and fluctuates constantly below the bar of the signifier, as an effect of the concatenation of signifiers among themselves.

Between the signifier and the signified, there is always a fluid, dialectical connection. The signified and the signifier are two distinct networks that never coincide. Meaning is constituted in the articulation between signifiers and not in the representative relationship of a signified with a signifier.[5]

The web of language covers all of reality, but Lacan warns that we must not delude ourselves about the idea that language is shaped by a simple and direct apprehension of reality. It is rather the structure within which the subject is constituted as such.

In the text of the 1960 "*Subversion of the subject and dialectics of desire*," Lacan uses the expression that *the signifier is that which represents a subject for another* (Lacan, 1966). This means that the subject can only be placed within the signifying chain, in which one is represented by one signifier for another signifier. One's own position is the effect of the signification. This minimal concatenation recalls, as can be easily observed, the "unlimited semiosis" *à la* Peirce, and it is in contrast with structuralist semiotics. In fact, it is not about a static positioning within a Symbolic structure; rather it is about incessant and continuous movement to another signifier. The reference to the subject represents a subversive operation carried out by Lacan with respect to the conceptual framework of structuralist linguistics. Indeed, in structuralism, the reference to the subject has no value (i.e., the value of a subject is defined by position, like mother, father, child, leader, followers, etc.), while for Lacan the logics of the signifier is kept in relationship with that of the subject by means of an ongoing and a ceaseless movement.

---

[5]This distinction between the signified and the signifier has not only theoretical but also profoundly clinical value since it turns out to be very useful in the analysis of language phenomena in psychoses. Within the psychosis, everything becomes a "sign" and "meaning." In fact, we observe a stop in the flow of meanings; there is no longer a reference from one meaning to another, but the presence of a meaning that refers to nothing but itself. In the symbolic order, each element counts as opposite to another, if the words are made up of pairs of opposition; in psychosis, on the other hand, the sign, in fact, is no longer dialectical, but it is univocally united to a signification and unlike the signifier it is not valid as opposed to another sign. It has a value in itself (Bonifati, 2000).

Language is the condition of the unconscious, and the signifying order causes the subject as a divided subject: when the subject speaks, the level of the utterance (what the subject says) can never coincide with that of the enunciation (the place from where the subject says what he says). The level of enunciation constitutes that part of the subject's discourse, which constantly escapes the possibility of grasping the subject, since it is constitutively separated from it by repression (Miller, 2021; Di Ciaccia & Recalcati, 2000). The subject can never consist of a single signifier, but it is represented by a signifier in another signifier. This means that the subject is divided, it is not an identity, it does not consist of any substance; rather the subject is what underlies this constant infinite referral of signifiers.

A further element of affinity between Peirce's semiotics and Lacanian theory is the possibility of making *sense* through the closure of the process dynamics of the semiotic chain. This comparison is rather delicate and not immediate as it is not exactly superimposable. According to Peirce, a sign by producing a series of immediate responses (the so-called *Energetic Interpretant*) gradually establishes a habit (*habitus*), a regularity of behavior in its interpreter. A habit is in fact understood as a tendency to act similarly under similar circumstances in the future. The *Final Logical Interpretant* of a sign represents the habit as a stabilized result of semiosis. From his perspective, Peirce combines realism and pragmatism by reaching the conclusion that reality is not a mere given, it is rather a result. The implication of this argument is very profound: The category of "habit" (*habitus*) has a double meaning, psychological and cosmological, since the laws of nature are the result of acquired habits and all things have a tendency to assume habits.

Lacan also poses the problem of what stops this continuous sliding of meaning through the chain of signifiers. The significant and the signified constitute two distinct networks, but this continuous referral from one signification to another indicates that meaning always goes toward something, toward another signification, and therefore toward the closure of the signification. Lacan affirms during the *Seminar III* that a sentence becomes alive only when it presents a sense. A sentence exists only if completed, and its sense comes from the end (Lacan, 1981). The point where the signifier coincides with the signified is defined by Lacan as *point de capitonnè* (using the metaphor of the mattress where the two surfaces are joined by knots, precisely called "*point de capitonnè*[6]"). This is the point where the signifier and the meaning intertwine, a point of convergence that allows us to place everything that happens in the discourse retrospectively and prospectively.

[6]The capitonnè knot is the technique used for the padding of sofas, armchairs, or headboards that spread around 1800. This padding is worked entirely by hand and quilted to form cushions arranged in a network of squares or lozenges (rhombuses). The quilt fabric is held in place by buttons or studs, for which the two flat surfaces of the cushion—the upper and the lower one—are held together by a series of knots (De Luca Picione, 2023a, b).

This expression is used by Lacan to recall the fact that there is a special signifier—the *Name-of-the-Father*—that functions as a point of *capitonnè*, which stops the slipping and sliding between the plane of the signifier and that of the signified.

We recall that the signifier of the *Name-of-the-Father* does not coincide with the real father, rather it corresponds to the paternal function, that is, that Symbolic function which acts as a metaphor of signification and obliterates the engulfment of the individual by the maternal desire. The *Name-of-the-Father* is therefore a psychic operator who acts semiotically and enables the subject to access the Symbolic function, i.e., the possibility of being able to give meaning to the experience.

The *Name-of-the-Father* allows the subject to access the Symbolic register and to enable his dimension of desire through the phallic signification. By stopping the signification, the capitonnè point realizes the possibility of generating signification in terms of *après-coup* (posteriority), that is, it is the last signifying element of the chain that gives meaning to it.

Metaphor and Metonymy: Effects of the Semiotic Dynamics of the Unconscious

The two semiotic perspectives—of de Saussure and of Peirce—therefore find themselves declined in an original way in Lacanian theory and clinic since the 1950s.

The two fundamental laws that structure the field of language are those of metaphor and metonymy ("*effects of meaning*"). Lacan draws this thesis from Jakobson's linguistics (1963), but it already finds a complete development in Freud's *Traumdeutung* (Freud, 1900). The concepts of displacement and condensation are the processes through which Freud defines the operational modalities of the dreaming work (namely displacement: transposition of a meaning from one element to another; condensation: several meanings cohere into a single signifier). Lacan operates assimilation of the mechanisms of the primary unconscious process (condensation-displacement) according to Freud (1911) with the mechanisms of synchronic and diachronic selection (metaphor-metonymy), which according to Jakobson constitute the foundations of the action of language.

Jakobson's semantic guidelines are the syntagmatic axis (functioning *in praesentia*) of metonymy and the paradigmatic axis (functioning *in absentia*) of metaphor. In the first case, it is a relationship of *contiguity*—or metonymic way—that connects two or more elements all present in a given series (we have the connection, the combination between one signifier and another). In the second case, we find a relationship of *similarity*—as metaphorical way—that connects one or more elements present with others that are absent from the series (there is a substitution movement in which a signifier takes the place of another signifier producing an unprecedented effect of signification).

While metonymy indicates a flight of meaning, an infinite flow, then the metaphor polarizes it, arrests it, and creates it in the form of a Symbolic cipher. The metonymic structure installs by means of the connection of the signifier with another signifier a *negative subtraction of sense*, a continuous sliding of meaning and the postponement of meaning (a sort of resistance of meaning). The metaphorical structure determines the possibility of a *positive production of the sense*.

The metaphor is capable of producing meaning; it arrests the perpetual metonymic escape through a significant substitution. For this reason, Lacan associates the paternal function (the *Name-of-the-Father*) with the metaphor. He conceives the *point of capitonnè* as the arrest of signification according to the scheme of retroaction (namely the sense of a sentence is fulfilled only with the last word that concludes and that allows us to grasp its effective meaning, precisely according to a retrospective temporality—*après coup*).

Further, Lacan assimilates the symptom to the metaphor. The symptom shows itself as homologous to the metaphor as it implies that a signifier replaces a repressed meaning by producing a sense new for the subject (in psychosis, we have metonymy but no metaphor) (Di Ciaccia & Recalcati, 2000. Bonifati, 2000). Conversely, Lacan assimilates desire to metonymy. Desire reveals a homology with metonymy as it is characterized as an infinite movement of relaunch from one object to another.

By these two tenets of working (metaphor and metonymy), language has an evocative power; it covers reality without being it and is based on a loss, the loss of the object. Lacan states that the word kills the Thing (*das Ding*) but at the same time allows its symbolization. Distancing oneself from the object, the word allows for the advent of language. What is absent can be named. The word presentifies the thing even when the thing is not there, concretely present.

The word arises from this alternation, from this absence-presence dialectic of the object. It is the world of words that creates the world of things. Language is not based on a one-to-one relationship between the signifier and the signified; the signified is not represented by the signifier but is given only in the articulation of the chain of signifiers. The signification always refers to another signification. This highlights the so-called *function of unrealization* of the signifier—*effect of fiction*—denouncing how language does not have a referential power.

By accessing the alternation of presence and absence of the thing through symbolization, the child gains access to language; they begin to engage with the concrete discourse system of their environment. The child overcomes the confusing succession of things present in their immediacy and begins to acquire a certain mastery over reality, placing themself in it as the subject of desire. Only starting from the loss of the object, from its abolition, the child can begin to desire and start the metonymic chain of signifiers.

Anti-semiotic Movements in Human Experience: The Impossibility of Making Sense, Jouissance, Loss of Subjectivity, the Real

In the progress of his theoretical reflection and clinical practice, in the 1960s–1970s, Lacan elaborated the passage from the *statute of the Other* of the register of the Symbolic to the *statute of the One* of the register of the Real. In other words, we pass from the *axiomatic of desire* based on the relationship with the Other to the *axiomatic of jouissance*, fundamentally headless and autistic in its relationship with the *small object a*.

In fact, Lacan begins to recognize that even the Symbolic *Other*, A, is marked by a lack. He expresses this situation with the expression S(A̸) to indicate the *signifier of the lack of the Other*. The Other is lacking, just like the subject. There is no Other that is both complete and consistent at the same time. This lack in some way regards the very structure of the signifier, which is differential—namely it is defined only by difference from another signifier—and thus excludes the absolute reference (De Luca Picione, 2019a, b, 2020a, b; Palombi, 2019; Zizek, 2015). The implications of this passage are profound: the Symbolic register progressively loses its robustness and completeness, yielding ever greater incidence to *Lalangue* (Lacan, 1975), that is, an asemantic form of signifying material which no longer has the character of differentiality of the Symbolic register but that is impregnated with *jouissance*.

Lalangue is the domain of melody, rhythm, gestures, bodily expression, and kinesthetic and contact sensations. It represents the first experience with language that implies the dimension of trauma, and as such, it has the character of enjoyment (*jouissance*) of reality. In this stage of theoretical and clinical evolution, Lacan suggests that since the outset the newborn is affected by the traumatism of language (before it is perceived as Symbolic). *Lalangue*'s experience makes the Real and the Symbolic consubstantial. Lacan in his complex essay *L'étourdit* (Lacan, 1973a, b) affirms the dimension of ambiguity in language, which is generated between the confusion and overlap between the *Language of the Symbolic* and the *Lalangue of the Real*.

No longer the symptom does act on the side of the signifier, as a metaphor, where a signifier whose meaning is removed is replaced by another signifier.

Now the symptom also acts in its "*letter*" aspect. The *letter* is defined, in *Lituraterra* (Lacan, 1971), as the precipitation of the signifier. The *letter* is deposited as the Real side of the signifier, in opposition to the Symbolic side. The *letter* refers to nothing but itself. The *letter* wants to make *One*; it is not articulated in the signifying chain.

According to Lacan, the subject (or rather the living being who is about to become a subject) draws a Significant (S1) from the hum, the murmur, the swarm (*essaim*) of the *Lalangue*, and makes this S1, with its traumatic effect, the cause of its satisfaction drive. The first signifier, a special signifier, S1 is a unary trait ("*Einzerzug*"—Freud, 1921). This S1 absorbs in itself the libidinal value of the experience to which it is associated and works as an engine of relentless and headless jouissance.

In *Seminar XX Encorè* (Lacan, 1975), we therefore observe a shift of great importance with epistemological and clinical effects that absolutely cannot be overlooked: the replacement of language with *lalanguae*. As Miller explains, behind language there is *lalanguae*; there is something else that does not function like language. Human being imagines (in the sense of the imaginary register) that language and speech serve to communicate. *Lalangue*, on the other hand, reveals that language is used for much more than communication and dialogue. *Lalangue* is the concept which means that the signifier primarily serves the enjoyment of the body, repeating the compulsion to repeat the initial trauma (Miller, 2004–2005).

Conclusions: From the Semiotics of Meaning to the Anti-semiotics of Jouissance

In this last scenario increasingly centralized on *jouissance* rather than on desire, the statute of the signifier the *Name-of-the-Father* bears a loss. This signifier increasingly loses its universal function of guarantor, of connection with the Symbolic structure of all signifiers, in order to assume a function of complement. The Other is barred; there is no guarantor for it. The *Other of the Other* does not exist, we do not have an ultimate guarantee, and the ultimate signifier of the Other is missing. Hence, the *Name-of-the-Father* itself does not exist as absolute, as given, and as universal. Each subject is forced to invent it and create something that can take its place. There is in this theoretical turning point a total revolution centered on the notion of *singularity*, understood as the human search for a substitute capable of juggling life by looking for possible forms of knotting of the three registers (the Real, the Symbolic, and the Imaginary). In fact, every person must find a way to keep the three registers together because one cannot live without their mutual interaction (De Luca Picione, 2019a, b, 2020a, b, 2023a, b).

Human beings find various ways of keeping the three registers together, adding in some way a "supplement" capable of keeping the knot together and creating a singular nomination (which responds as a possible solution to the generalized foreclosure of the *Name-of-the-Father*). The contemporary clinic shows the pluralization and singularization of the *Name-of-the-Father*.

During the *Seminar XXIII—Les Sinthome* (Lacan, 2005a, b) Lacan defines these forms of singularity with the term "*sinthome*." The *sinthome* word comes from the archaic sixteenth-century spelling, and it is used to differentiate it from the medicalizing conceptualization of the *symptom*. The sinthome is a subjective form of writing, and its origin is located in the Real, whose function is to constitute an act of Symbolic naming. The sinthome is precisely the story of the subject, of the way in which the subject manages to live (or survive) in reality by creating forms of singular knotting between the three registers.

Miller argues that the sinthome is always inscribed for everyone in the father's resignation. It is precisely in this margin opened up by the father's resignation that the signifier is the cause of jouissance. The sinthome represents a healing, therapeutic, and restorative factor. The sinthome appears as an operator of consistency that allows the Symbolic, the Imaginary, and the Real to continue to stand together (Miller, 2004–2005).

During the *XXIV Seminar, L'insu que sait de l'une-bévue s'aile à mourre* (Lacan, 1976–1977), Lacan declares that knowing one's own symptom means knowing how to deal with it, knowing how to untangle and manipulate it. The *sinthome* is precisely a knowing how to do it, not in the sense of a universal formula dictated and known by the Symbolic. *Knowing how to do it* means being able to do something starting from this knowledge which is nothing more than a misunderstanding, a scam, and something that breaks into the blurred and littoral borders of reality.

Lacan shows the example of the Irish writer James Joyce's life and literary work. His writing had a substitute and sustaining function in his life, allowing him to both nominate and knot the three registers. Joyce's *sinthome* is exactly the compensation for a paternal deficiency. Joyce has made of his *sinthome* a product of art, of his singular unique art. The symptom is not to be healed; rather the sinthome is presented so that the subject makes use of this singularity (Miller, 2004–2005). We find a very relevant clinical implication. The subject can find a use starting from this *scrape* of jouissance, which cannot be assimilated to the Symbolic. That nonsense element can become an asset.

Miller (2004–2005) explains to us that it is a question of isolating a remainder, a core, and a detached piece, which is not at all in the semiotic relationship of the signifying chain. There are therefore no longer formations of the unconscious to decipher and interpret. We are no longer in the order of a hidden unconscious truth to be identified. We are no longer in the order of a masking to be revealed through a perfect and definitive interpretation. We are no longer in the order of a buried knowledge to be brought to light through the archaeological excavation of a psychoanalysis devoted to the ideal purity of the mnemonic function. We are no longer in the order of a symptom/metaphorical signifier to be deciphered in its meaning.

We are now in the order of a Real, that is, of something without sense relationship that makes a hole of *jouissance*, without any sense, without any history in terms of an imaginary narrative that finds specific causes for each effect. The Symbolic is definitively recognized as fallacious or as laundered in its function of definition and total naming of the Real.

Through the uncanny, inscrutable crossing of the Real, each subject builds his own *sinthomatica* element, by identifying the singular form of condensation of jouissance and desire in order to make a social bond starting from one's own hole and from one's own *scrape*. In this perspective, without being completely erased in its importance, the Symbolic register and its semiotic processuality constantly crash against the anti-semiotic incandescence of the Real.

Semiotic constructions no longer find stable place; any process of sense-making loses its centrality and full decipherability. Clinical practice is now based not so much on the interpretation and detection of meaning and truth, but on the possibility of being able to find a unique use for each subject of the nonsignificant gap of the Real.

In conclusion, it then becomes necessary to always have to deal with a double articulation: the semiotic side and the anti-semiotic side of human experience. The former generates a *signifying effect*; the latter produces a *jouissance drive*. This difference refers to the distinction that Lacan proposes in *Lituraterra* (Lacan, 1971) between the *frontier* and the littoral. The frontier marks what it distinguishes and clearly separates among identities. While the littoral is what is fading, it is what opens up to the impossible, to a "beyond" that is never reachable.

The *signifier* therefore works according to the logic of the *frontier*. Frontier makes a distinction, and by functioning as an operator of difference, it creates the possible conditions for making links, for relating distinct things, and for creating chains of signifiers according to a differential logic. The *letter* finds its logic in that of the *littoral*, that is, an impossible reference to anything other than its materiality.

The signifier is traced in the functioning and dominion of the *Other*; the letter wants to do nothing but *One*. The signifier refers to another signifier by promoting the dynamic chain S1➔S2; the letter is encysted in the repetition of an S1 as a unary trait, a source of enjoyment starting from the original trauma that the living subject experiences.

Human experience is founded in this incessant tension between a semiotic dynamics and an anti-semiotic thrust.

References

Bonifati, L. (2000). *La psicosi in Jacques Lacan. Da Aimée a Joyce*. FrancoAngeli.

Cosenza, D. (2003). *Jacques Lacan e il problema della tecnica in psicoanalisi*. Astrolabio.

De Luca Picione, R. (2015). *La Mente come Forma. La Mente come Testo. Un'indagine semiotico-psicologica dei processi di significazione*. Mimesis.

De Luca Picione, R. (2017). Il fantasma in psicoanalisi, un dispositivo che articola la "statica" e la "dinamica" temporale della significazione. *European Journal of Psychoanalysis*. ISSN: 2284-1059. Available on line: http://www.journal-psychoanalysis.eu/il-fantasma-in-psicoanalisi-un-dispositivo-che-articola-la-statica-e-la-dinamica-temporale-della-significazione/

De Luca Picione, R. (2019a). *La topologia e la psicoanalisi. Scritture (im-) possibili del buco e della soggettività*, "La Psicoanalisi. Studi internazionali del campo freudiano", nn. 63/64, 205–238.

De Luca Picione, R. (2019b). *Il nodo borromeo nell'insegnamento di Jacques Lacan. Un annodamento fecondo tra psicoanalisi e topologia*, "L'Inconscio. Rivista Italiana di Filosofia e Psicoanalisi", 7(1), 240–265.

De Luca Picione, R. (2020a). *L'impresa topologica di Jacques Lacan. La psicoanalisi tra superfici, confini, buchi e nodi*. Mimesis.

De Luca Picione, R. (2020b). La singolarità del «sinthomo» e la supplenza dei «Nomi-del-padre» nell'insegnamento di Jacques Lacan. *L'Inconscio. Rivista Italiana di Filosofia e Psicoanalisi, 9*, 60–88.

De Luca Picione, R. (2023a). *Il nodo e la Psiche. Topi e dinamiche del nodo nella costruzione psichica*. Paginaotto.
De Luca Picione, R. (2023b). Semiotiche e polisemie del taglio in Lacan. Psicoanalisi in divenire. In M. Milanaccio (Ed.), *Il taglio lacaniano* (pp. 29–41). Paginaotto.
De Luca Picione, R., & Freda, M. F. (2022). The otherness in the constitution of the psyche: Arguments from psychoanalysis and cultural psychology. In P. Fossa (Ed.), *New perspectives on inner speech* (pp. 23–40). Springer.
De Luca Picione, R., Fossa, P., Molina, M. E., & Lauro-Grotto, R. (2022). Looking at oneself in the mirror of the others. Modelisation and implications of a study on human re-flexivity starting from semiotics and psychoanalysis. *Rivista Di Psicologia Clinica, 1*, 85–121.
De Saussure, F. (1916). *Course in general linguistics*. Payot.
Di Ciaccia, A., & Recalcati, M. (2000). *Jacques Lacan*. Bruno Mondadori.
Freud, S. (1900). *The interpretation of dreams*. In *The standard edition of the complete psychological works of Sigmund Freud* (Vol. IV–V). The Hogarth Press.
Freud, S. (1911). Formulations on the two principles of mental functioning. In *The standard edition of the complete psychological works of Sigmund Freud* (Vol. XII). The Hogarth Press.
Freud, S. (1920). *Beyond the pleasure principle*. In *The standard edition of the complete psychological works of Sigmund Freud* (Vol. XVIII). The Hogarth Press.
Freud, S. (1921). Group psychology and the analysis of the ego. In *The standard edition of the complete psychological works of Sigmund Freud* (Vol. XVIII). The Hogarth Press.
Hjelmslev, L. (1963). *Prolegomena to a theory of language*. University of Wisconsin Press.
Lacan, J. (1966). *Ecrits*. Editions du Seuil.
Lacan, J. (1971). Lituraterre. *Littérature*, 3–10.
Lacan, J. (1973a). *Livre xi. Les quatre concepts fondamentaux de la psychanalyse (1964)*. Seuil.
Lacan, J. (1973b). *L'etourdit: Scilicet 4*. Seuil.
Lacan, J. (1975). *Livre xx. Encore (1972–73)*. Seuil.
Lacan, J. (1976–1977). *Livre xxiv. L'insu que sait de l'une-bévue s'aile à mourre* (pp. 12–15). Ornicar?.
Lacan, J. (1981). *Livre iii. Les psychoses (1955–56)*. Seuil.
Lacan, J. (1994). *Livre iv. La relation d'objet (1956–57)*. Seuil.
Lacan, J. (2005a). *Livre vii. L'éthique de la psychanalyse (1959–60)*. Seuil.
Lacan J. (2005b). *Livre xxiii. Le sinthome (1975–76)*. : Seuil.
Lévi-Strauss, C. (1949). *Les Structures élémentaires de la parenté*. Presses Universitaires de France.
Miller, J. A. (1999). Les six paradigmes de la jouissance. *La cause freudienne, 43*, 7–29.
Miller, J.-A. (2004–2005). *Pièces detachèes. La cause freudienne, nn.*, 60–66.
Miller, J.-A. (2021). *Capisaldi dell'insegnamento di Lacan. L'orientamento lacaniano*. Astrolabio Ubaldini.
Pagliardini, A. (2016). *Il sintomo di Lacan: dieci incontri con il reale*. Galaad Edizioni.
Palombi, F. (2019). *Jacques Lacan*. Carocci.
Peirce, C. S. (1935). *Collected papers of Charles Sanders Peirce*. Harvard University Press.
Recalcati, M. (2012). *Jacques Lacan. Desiderio, godimento e soggettivazione. Vol. 1*. Cortina.
Recalcati, M. (2016). *Jacques Lacan. La clinica psicoanalitica: struttura e soggetto. Vol. 2*. Cortina.
Tarizzo, D. (2003). *Introduzione a Lacan*. Laterza.
Zizek, S. (2015). The limits of the semiotic approach to psychoanalysis. In R. Feldstein & H. Sussman (Eds.), *Psychoanalysis and...* (pp. 89–110). Routledge.

Raffaele De Luca Picione, Ph.D., Psychoanalyst, Full Professor of Dynamic Psychology, Scientific Director of Research Laboratory on Liminality of the Psychic and Collective processes, Giustino Fortunato University (Benevento, Italy).

Chapter 3
Bela Lugosi's Haunted Mirror: Spontaneous Deployment of Lacanian Concepts in Rending Paranormal Experiences

Anna Madill

Lacanian theory can be opaque and difficult to understand. Moreover, while its concepts were developed in the context of therapeutic practice, it can be hard to see how Lacanian theory illuminates the experiences of everyday life. Hence, the first aim of this article is to provide an example of the spontaneous deployment of Lacanian concepts in the rendition of disturbing experiences by narrators naïve to psychoanalytic theory. In so doing, I seek to demonstrate how at least some of Lacan's key concepts can resonate strongly with mundane accounting practices expressing and explaining the 'felt sense' or 'lived reality' of trauma.

The second aim is to explore the applicability of Lacanian theory for understanding experiences of the paranormal. Stories help us communicate our experiences to others and, in turn, to make sense of the world through shared narrative conventions (Bakhtin, 1981). Stories of the paranormal have a stockpile of genres from which draw, such as gothic, horror, and true crime, alongside the usual devices of conversational interaction when spooky experiences are discussed with others (Wooffitt, 1992). Many paranormal tales are presented, and received, as fictional entertainment. Others, however, espouse to be true, although this, itself, is a not uncommon strategy to enhance the impact of creative works.

The text on which this analysis is based is a piece of television entertainment which tells a tale of the paranormal around an artefact with contested provenance (e.g. Biddle, 2019). As such, it sits in the liminal space between truth and fiction as, arguably, do the formations of the unconscious. Hence, in undertaking my analysis, I will take my cue from Bond (2013) who describes his use of Lacanian theory with regard to crime scene photographs as 'above all, not a search for some (lost) object—or some neatly asserted outcome—but an exercise in thinking psychoanalytically' (p. 174).

A. Madill (✉)
School of Psychology, University of Leeds, Leeds, UK
e-mail: a.l.madill@leeds.ac.uk

S. H. Klempe, A. Madill (eds.), *French Psychoanalysis Revisited*, Annals of Theoretical Psychology 20, https://doi.org/10.1007/978-3-031-68534-7_3

Material

The material is taken from a six-episode television mini-series called *Deadly Possessions* first aired on 2 April 2016 on the *Travel Channel*. This is an off-shoot of the popular networked series *Ghost Adventures*. In *Deadly Possessions* the host and producer—Zak Bagans—interviews members of the public who are offering him 'haunted' or 'cursed' artefacts for his museum, *The Haunted Museum*, in Las Vegas. Hence, the mini-series functions both as entertainment and as an advert for the museum.

The material is a 27-minute clip representing the first half of episode 4. It was selected because the content appears to invoke strongly the Lacanian *objet petit a*, the concept often considered Lacan's most significant contribution to psychoanalysis (Kirshner, 2005). As a piece of programming, the material as aired is edited and is artificial to the extent that the guests are tasked with presenting an interesting story about their artefact and the host with creating engaging content in line with the conceit of the series. Moreover, the show creates tension through the setting of the museum; muted lighting; eerie soundscape; inserting old photographs and film clips, where relevant; and using short video recreations dramatizing aspects of the narrated story. Where necessary for the analysis, stills from the sequence are included within the conditions of Fair Use.

Synopsis

In the selected material, Cindy Lee relates a story about the murder of her Uncle Bob, Frank Roberts Saletri. She tells us that her uncle worked with the actor Bela Lugosi and lived in his old house. In 1982 her uncle was murdered in the bedroom of this house: tortured with a screwdriver and then shot in the head. The murder has never been solved. Cindy also tells us that the mirror from this bedroom now belongs to her family. Although not entirely clear, the mirror seems to have been taken by Cindy's older daughter when she left home but then returned to Cindy's house and placed in her spare bedroom. Cindy and her younger daughter, Irene, recount aspects of the older daughter's experience with the mirror while she was living alone. This involved seeing a 'dark entity' in the mirror, hands reaching out of the mirror, and teeth biting her neck while she curled her hair in front of it. Traumatized, she returned to her mother's house. Irene also tells us about a bad dream she had while sleeping in the spare room not realizing the mirror was in the corner. She dreamed of being attacked and awoke with scratches on her body. Cindy wants to leave the mirror behind, and Zak agrees to give it a 'good home' in his Haunted Museum.

Throughout, Zak provides relevant paranormal lore and posits paranormal explanations for the disturbing experiences surrounding the mirror. Zak then recruits three of his colleagues in a scrying experiment to stare into the mirror in the isolation room of the museum. They have various strange experiences including seeing a mysterious light in the mirror. In the final sequence, Zak documents a flood in the museum basement the morning after the scrying experiment and connects this mishap to his new ownership of the mirror.

Method

The material was transcribed verbatim with descriptions added where necessary to understand the text, such as where or at whom Zak is looking, and indication of visuals, particularly vis-à-vis the mirror (see *supplementary material*). A diagram was also created of the personages mentioned, relationships between them, relationship to the mirror, and the location in which the mirror is relevant to them. The diagram helped to identify associations between elements of the story and the filmed sequence but also people made pertinent by their absence. The transcript was then read and reread carefully while making notes on resonances with key concepts in Lacanian theory.

As in psychoanalytic practice, the narrative was approached from the position of 'listening' for the way in which unconscious desire organizes speech despite, even *in spite*, of the conscious intension of the speaker. This meant following associations made in the narrative, identifying assumptions that must be made for the narrative to work, and 'hearing' where 'it' speaks the truth of desire through reading for literal meaning which goes against the grain of probable intent. In this way an interpretation is offered of the points of contact between the story told and Lacanian theory. These are argued to mark the phenomena of trauma which are, by definition, almost impossible to articulate and so find expression in layered and oblique registers or repertoires of meaning. My approach accepts the necessity of narrating experiences of the paranormal via genre conventions, exploiting even to a high degree of theatricality the visual medium of popular television programming. With regard to the latter, some analysis is undertaken with regard to impacts of the camera work. However, issues of truth and fiction are conceptualized analytically as the single side of a Mobius strip as seen from different perspectives or at two different points in time, in which *accounting* for and *creating* reality are inextricably linked.

Analysis

The analysis draws predominantly on central concepts of Lacanian theory. The mirror stage and the *objet a* are related in that the *objet petit a* was expounded through Lacan's exploration of the implications of the mirror stage (Proto, 2013). The analysis also draws on Freud's (1918) notion of the primal scene as developed by Lacan (1953 [1979]) and Freud's (1919) exploration of the uncanny which has theoretical coincidences with Lacan's mirror stage, particularly with regard to the specular or doubled other, the fragmented body, and the alter ego (Twohig, 2003). Reference is made throughout to the three orders posited by Lacan in which phenomena are registered. Simply put: the Imaginary is the realm of images, particularly important being the image of the body; the Symbolic is the realm of the signifier and of meaning; and the Real is what cannot be incorporated into the Imaginary or Symbolic however, rather than preceding these two orders, is constituted alongside them and marks their edge. Finally, the analysis is considered in relation to the *fundamental fantasy* as structured differentially according to psychological structure vis-à-vis the *objet a* and the *Other*.

The Mirror Stage

The central artefact of the text under scrutiny is a mirror inherited through a family line and relevant in the story to three of its generations: from uncle, to niece, to the niece's daughters. The mirror is important in Lacanian theory both as a physical surface and as a metaphor of the way in which human subjectivity develops in a process of being reflected back by others. Specifically, the mirror stage is a posited juncture during which the child between the ages of 6 and 18 months develops a sense of having an integrated body and, eventually, an ego (Lacan, 2006 [1949]). However, this 'little other', or *petit autre*, in the mirror is external and whole while the child experiences him- or herself as a disparate cacophony of feelings, sensations, and uncoordinated body parts. In most the propitious scenario, the first *Other*, usually the mother, joins the child in jubilation over recognition of its image and confirms it to be the child's own, and the child's independent existence and positive value are confirmed consistently in the reactions of significant others. In this way, if fortunate, the child establishes a strong sense of psychological and physical integrity and worthiness of love. However, this sense of integrity constituting the ego is installed from the outside and may remain fragile. In the text under consideration, we see this sense of integration come under pressure.

Cindy tells us about the traumatic origin of the Bela Lugosi mirror in the family story within the context of the torture and murder of her Uncle Bob: 'somebody took a screwdriver to his knees and elbows. And they shot him and then they tried to dig out the bullet with a screwdriver' (lines 45–47). The mirror, which we are told was in the room at the time, is therefore associated with a reflection of bodily rupture and death. In fact, for both Cindy's daughters, the mirror catalyses experiences of a compromised body: of being bitten (line 119) and of being scratched (line 236) but also of fragmented body parts including hands (line 156) and a face (line 239).

Uncle Bob's death is also traumatic in being sexualized. The screwdriver and bullet are penetrating phallic objects, he was killed in his bedroom, and the murderer indulged himself there sadistically. Importantly, Cindy adds that it 'wasn't a forced entry' (line 58), with the, most likely unintentional, connotation that the meeting had been anticipated by her uncle as a consensual sexual liaison. Moreover, she states, with hearable sexual innuendo, 'I think it was a close friend and whatever else went on- who knows' (lines 58–59). The sexual aspects of the mirror's traumatic history are played out also in the disturbing experiences of Cindy's daughters. They too are attacked sadistically in its presence, phantasmagorically while Cindy's older daughter attends her feminine toilette (lines 113–114) and in a dream while Irene sleeps in her bed (line 235–237).

These disturbing experiences do not occur with any mirror. They occur with a mirror associated strongly with a traumatic event in the family history: what might be conceptualized psychoanalytically as a family myth constituted around a primal scene.

The Primal Scene

Freud (1918) first conceptualized the primal scene as a repressed early memory, fantasy, or reconstruction of having witnessed parental coitus misunderstood as an act of violence. Later, Freud (1937) reformulated his understanding of the primal scene as a traumatic, usually sexually arousing event, in the life history of the individual or, importantly here, of their forebears. Essentially, the primal scene provides the unconscious co-ordinates for our constitution as sexed beings around the primacy of the father's relationship with the mother. The primal scene can be interpolated into a family myth which is played out fatalistically in a cycle of repetition compulsion. Lacan (1953 [1979]) identified this as the 'neurotic's individual myth', exploring its features through re-examining Freud's case of the Rat Man. In this, Lacan argued that family stories about his father's shameful gambling debt and marriage for money replayed in the Rat Man's immobilization constellated by a situation in which a repayment scenario occurred alongside the presence in his life of a rich woman-poor woman binary (Hewitson, 2013).

Lacan makes an important distinction between the Imaginary father, the Symbolic father, and the father-in-the-Real. The Imaginary father is the offspring's image of the actual man imbued with fantasies about his qualities. The Symbolic, or Oedipal, father is the function he plays situating his children in the social order as sexed beings separate from their mother. The role of Symbolic father need not be conducted by the biological progenitor, or indeed by a man, and can be fulfilled, for example, by an organization such as a school. Where the castrating symbolic capacity of the father is weak or absent, the child is particularly vulnerable to experiencing in some form the obscene primal father-in-the-Real (Lacan, 2003 [1938]). This is the father who features in the origin myth of culture posited by Freud (1913): the father of the primal horde not subject to the law but who assumes sole sexual access to all the women and, as a result, is murdered and eaten by the excluded 'band of brothers'. In this, Freud provides an explanation in the form of a myth for socialization which places a limit on *jouissance* and associated incest taboo.

The story of the murder of Cindy's uncle may function as a family myth involving a particularly archaic primal scene through echoing in striking ways the myth of the primal horde. First, Cindy says 'It's speculated like a mob hit' (line 35) with the implication of being a ritualized and fatal punishment on one man by a group of men. Second, cannibalistic resonances appear via association with the figure of the vampire—one of Lugosi's famed roles—in that 'Cindy Lee's uncle was killed inside Bela Lugosi's old house' (lines 50–51). Third, sexual elements are involved, as discussed above, and, again, via the association with the vampire which Swales and Owens (2020) argue portrays repressed sexual *jouissance*. Hence, the story of the murder of Cindy's uncle can be understood as a particularly horrific and archaic family primal scene involving the murder of the obscene father-in-the-Real.

At this point it is useful to consider a diagram of the personages mentioned in the narrative to help identify important relationships and absences (Diagram 3.1).

The text under consideration is not only a narrative of the paranormal; it draws also on the genre of true crime given that Saletri's murder is documented in numerous places (e.g. McMillan, 1986). In this respect, it is interesting that the story itself, like many 'true crimes', is constructed around two key absences or holes: (i) the victim, i.e. Uncle Bob, in that he has been murdered or 'taken out', and (ii) the killer, in that he has never been identified or, hence, named.

There are additional absences of psychoanalytic import. Logically, the father of Cindy's daughters is missing from the narrative, as are Cindy's own parents who are her genealogical connection to Uncle Bob. Moreover, Cindy's older daughter is missing because, we are told, she is too traumatized to be part of the show, and she is never named. The latter is significant in Lacanian terms because the *name-of-the-father*, or *paternal metaphor/function*, is a mode through which the Symbolic cuts the dyadic relationship between mother and child. This occurs by making both beholden to a third term or '(sur)name' representing socially inscribed obligations and position. This points to a fragility in the family Symbolic through absences along the paternal line and, hence, in the paternal function. As explained above, this can create a vulnerability to experiencing the obscene father-in-the-Real, here conflated with a number of constellated associations (as outlined later), including Uncle Bob's murderer who, in an overdetermined manner, is unassimilable to the Symbolic through also remaining unnamed (Diagram 3.2).

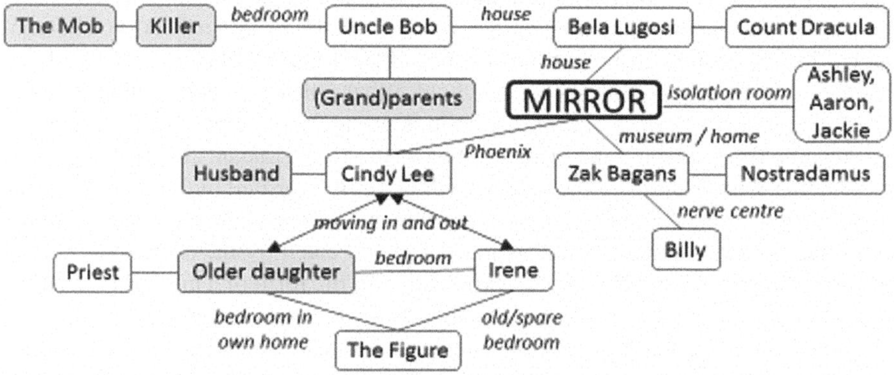

Diagram 3.1 Personages, the relationships between them, their relationship to the mirror, and the location in which the mirror is relevant to them (shaded indicates pertinent absence)

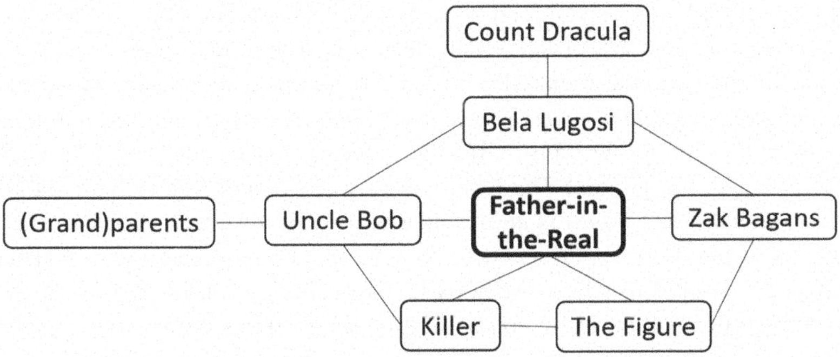

Diagram 3.2 Constellated associations around the father-in-the-Real centred on the mirror

As an artefact connected directly to Uncle Bob's murder, the mirror appears to condense for the family a sadistic, sexually charged, primal scene around a vicious and unassimilable uncle/killer constellation, extending metonymically to other elements. This resonance of death is magnified also in the physicality of the mirror in that it is the shape and size of an archetypal tombstone. And the mirror is brought to Zak because it is having a disturbing effect, which includes the frightening image it sometimes reflects. For example, we are told that Cindy's older daughter 'could see like a dark entity' (lines 115–116) or alien figure in the mirror which causes her anguish. In fact, a central theme organizing the text is the potential of the mirror to manifest what is dreadful and should not be there, and Lacan's concept of the *objet a* provides a way of understanding what might be in play.

The Objet a

The *objet a* is Lacan's development of Freud's and Klein's concept of the 'lost object'. In Lacanian theory, in order for the child to be situated securely in the Symbolic, they must be subjected to 'castration' and cut away from symbiosis with the mother. Castration is experienced unconsciously as losing parts of one's own body, for example, the mother's breast theorized to be experienced by the infant as completing their mouth. In Seminar X on 'Anxiety', Lacan (2014 [1962–1963]) builds on Freud's classical notion of the oral, anal, and phallic objects/stages by adding two more, i.e. the *gaze* and the *voice*, the latter associated with the super-ego. Designating voice the 'deepest phase' (*ibid.*, p. 295), Lacan places the sequence in an arc representing the idea of 'repetition with a difference' pivoting at the phallic object, in which the *gaze* contains always a regressive movement to the anal object and the *voice* to the oral object. For example, Harari (2001) provides a relevant illustration for the oral-voice/super-ego axis reminding us that '(t)he super-ego detected by Melanie Klein [...] is ruled by the devouring tension marked, for example, by the vampirism of the Desire of the Mother' (p. 196).

Although the phallus is retained as a special form of the *objet a*, in his subsequent seminar Lacan (1978 [1964]) considers only four main modes of loss. Each is highly libidinalized and associated with a drive, an erogenous zone, a tangible *part object*, and an intangible *objet a* (Vanheule, 2014): (i) oral drive, mouth, breast, and 'taking in nothing'/*The Nothing*; (ii) anal drive, anus, faeces, and *The Gift*; (iii) scopic drive, eye, image, and *The Gaze*; and (iv) invocatory drive, ear, sound, and *The Voice*. Hence, the *objet a* is an absence within an unconscious constellation of *part objects* of the body experienced as detachable and associated with its rims, i.e. with entry and exit points where the body is permeable and eroticized. In this regard, it is not insignificant that, in his exposition of the mirror's paranormal power, Zak refers to it as a rim between two spaces, i.e. as a 'portal' (lines 97, 291, 320, and 361) and as a 'doorway' (line 345). The unconscious experience of loss creates desire for the return of the *objet a*, and, all going well, the young person enters the Symbolic motivated to re-find them in socially acceptable ways. However, a central feature of the *objet a* which makes it extremely paradoxical is that, while exerting a profound effect through causing desire, it never existed and never will exist in tangible form.

The *objet a* can be experienced in each of the three orders and, because it is properly a lost object, its appearance is signalled by anxiety. In the Imaginary, the *objet a* is the *petit autre* in the form of the uncastrated double, the rival who is feared to be the actual object of the desire of the mother. Indeed, in the Imaginary, the *objet a* is ambiguously close and when it appears to manifest is experienced as persecutory. In the Symbolic, the *objet a* is 'the agalama, the precious, "hidden", "object" that the *Other* possesses and that the subject seeks out for pleasure and plentitude' (Proto, 2013, p. 4). In the Symbolic, the *objet a* is always too far away and out of reach. In the Real, the *objet a* is unassimilable and is experienced as *surplus jouissance*: enjoyment to the point of suffering. Paradoxically, this is because the Real *objet a* is always too close and cannot be 'shaken off''.

A fracture line in the Symbolic will be magnified in the Imaginary because, by definition, 'the dyadic relationship between subject and mirror excludes the paternal metaphor' (Proto, 2013, p. 9). And, as we have seen, Cindy's daughters are subjected to terrifying images manifested in association with the Bela Lugosi mirror. It is interesting to consider how, in contrast, Zak, who has no personal history with the mirror, actively pursues manifestations in it with curiosity. Moreover, in its various manifestations as *objet a*, Bela Lugosi's mirror is construed as a desiring object: as a thing that wants to consume (line 99) and is angry (line 23 and 314). In this way, the mirror provokes fear in the Lacanian terms of encapsulating the 'desire of the (m)*Other*' which is always impenetrable and potentially deadly. Experienced as having its own volition, the mirror also evokes aspect of the uncanny identified by Freud in terms of whether a seemingly ordinary object may not indeed be animate.

In his study of the uncanny, Freud (1919) examines the complex range of meanings of the German words *heimlich* and *unheimlich*. The most relevant to the current analysis are that the former can mean belonging to the house, domestic, and familiar and the latter deceitful, malicious, and revealing what is concealed, even to oneself. Freud demonstrates that these apparent antonyms have overlapping meaning around the idea of the *estranged familiar*. This ambiguity is at play in the text and, in important respects, involves the mirror as an inherited object in circulation through Cindy Lee's family. In literal terms, the mirror is *heimlich*: it is of the *house*. As Cindy tells us: 'The mirror used to be in Bela Lugosi's *house* [...] My uncle lived in there' (lines 26–28). As an inherited artefact, it is also possible to describe the mirror as belonging to the *house* of Lee. This clearly evokes the idea of the mirror being not only *familiar* but *familial*. The relationship between ego and counterpart in the mirror is a narcissistic one which is, here, inflected by a family myth involving a particularly horrific primal scene. We therefore arrive at the idea of the mirror as *unheimlich*, the estranged familiar. Again, it is useful to contrast this with Zak's attempted *familiarity* with the mirror promising to 'give it a good home' (lines 283–284), his use of the word 'home' implying domestication. We now explore the uncanny Bela Lugosi mirror in relation to the different modes of *objet a* from key points of view in the text (Table 3.1).

The Oral Object The mirror is an oral object for Cindy's eldest daughter and, arguably, the *objet a* in its most archaic form. She experiences bites to her neck as she combs her hair in the mirror. Hence, there is a metonymic association from the mirror, to Uncle Bob, to Bela Lugosi, to Count Dracula (Diagram 3.2). Through their propensity to bite and suck out the life blood, vampires encapsulate the *sadistic* oral object associated with sexuality and death. Moreover, the literary trope that a vampire has no reflection ratifies it as an *objet a* of no concrete substance. However, as argued throughout, the chain of associations extends also to the father-in-the-Real (Diagram 3.2). In this regard, it might be suggested that Cindy's eldest daughter experiences the mirror as an oral *objet a* in the Real and, hence, as a certain mode of hallucination:

> The subject calls upon the Father to guarantee the law that situates both the subject and his desire in the Other, but encounters only a void. The foreclosure of the Name-of-the-Father gives rise to the fantasmatic presence (present in the Real) of a malevolent authority, suspected of having intrusive or criminal intentions, desiring to commit sexual abuse or homicide. Unlike a repressed signifier, a foreclosed signifier is not absorbed into the unconscious and therefore does not reappear in the psyche in the form of a neurotic symptom. It returns, rather, in the real, usually in the form of a hallucination. (No Subject—Encyclopedia of Psychoanalysis, paras 7–10)

Zak leverages also the oral potential of the mirror to build his exposition of its paranormal powers. Specifically, he speculates about the ability of the mirror to

Table 3.1 The mirror as objet a from key points of view

Mode	Cindy	Irene	Eldest daughter	Zak	Aaron	Ashley	Audience
Oral			Real	Imaginary			
Anal	Real			Symbolic			
Gaze		Imaginary	Imaginary	Imaginary, Real	Imaginary, Real	Imaginary	Real
Voice				Imaginary	Imaginary		

'consume' aspects of what is reflected in it: 'did that mirror capture that killer's energy- that killer's soul? [flash of a mirror in theatrical re-enactment] Possibly your uncle?' (lines 78–80), and he asks of it, 'What is inside of you?' (line 355). In this, Zak's orientation towards the mirror suggest that he experiences it as an oral *objet a* in the Imaginary: that is, as encapsulating an image of the rival who is ambiguously close and persecutory.

The Anal Object The mirror is an *anal object* for the mother, Cindy. It is an unwanted gift representing in physical form trauma inherited through the paternal line, and she states: 'This item has caused my family so much anguish that I no longer feel safe with it' (lines 12–13). Metaphorically, the mirror represents Cindy's murdered uncle and, metonymically, his killer, but also Cindy's parents who are absent from her narrative but through whom the mirror must have come into her possession (Diagram 3.2). Understandably, she wants to get rid of this *anal object* and articulates perfectly the psychological dilemma presented: 'I can't sell it. I can't give it. But if it kinda gets left behind' (lines 272–273). Hence, she conveys the felt sense of the mirror as an *anal object* in the Real, stuck to her in way that cannot be passed on to someone else in a deliberate act. While the killer remains unidentified, she can regain a proper distance from the unassimilable Real of the family trauma only through a re-enactment of Symbolic castration in which the object is 'lost'.

The intangible *objet a* of the anal drive is the *gift*, and, hence, the mirror is an *anal object* also for Zak in that he is willing to receive it for his museum collection. In fact, he says of the mirror: 'this may be my favourite possession to date' (lines 352–353), and 'I believe this mirror to be the most dangerous possession that I own' (lines 486–487). So, for Zak, the mirror is an *anal objet a* in the Symbolic: that is, a powerful, alluring, and charismatic item that will belong to him.

It is interesting to consider the double meaning of the word 'possession'. Proto (2013) states that 'in the *Real* the *objet a* is "possessed" by the subject' (p. 8). This possession, however, is experienced in a traumatic way as one of being unable to shake off a foreign body—the *surplus jouissance* of a piece of shit—and, hence, is also of being *possessed by* this object. This is conveyed by Cindy in her allusion to the mirror as an unwanted gift/inheritance that cannot be given away. Moreover, although Zak refers to the mirror as a 'favourite' possession, he also notes it to be 'the most dangerous', and the polluting aspects of this *anal object* manifest in the dirty, possibly electrified, water of the flooded museum basement he attributes to it: 'All this water. You don't want to touch that' (lines 481–482). However, for Zak, this helps convey to the audience the high status of the object now in his haunted museum.

The Object Gaze Of all the modes of the *objet a*, the *object gaze* of the scopic drive is the most prominent in the material analysed.

Cindy's older daughter seems troubled by the *object gaze* in the Imaginary. In the Imaginary, the *objet a* is experienced as the persecutory *petit autre* of the mirror image, and we are told Cindy's older daughter says a 'figure would come through the mirror [re-enactment with flash of mirror] [...] and attack her' (lines 120–123). As an *objet a*, this figure is never fully discernable and manifests predominantly as *part objects*: 'described the hand [...] [re-enactment with flash of mirror] almost there reaching' (lines 155–158). Moreover, Cindy reports how her older daughter continued to be persecuted by the *object gaze* in the Imaginary, catching something out of the corner of the eye, 'second-guessing things [re-enactment with flash of mirror] where you think you see things' (lines 197–198). Cindy's description of her nameless daughter's experience may provide examples of how, *in extremis*, 'the father's signifier (i.e. the Law, the Oedipus complex, the Symbolic Order etc.) only survives as an *imago* of the father' (Proto, 2013, p. 9) and not a properly installed *name*-of-the-father.

Irene, too, experiences the *objet gaze* in the Imaginary. While sleeping, unbeknownst in a room with the Bela Lugosi mirror, Irene tell us she had an 'awful dream of something attacking me- scratching me- holding me down' (lines 236–237). Like her older sister's experience, Irene's dream is of aggressive *part objects*: 'I just remember this vision of hands. This very dark face' (line 239). The attack manifests also in the Imaginary with Irene's discovery of scratches on her body: 'Even the middle of my back where I was not able to reach' (lines 242–243) and, presumably, cannot directly see. But Irene has been seen by the *objet gaze*. In fact, one might say it has had her 'in its sights'. However, despite these disturbing experiences, Irene keeps a foothold in the Symbolic, describing herself as 'more scientific' (line 253) and maintains a containing distance from the *objet a* though allowing it to remain a puzzle to rationality: 'it just didn't add up' (line 260). Even so, both Cindy's daughters appear to be struggling to find a stable and independent space in the Symbolic, moving in and out of their mother's house, intermittently sharing a bedroom or sleeping in the spare room.

The *object gaze* in the Imaginary register is also utilized during the show with Zak filmed looking into the mirror seeking out an anomalous human figure or *petit autre*: 'I just look in here [cut to Zak on viewer's far left looking into the camera / mirror; Zak is now speaking in the visuals] trying to see if somebody will appear behind me' (lines 332–334).

Chabot (2019) refers to contemporary burgeoning of paranormal investigation media as an epistephilic drive in the register of seeing, specifically 'a desire to visualize the imperceptible' (p. 1), in other words, a desire to *know* through the desire to *see*, in a terrain where, typically, it may be difficult to believe one's eyes. As Black (2014) states, it is in such circumstances that '(t)he subject is itself caught up, manipulated and captured, by the field of vision' (p. 362–3). Our short extract from *Deadly Possessions* demonstrates the host and his colleagues leveraging the 'epistephilic drive in the register of seeing', 'capturing' the audience in the 'field of vision' in terms of both *accounting* for and *creating* the reality presented in the show.

In terms of *accounting* for the phenomena described by Cindy and Irene, Zak connects the mirror with the *object gaze* in the register of the Real. Early on Zak introduces the idea of the mirror that watches, stating in a voiceover: 'Cindy Lee's uncle was killed inside Bela Lugosi's old house [flash of a mirror in theatrical re-enactment] with the mirror watching' (lines 50–52). This evokes Lacan's story of the floating sardine can in which he explicates a moment of realization with regard to the *object gaze*. While his companion pronounces that 'The can doesn't see you',

Lacan disagrees: 'the can was looking at me, all the same. It was looking at me at the level of the point of light, the point at which everything that looks at me is situated' (Lacan in Jay, 1993, p. 365). It is this *gaze* that Zak imputes to the watching mirror, specifically the *Real gaze* as the point from which one is seen but from exactly where one can never discern.

On the other hand, the mirror as a haunted object capable of 'looking back' is *created* during the *content* of the show in a scrying experiment (lines 65, 67, 95, and 413): an occult technique for making the 'un-seeable' visible in a reflective surface. Zak recruits three colleagues—Aaron, Ashley and Jackie—to sit one-by-one in the isolation room explaining that 'I want you to stare into this mirror and I want you to look at yourself in this mirror until I call you up' (lines 391–392). The image in the mirror has a disturbing effect, and the *object gaze* manifests in the Imaginary for both Aaron and Ashley. Ashley says, 'I almost feel like I'm looking at somebody else' (line 411), and, while Aaron identifies with his image in the mirror, it is of an alter-ego compromised by age: 'I just found myself old-really old' (line 426). Moreover, they both glimpse a mysterious light in the mirror for which there is no objective source. At this point, Aaron experiences also a presence: 'then all of a sudden I saw this light like someone came in' (line 451), and he demands of it 'Come out and show yourself' (line 422). Hence, characteristic of the appearance of the Real *object gaze*, Aaron becomes aware of himself as conspicuously visible by the uncanny *Other* and from a vantage point he cannot perceive: 'You saw me. Let me see you' (line 431).

The Bela Lugosi mirror as a haunted object is *created* vis-à-vis the *object gaze*, not only in the *content* of the show but in the production of an uncanny effect via its *form*.

First, the whole sequence is filmed with an oval of light centre screen (Images 3.1, 3.2, 3.3, 3.4, and 3.5). This creates an atmosphere of mystery through obscuring the image but, importantly, produces an effect of the object *gaze* through creating a desire to see the focal point more clearly. Specifically, the oval of light suggests an ever-present eye, and flashing images of eyes and the oval top of the mirror as an eye-like pattern are interspersed throughout the piece. This oval part-image of the mirror is like a cataracted eye with strange alien irises in red vertical stripes (Image 3.1). And the blind eye of an unfathomable presence is a paradigmatic manifestation of the Real *gaze*. Hence, through this *form* of filming and editing, the viewer, too, is caught in the dangerous ambiance of the mirror.

Second, the sequence presents us throughout with images of doubles echoing the *objet a* in the Imaginary as the *petit autre* in the uncanny form of the uncastrated double. Hence, Cindy and Irene are filmed next to the mirror such that their reflection can be seen disconcertingly askew (e.g., Image 3.2). Moreover, in the scrying experiment, Aaron and his reflection are shown in the same shot (Image 3.3), Aaron and Jackie are edited as if staring into the mirror side by side, and multiple images of Aaron appear on monitors.

Third, at points, Zak is himself installed as the *object gaze*, and a mutually supporting uncanny dialectic is played out between Zak and the mirror. Zak's instantiation as *object gaze* in the Imaginary can be discerned, while his colleagues are in the

Image 3.1 Image of the top curve of the mirror used in clips throughout (11 min 05 s)

Image 3.2 Askew doubling of Irene in the mirror (10 min 00 s)

isolation chamber. Zak tells us that he will be 'in nerve centre with Billy where I can monitor them closely' (lines 404–405). In this way, Zak is able to see his colleagues on the monitors while being himself, but as another *petit autre*, unavailable to their sight. However, importantly in terms of *form*, Zak speaks directly to camera. Many television programmes involve direct address to the viewer, and this is utilized to some extent in *Deadly Possessions*. However, arguably, this specific instance may create an effect of the *object gaze* in the Real for the audience, i.e. of being seen

Image 3.3 Direct doubling of Aaron in the mirror (23 min 33 s)

Image 3.4 Zak looking into the camera lens/mirror (18 mins 07 s)

from an impossible specular place inside the screen. That is, first, Zak is at the same time installed as *object gaze* vis-à-vis his colleagues, and, second, it is the only time in the sequence as a whole that he speaks to camera.

This effect is magnified in a short sequence towards the end in which Zak contemplates the mirror on his own (lines 317–363). He is filmed looking searchingly almost directly into the camera, giving the impression of scanning the mirror's reflective surface. However, in the moments Zak looks into the camera, the Real

Image 3.5 Zak walks away in/from the mirror (18 min 45 s)

objet gaze is installed for the viewer disconcertingly in two seeming opposing places at once. First, Zak is the *gaze* as he stares blindly out at the viewer and seemingly into the mirror (Image 3.4). That is, he transforms the viewers' safe position as 'watcher' to that in which their own presence is being searched out visually from inside the television. Second, the viewer is also installed as the Real *gaze* as they watch Zak seeming from the impossible specular place within the mirror that Zak cannot see.

The Object Voice Interestingly, it is only after Zak has taken possession of the mirror that the *object voice* appears in the narrative. Miller (2007) clarifies that '(t)he voice is everything in the signifier that does not partake in the effect of signification' (p. 141). Hence, the *voice* manifests while Aaron is in the isolation room and Zak finds it hard to understand some of what he says, importantly, about the uncanny mirror: 'What did he say?' (line 425). Another feature of the *voice* is that it is assigned to the *Other* and, like all forms of the *objet a*, has a libidinal charge. This occurs for Aaron when he hears noises in the isolation room and takes them as a sign of presence associated with the mirror: 'There's a weird feeling in here guys. I heard something right here just like scuffle' (lines 441–442).

The *voice* also features in Zak's filming of the basement flood in that he draws attention to noises for which he cannot account and attributes the scenario to the mirror being in his possession: 'Oh gosh. *Bleep.* [unexplained noises] Holy *bleep*. Just heard sounds coming from right here. [unexplained noises] Hear that? [unexplained noises] Loud noises coming from in here. [unexplained noises] Just capturing it' (lines 478–481). In both these instances, the *object voice* appears to manifest in the Imaginary. In the first example, this can be surmised because Zak and Aaron are contemporaries who exhibit, at times, some friendly tension, and, in both, objectively audible sounds create a 'fantastic image' of the mirror's persecutory power. Finally, the *voice* can also manifest in situations where vocalization is detached from the body from which it belongs (Zizek, 2012), such as in Zak's voiceovers, during which he is instantiated into the position of *objet a*.

The Fundamental Fantasy

In Lacanian terms the subject and object must be separated, yet remain in relationship, for the individual to sustain the *fundamental fantasy* framing their reality. Hence, when the object appears, this marks a terrifying failure of the *fantasy* (Troubé, 2015). The *fundamental fantasy* is unconscious and underlies the structure of the individual as obsessional neurotic, hysterical neurotic, or perverse. All are variants of the, typically masculine, obsessional neurotic's *fantasy* captured in the matheme $<>a. This can be read as the subject of the unconscious in relationship with the *objet a*, the *fantasy* being to make this impossible relationship direct, complete, and fully satisfying. As the basic *fantasy*, $<>a has been a central theme of this analysis. It is, however, the other types of *fundamental fantasy* that are illustrated more specifically in the examined text as differential structural positions taken towards the *objet petit a* and the 'big' *Other* representing Symbolic authority. To be clear, the following is not a commentary on the people in the show but is an analysis of the structural position they appear to inhabit within the sequence as aired.

Hysteric Within the text, Cindy and Irene illustrate the typically feminine hysterical neurotic position. The *fantasy* of the hysteric is represented by the matheme a<>Ⱥ which can be read as the hysteric as object in relationship with the *Other* as barred or structurally incomplete. That is, as Bryant (2013) explains: 'the hysteric wants to be the solution to the master's lack or incompleteness. Therefore [s]he uses [her/]his fantasy as way of maneuvering the Other to reveal a lack of incompleteness in the Other so that [s]he might come to fill that lack' (para 13). Accordingly, it is Cindy and Irene who offer up to Zak the *objet a* he is understood to desire and, hence, to lack. Cindy and Irene also demonstrate a relationship with the *Other* as 'master' through being able to situate the mirror in the Symbolic and provide it meaning by way of a family myth. Finally, the neurotic mechanism of repression is suggested by Cindy's inability to do more than allude to the sexual elements of the family myth, while she is able to describe its violence, and in Irene's typically hysterical conversion symptoms whereby unconscious conflicts are inscribed on the Imaginary of the body.

Perverse The sequence itself includes elements of the typically masculine perverse position. Central to the perverse position is the instantiation of a fetish object which provides *jouissance* but through covering over the structural absence of the *objet a*. Indeed, arguably, the series *Deadly Possessions* is focused on such fetish objects and, as is typical of the perverse mode of operation, 'creates a scenario in which *all* *is not as it seems*' (Bond, 2013, p. 86). Moreover, the actual sequence under analysis has a perverse structure in which the object is first idealized and subsequently portrayed as polluting.

The perverse *fantasy* is represented by the matheme a<>$ which can be read as the perverse person as object in relationship with the subject of the unconscious. Specifically, the perverse person acts as the object instrument of the *Other*'s *jouissance*, effectively seeking to provide an experience of the *objet a* as 'too much'. The analysis has indicated ways in which Zak is instantiated in the text at points as *objet a* in the form of the *gaze* and the *voice*, and, as host, he does have the role of acting on behalf of the enjoyment of the audience. Moreover, Zak is the only person presented as taking a masterful position vis-à-vis the mirror: he stands to look into it, touches it while looking, and walks away from it (lines 317–363). Importantly, this sequence ambiguates in a highly uncanny way the position from which Zak is being filmed walking away (Image 3.5). Is Zak being filmed: merely from behind the mirror? from within the mirror with the audience instantiated as Real *gaze*? from behind in the mirror as mere reflection? or as existing 'in' the mirror only as the *gaze* of the father-in-the-Real? (Diagram 3.2).

Psychotic Unlike people of neurotic or perverse structure, those with psychotic structure have no *fundamental fantasy* and are stuck in primary development because 'the *Other* doesn't answer, or failed to answer sufficiently' (Verhaeghe, 2004, p. 351). Within the text Cindy's older daughter illustrates the psychotic position, indeed, as mentioned by her mother: 'She got where she was second-guessing things [re-enactment with flash of mirror] where you think you see things and are you psychotic or is that real?' (lines 197–199). According to Lacan, people of any structure can experience paranoia and hallucinations. However, 'in psychosis elements from the unconscious are not experienced as coming from within – as in neurosis, where symptoms express warded-off truths – but as strange messages that come from without […] themes of the subject's existence do not enter into the law of the Symbolic, but emerge in the Real as puzzling and overwhelming problems that seize the subject from the outside' (Vanheule, 2014, p. 71). In this way, unlike Cindy and Irene, Cindy's older daughter is mute with regard to storytelling about the mirror, and we are told that she has experienced the disturbance directly in her waking life unmediated by the buffer of a functioning Symbolic family myth.

Reflections

The first aim of this article was to provide an example of the spontaneous deployment of Lacanian theory by naïve narrators in their rendition of some disturbing experiences. It is argued, and hopefully has been demonstrated, that phenomena related to Lacan's mirror stage and to his theory of the *objet a*, amongst others, are paralleled in the mundane sense-making practices in the examined text which attempts to express and explain the 'felt sense' or 'lived reality' of trauma. The mirror as *objet a* must be lost: cut from the Imaginary body of the family. Only then, whilst the killer remains unnamed, can Cindy and her daughters attempt to normalize the family Symbolic disrupted by the horrific murder of Uncle Bob constituting the archaic primal scene of the family myth.

The second aim was to explore the applicability of Lacanian theory for understanding experiences of the paranormal. Here it is useful to reflect on Lacan's (2007 [1959–1960]) aphorism 'every truth has the structure of fiction': that reality itself is fantasmatic, its co-ordinates ordained by the *fundamental fantasy*, or structural lack of a *fundamental fantasy*. Reality, which when put under pressure through trauma, can become distorted by intrusions of the Real. The analysis presented has made intense use of this stance. That is, texts such as *Deadly Possessions* are argued to play hard in the space between truth and fiction, for example, *accounting* for and *creating* a reality of Bela Lugosi's mirror as a haunted object: as an *objet a*—essentially a Real *object* with Imaginary and Symbolic iterations. It is useful, however, to consider also Johnston's (2008) suggested reversal that fiction may have the structure of a truth: i.e. that the truth of desire is embedded in the stories we tell ourselves and others, whether or not the artifice is deliberate as in an edited sequence of television programming. Hence, the value of paranormal reality TV is likely less in how closely they correspond to the facts but what they reveal about the workings of desire.

Additional Supporting Materials The transcript of Deadly Possessions, Series 1, Episode 4, 0:29-27:15 (of 51:13) can be provided by the author on request.

Acknowledgements This analysis benefitted enormously from insights provided by the Lacan Reading Group of the University of Leeds, UK, in particular Dr Brendon Nicholls and Dr Nicolas Ray. I am also grateful to Professor Hoare Klempe for organizing and securing funding for the workshop on *New Perspectives on French Psychoanalysis* at the Norwegian University of Science and Technology in December 2022 and for the feedback I received at this event. This article formed the basis of an online presentation for *Lacan in Scotland* organized by Dr Calum Neill which can be viewed at http://tinyurl.com/2j93bzhp.

References

Bakhtin, M. M. (1981). *The dialogic imagination: Four essays* (M. Holquist, Ed.; C. Emerson & M. Holquist, Trans.). University of Texas Press.

Biddle, K. (2019, January 10). A closer look at the Bela Lugosi 'haunted' mirror. *Skeptical Inquirer*. https://skepticalinquirer.org/exclusive/a-closer-look-at-the-bela-lugosi-haunted-mirror/

Black, A. (2014). Lacan's encounter with a Buddhist statue and the gaze as *objet a*. *Psychoanalytische Perspectieven, 32*(4), 339–366.

Bond, H. (2013). *Lacan at the Scene*. MIT Press.

Bryant, L. R. (2013). *Lacan and the 4 (or 16) fantasies*. Larval Subjects. https://larvalsubjects.wordpress.com/2013/03/26/lacan-and-the-4-or-16-fantasies/

Chabot, K. (2019). *Transmedial ghosts: Paranormal investigation from photography to YouTube*. PhD thesis, University of Toronto.

Freud, S. (1899). *The interpretation of dreams*. Franz Deuticke.

Freud, S. (1913). Totem and taboo. In J. Strachey et al. (Trans.), *The standard edition of the complete psychological works of Sigmund Freud, Volume XIII (1912–1913)*. Hogarth Press.
Freud, S. (1918). From the history of an infantile neurosis. In J. Strachey et al. (Trans.), *The standard edition of the complete psychological works of Sigmund Freud, Volume XVII (1917–1919): An infantile neurosis and other works* (pp. 1–124). Hogarth Press.
Freud, S. (1919). The Uncanny. Trans. James Strachey. *Art and literature: Jensen's Gradiva, Leonardo da Vinci and other works* (pp. 335–376). Penguin.
Freud, S. (1937). Constructions in analysis. In J. Strachey et al. (Trans.), *The standard edition of the complete psychological works of Sigmund Freud, Volume XXIII (1937–1939): Moses and monotheism an outline of psycho-analysis and other works* (pp. 255–269). Hogarth Press.
Harari, R. (2001). *Lacan's seminar on 'Anxiety': An introduction*. Other Press LLC..
Hewitson, O. (2013). *Reading 'The Neurotic's individual Myth' – Lacan's masterwork on obsession*. LacanOnline.com. https://www.lacanonline.com/2013/09/reading-the-neurotics-individual-myth-lacans-masterwork-on-obsession/
Jay, M. (1993). *Downcast eyes: The denigration of vision in twentieth-century thought*. University of California.
Johnston, A. (2008). *Zizek's ontology: A transcendental materialist theory of subjectivity*. Northwestern University Press.
Kirshner, L. A. (2005). Rethinking desire: The objet petit a in Lacanian theory. *Journal of the American Psychoanalytic Association, 53*(1), 83–102.
Lacan, J. (1978 [1964]). *The four fundamental concepts of psychoanalysis: Jacques Lacan (Seminar XI)*, edited by J.-A. Miller, translated by A. Sheridan, W. W. Norton & Co.
Lacan, J. (1979 [1953]). The neurotic's individual myth. Edited by J.-A. Miller, translated by M. N. Evans. *The Psychoanalytic Quarterly*, *48*, 405–425.
Lacan, J. (2003 [1938]). *Family complexes in the formation of the individual* (C. Gallagher, Trans.). Karnac Books.
Lacan, J. (2006 [1949]). The mirror stage as formative of the *I* function as revealed in psychoanalytic experience (B. Fink, H. Fink, & R. G. Ecrits, Trans.) (pp. 93–81). Norton.
Lacan, J. (2007 [1959–60]). *The Ethics of Psychoanalysis: Jacques Lacan (Seminar VII)*, edited by J.-A. Miller, translated by D. Porter. Routledge.
Lacan, J. (2014 [1962–1963]). *The Seminar of Jacques Lacan, Book X, Anxiety*, edited by J.-A. Miller, translated by A.R. Price. Polity.
McMillan, P. (1986, January 23). Sister of slain lawyer offers $10,000 reward. *Los Angeles Times*. https://www.latimes.com/archives/la-xpm-1986-01-23-me-27803-story.html
Miller, J.-A. (2007). Jacques Lacan and the voice. In V. Voruz & B. Wolf (Eds.), *The Later Lacan: An introduction* (pp. 137–146). Suny Press.
No Subject – Encyclopedia of Psychoanalysis. Talk: Foreclosure. https://nosubject.com/Talk:Foreclosure#:~:text=Unlike%20a%20repressed%20signifier%2C%20a%20foreclosed%20signifier%20is,real%2C%20usually%20in%20the%20form%20of%20a%20hallucination. Accessed 28 Nov 2023.
Proto, F. (2013). Fatal objects: Lacan in Baudrillard part II (The third simulation stage: Postmodernity). *International Journal of Baudrillard Studies, 10*(2).
Swales, S. & Owens, C. (2020). Psychoanalysing abivalence with freud and lacan: On and Off the Couch. Routledge.
Troubé, S. T. (2015). From the uncanny to the delusional atmosphere: A loss of reality common to neurosis and psychosis? *Journal of Psychoanalytic Studies, 19*, 32–42.
Twohig, V. N. (2003). *Extimacy and the evocation of the uncanny: Between Freud and Lacan*. Higher Diploma.
Vanheule, S. (2014). *The subject of psychosis: A Lacanian perspective*. Palgrave Macmillan.
Verhaeghe, P. (2004). *On being normal and other disorders: A manual for clinical psychodiagnostics*. Other Press.
Wooffitt, R. (1992). *Telling tales of the unexpected: The organization of factual discourse*. Harvester Wheatsheaf.
Zizek, S. J. (2012). Forward: The camera's posthuman eye. In H. Bond (Ed.), *Lacan at the scene* (pp. xi–xv). MIT Press.

Anna Madill specializes in qualitative methods, with particular interest in visual approaches. She is Chair in Qualitative Inquiry and former Interim Head of the School of Psychology, University of Leeds, UK. Anna is Fellow of the British Psychological Society and Fellow of the Academy of Social Sciences. She cofounded and chaired (2008–2011) the British Psychological Society Qualitative Methods in Psychology Section. Some of her research projects can be found at https://projectresilience.co.uk/,

Chapter 4
The Möbius Strip as a Theory of Narrative?: From Bessie Head's Early Journalism to *The Cardinals*

Brendon Nicholls

We should begin with a Lacanian topology. The figure of the Möbius strip is well-known. A single strip of paper is given a twist and attached end to end. The result is a loop that has, paradoxically, only one surface. Since much of my argument rests on the spatial paradoxes of the Möbius loop, the reader may wish to manufacture their own Möbius strip at this point.[1] Cut a long band of paper. Label topside left A and topside right B. Directly overleaf under A; write C. Directly overleaf under B; write D. Draw ants on each surface, walking in the directions indicated below.

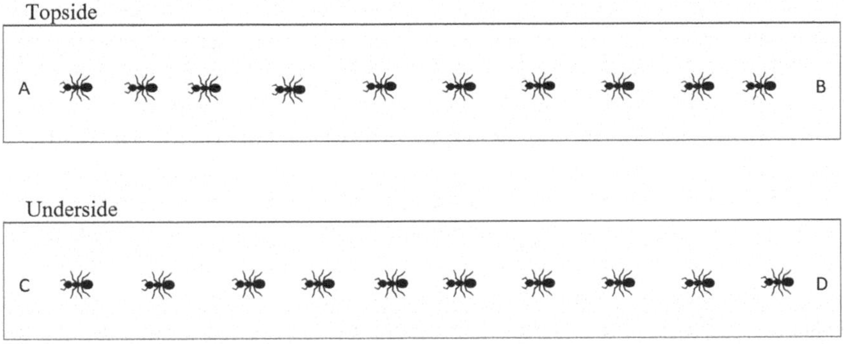

[1] I am grateful to Nick Ray for drawing my attention to the pre-existing precedent of John Barth's "Frame-Tale", from *Lost in the Funhouse* (1968). The reader who cuts out the Mobius strip from Barth's book renders pagination and medium of expression obsolete, because print on the page (in fiction) is made "tape" (the Möbian loop) by recursive prose.

B. Nicholls (✉)
University of Leeds, Leeds, UK

Senior Research Associate, Department of Literary Studies in English, Rhodes University, Grahamstown, South Africa
e-mail: b.l.nicholls@leeds.ac.uk

S. H. Klempe, A. Madill (eds.), *French Psychoanalysis Revisited*, Annals of Theoretical Psychology 20, https://doi.org/10.1007/978-3-031-68534-7_4

Affix C under A and D under B with lengthwise glue or tape, so that ants walk on both sides of a surface (alternatively, draw ants on two surfaces of a single strip with A above C and B above D). Now, half-twist A to the underside, and attach the two ends to create a loop, so that A and B meet face to face and are no longer visible. Affix the join with glue or tape so that only a loop remains. This is your Möbius loop, with its topological paradoxes. Follow the path of the ants on your loop—perhaps by tracing your finger over them—to witness the first paradoxical effect.

In *The Basic Topology of Jacques Lacan*, Jeanne Lafont describes this first paradoxical effect of the Möbius strip as follows:

> After the sleight of hand we have just described [in attaching the twisted ends of paper], the topside and underside of this strip of paper are found to be continuous. The common usage of "head or tails" is subverted. The topside and the underside are continuous with one another. A little gentleman or an ant that walked along one of the sides of this surface would find himself upside down on the other side without even perceiving this incongruity. (Lafont, 1986, p. 15)

In this example, Lafont has in mind Maurits Escher's (1963) rendering of the Möbius strip in "Möbius Strip II (Red Ants)". Similarly to your loop, several ants pass along the strip's surface. They start at any original point and then pass that point on the "obverse" surface, only to repass that same point on the "original" surface. Since we are talking about a single surface, there is properly speaking no "original" or "obverse". In my view, one way of thinking about these "ants" would be to imagine their ceaseless journey along a surface and their momentary contiguity with one another, as approximate to the path of the signifier along the signifying chain. (The reader of Barth's "Frame Tale" (1968, pp. 1–2) will know that it begins "Once upon a time there was a story that began" and that it loops over the Möbian "overleaf" to continue "Once upon a time there was a story that began" and so on, *ad infinitum*.)

By implication, we might consider the activity of literary reading as the straightforward spatial progression along an infinite signifying chain. Considered spatially, meaning-making or interpretation by the (active) reader would necessarily foreshorten or truncate the path of the signifier. This foreshortening would be one way to ensure that the obverse side of the Möbian journey is reached via a metaphorical leap to the ostensible undersurface. This metaphorical leap is equivalent to literary meaning-making "across" or beyond the page, or across the signifiers of a literary passage. Comprehended spatially, metaphor becomes a foreshortening of signs' spatial sites and their temporal moments. Within the ordinary grammatical and syntactical laws of English (or French, or Zulu), this foreshortening can only be achieved by disregarding the deferrals and delays emplotted along the metaphorically-substituted signifier's habitual path.

To illustrate the point I am making about spatialized metaphor, let us imagine a scenario:

> A young boy's father makes him a kite. They spend time together flying this made thing in autumn during the boy's first year of school.

> Years later, the boy, now a man, has an idea in a management meeting. "Let me fly a kite for a moment …" he begins.

It is clear from this example that, if associatively invested in its childhood antecedents, the metaphor "to fly a kite" meaning to "moot a new or speculative idea" would rely upon the omission of the entire apparatus of psychic investments in the father, schooling in the formation of ideas, language acquisition, the subject's developmental timeframes, other kites or ideas the boy has known and loved, along with a bit of clichéd managerial "blue skies thinking" in the mix. In psychic terms, there is no way of telling which kite has just (been) flown. The alert reader might even at this point contemplate the rising musical strains of *Mary Poppins*' conclusion in the latter moment of the management meeting, for instance. Nevertheless, in whatever substitutable equivalence it claims, the metaphor instantly foreshortens a very extended signifying chain. For the metaphor to hold as psychic "truth" about the subject, it must stave off adjacent contingency (in this instance, the dancing chimney sweeps or the duck umbrella in *Mary Poppins*, perhaps).

To demonstrate the foreshortening mechanism of metaphor spatially—and its refusal of metonymic adjacency—the reader may wish to return to our ants. Pick any ant. Pick any corresponding ant on the "obverse" surface, or even on the "same" surface several ants along. Witness how many ant steps, how many signifying instances, would need to be disregarded along the Möbian path to achieve any immediate metaphorical substitution. This is the foreshortening of the signifying chain. This is the psychoanalytic symptom. This is also literary meaning-making—rearranging contingent signifiers into coherent effects, jumping overleaf across the signifying surface on the page, flicking backwards through past pages to regloss now resonant events along the signifying chain ("In which moment might my speculation fly?" our literary reader might ask in their moments of inquisitive resequencing).

The interest value of the Möbius strip is that it subverts our usual understandings and representations of space. It abolishes ideas of top and bottom, of surface and depth. The Möbius strip accomplishes this abolition not by resorting to three-dimensional representation but by introducing the crucial fourth dimension of time. Lafont explains:

> Only a temporal event differentiates the topside and the bottom side, which are separated by the time it takes to make a supplementary turn. The dichotomy between the two notions, underside and topside, only reappears at the price of the intervention of a new dimension, that of time. Time, as continuity, makes the difference between the two faces. If there are no longer two measures for the surface, but only an edge, time imposes itself as accounting for the strip. (Lafont, 1986, p. 15)

Sustaining my previous suggestion that the ant's path around the strip would be approximate to the path of the signifier along the signifying chain, it is clear that what distinguishes signifiers from one another—especially if these signifiers are visibly the "same"—would be their differentiated placement from one another in space and time. In other words, a signifier that is visibly identical to another on the obverse surface (for instance, the signifier "ant") would exhibit the key differences of spatial distance and temporal deferral. The "temporal event" in Lafont's phrasing might be thought of as delay or deferral. Contrariwise, it might be thought of as suspense or prolepsis. Deferral, delay, prolepsis and suspense are also habitual and constituent ingredients of (literary) narrative.

There is a second paradox that Lacan highlights in his thinking on the Möbius strip. If you cut along the length of the strip—cut along the path travelled by the ants, or by the signifier—you derive a loop with two twists and two surfaces (upper and lower) once again. In summary, the representational paradox of the Möbius band is the paradox of a single surface that flips into its apparently "obverse" corresponding surface. This paradox can be undone via an equally paradoxical interpretive cut along the band's entire length. At this point, the active reader may wish to pick up a pair of pointed scissors. Pierce a hole in the Möbian surface alongside any ant. Now cut alongside the path of the ants from head to tail all the way along the loop, crossing their path only once to join your start and end point cuts. Trace how many surfaces emerge in the remaining loop. An extended gap has now emerged in the path of the ants. Let us, for the time being, call this gap "lack". Let us, for the time being, call our new dual-sided loop the "resolved – and extended – Möbian topology".

The interpretive cut we have just undertaken resolves the single-surfaced paradox of the Möbius loop into its dual-surfaced paradox. Once again, this is the "resolved – and extended – Möbian topology". In analysis, the analyst's goal is the interpretive cut in which the analyst discovers the analysand's desire. Once again, Lafont phrases it helpfully:

> Let us note before concluding that it is on this paradox that Lacan bases one the central notions of the analytic cure: that of interpretation. The axiom "interpretation is the cut," allows us to discern how this type of intervention on the part of the analyst discovers the desire of the analysand, masked in his own *dire* ["saying," or in my preferred improvised translation, "statement"].
>
> The fact that the cutting of a Moebius strip makes a strip with four half-twists appear, which is not Moebian this time, introduces a final characteristic of the Moebius strip. (Lafont, 1986, p. 19)

In one possible schema, psychoanalytic interpretation is a lengthwise cut along the signifying chain that "surfaces" the analysand's unconscious signifying and "meaning-making" arrangements. In other words, interpretation surfaces the patient's unconscious binding of prior enchained—that is to say metonymic, contingently placed, laterally arranged—signifiers into symptomatic and deceptively "deep", metaphors. The interpretive cut resolves the originating Möbian paradox and with it the binding of symptom and subject. The interpretive cut resolves the illusorily double-sided Möbian surface into an actual double-sided surface containing an additional loop. Cut along its length, the Möbian paradox resolves into an adjusted topology that once again contains two, unbound surfaces (and a much more extended signifying chain).

The successful interpretive cut makes non-functional, or unbinds, the subject's symptomatic fantasy of sense-making. Put another way, analysis reveals to the subject his or her nonsensical constitutive statement. Analysis has an ultimate desubjectivizing consequence. The metaphorical substitution of the symptom cannot work, because the single surface required to make it function no longer exists. The interpretive cut of analysis meets the founding nonsensical statement [*dire*] of the subject and its initial foreshortening of the signifying chain, with a topologically achieved extension, including lack.

As we know from Lacan's work, the neurotic subject's desire pursues a lost object—which its paramour is presumed to possess—modelled in each case on a template derived from the infant's partial drives. The neurotic fantasy is of desire pursuing and securing the enigmatic and impossible lost object that will finally complete the barred, lacking subject. This enigmatic, impossible, lost object is *objet a*. The subject may pursue *objet a* through specular fantasies of confirmatory recognition, but *objet a* itself cannot be recognized in a specular encounter.[2] Ellie Ragland points out:

> At the level of perceptual effect, the Moebius strip subtends the gaze, which subtends the other drives as that into which one is already born. One does not gaze. One is gazed at, unconsciously seeing oneself as being seen.
>
> [...]
>
> Lacan compares the twist in the Moebius form to the twist in thought that allows one to drop ideas or associations into the memory bank of the unconscious where knowledge remains hidden. (Ragland, 2004, pp. 19–20)

In this twist between thought and the unconscious, the "inner 8" or "interior eight" shape in the centre of the Möbius loop is equivalent to the operation of *objet a* in motivating thought and signification (see Lacan, 2006, p. 731). The subject's fantasy circulates around the specific configuration of the *object a* that structures the subject's particular mode of lack. Desire addresses itself to the plenitude that the subject imagines may be discovered and retrieved in *objet a*. Strictly speaking, the subject cannot name or imagine *objet a*. It is an enigma or cipher of lack that constitutes the subject in the first place. The subject cannot imagine what it is lacking, because what is lacking inaugurates the barred subject in the first place. What the subject imagines it has lost (*objet a*) determines how the subject directs its statement or *dire*. Through the subject's statement, its desire (for the lost object) is both relayed toward, and perpetually deflected from, its aim.

For this reason, *objet a* models the dimensions of the subject's lack, the dimensions of absence around which the subject addresses its thought and desire through the signifying circuit. To be a subject is to circumlocute. The subject may state anything but its circumnavigation of its lack. Let us, through two passages in Lacan's seminar on *Anxiety*, return to our little signifying ant upon its circuit:

---

[2] The classical painting, Holbein's "The Ambassadors" in the National Gallery, London, contains a memento mori which is close to what *objet a* might amount to in a specular encounter, a distorted skull in the foreground. To see the skull and recognize it, the viewer would need to tilt and angle the picture plane 45 degrees away from the viewer on the right and 45 degrees upward on the left corner, thus distorting the two "Ambassadors" in the background who are the ostensible subjects of the painting.

> An ant walking along one of the apparent faces [of the Möbius strip] will pass over to the other face without needing to go over the edge. In other words, the Möbius strip is a surface that has just one face and a surface with just one face cannot be turned inside out. If you turn it over, it will still be identical to itself. *This is what I call not having a specular image.* (Lacan, 2014, p. 96)

The subject who does not have a specular image is the subject who does not lack; the unbarred subject already completed by *objet a*. For this reason, Lacan associates the ants tracing the Möbius strip's circumference with signifiers tracing the dimensions of the "inner 8". The inner 8 is the topological edge where *objet a* has been presumed to be removed from the subject. Showing his audience in *Seminar X* a Möbius strip, he states: "I've constructed it for you and I'll pass it around. It does hold a little interest because, let me tell you, this is the *a*. […] The *a* is put together like that" (Lacan, 2014, p. 97).

Our Möbian subject's experience is structured by misrecognition of its circumstance. The thinking ant walking along the loop conducts itself through signifiers, while being driven around the missing "inner 8" that the ant—the signifying subject—circumnavigates as it follows its Möbian path. Lacan explains:

> If the insect that wanders along the surface of the Möbius strip forms a representation of the fact that it is a surface, he can believe from one moment to the next that there is another face that he hasn't explored, the face that is always on the back of the face along which he is walking. He can believe in this other side, even though there isn't one, as you know. Without knowing it, he is exploring the only face there is, and yet, from one moment to the next, it does indeed have a back.
>
> [The missing *objet a*] is what forms the reality of the world the insect is walking about in. The little interior eight is well and truly irreducible. In other words, it is a lack for which the symbol cannot compensate. This is not an absence that the symbol can counter. (Lacan, 2014, p. 136)

In Lacan's thought, therefore, the spatial circumference of the "inner 8" of the Möbius strip—its empty middle space—gives dimension to the specificity of the subject's psychic arrangements. In other words, the signifying chain, composed of an arrangement of insubstantial signifiers, has an unconscious life that belatedly emerges as a latent meaning-effect via the transverse deferral of time. That temporal deferral contours the negative space of the "inner 8". The inner eight gives dimension to the patient's complex psychic life. Lafont explains this psychic life in terms of temporal movements:

> Let us remark that beginning with this drawing of the interior eight a notion finds itself at once decomposed into diverse acceptations (regression and progression) and unified as a concept. The multiplicity of readings of a concept is accorded its true richness; it is not that a concept has several senses, it is that it is the unique representative of a complex material analyzable in several effects. (Lafont, "Topology," 1986, p. 21)

The inner eight of the Möbius strip, then, is a complex of backward regression and forward progression in the signifying chain that constantly addresses its oblique loss, and iterates itself as a seeming conceptual unity—the subject that presumes to know and state itself. This conceptual unity orients and operates the subject, a subject that only "exists" to itself in its self-declaration through the signifier, and the metaphorical arrangements (progression and regression) that instate the subject's originating and sustaining "presence". Given such an arrangement of the subject, only the analyst's interpretive cut holds the potential to adjust this space.

In short, in Lacan's Möbian topology, the signifier is on a route to its illusory "obverse" signified. The signified, in turn, is another signifier achieved only in delay or development, whose psychic correlatives are regression or progression, and whose narrative correlatives are analepsis and prolepsis. Regression or progression and analepsis or prolepsis, as I hope I have shown, amount to the metaphorical mechanisms of the symptom.

We might illustrate progression and regression along the signifying chain by returning to Lafont, who gives the apposite example of the sentence, "A man is a man" (1986, p. 21). In Lafont's example, the two men are not one and the same. One man is an individual, and the other man is a general class of (plural) men from which he is taken. "A man is a representative of mankind" might be one convenient paraphrase. The temporal deferral in the sentence means that the initial signifier ("A man") does not subsequently signify itself ("a man").

This statement obviously unconsciously comprehends the differentiating category of womankind, or further, gender fluidity and multiplicity, within itself. What the first man ("A man") lands upon in the sentence is the symptom of his statement ("... is a man"), which is itself made expressively adequate by its implicit deferral. In other words, "men" are constitutively defined by extraneous signifiers through which their lack as substantive signs is relayed—"women" or "transwomen", or the differences between the individual instance ("man") and the general category from which it is taken ("mankind"), or what have you. Moreover, the same signifier repeats with a key temporal difference (in the subsequent moments of the utterance), a key spatial difference (in the arrangements of syntax), and a key referential difference (in the respective implied signifieds). The subject of the grammatical sentence perpetually pursues the aim of its object. The object it alights upon is not the same object the subject of the sentence initially sought. Although language regulates the contextual conditions of our momentary self-positing, it also always refuses to put us in our place. The signifier only ever returns to itself in an asymmetrical relation.

The single surface of the Möbius strip means that what is conscious is differentiated from its selfsame unconscious surface only by temporal progression. The unconscious is "structured [...] like a language" in Lacan's famous pronouncement (2006, p. 737). Crucial to Lacan's topology of the unconscious is the passing of time. If we imagine the Möbius strip's surface as a signifying chain, as I have already suggested, then what differentiates unconscious signifiers from conscious ones—which the subject's desire negotiates metonymically across the signifying chain—is simply the passage of signifier to signifier through time. The signifier's idiomatic formation as a constellation of motivated and symptomatic metaphors amounts collectively to a subjective hypothesis—the founding hypothesis in fantasy of a subject that imagines itself into being.

The subject's founding hypothesis is an unconscious wager in fantasy, designed to meet the unknowable demand of the Other. If the subject asks the primary question "What does the Other want of me?" the subject's speculative answer may well approximate "Perhaps I should become something like this?"

Lacan's formulation makes this clear in Seminar X on *Anxiety*. Lacan imagines the original scenario of an (infantile) subject unknown to itself. In Lacan's obscure allusion, the subject wears the mask of the Sorcerer from the Cave of the Three Brothers. Lacan alludes here to a French prehistoric rock drawing of a human sorcerer in the bodily form of an antelope.[3] Lacan's subject therefore wears a mask taken from a shape-shifting sorcerer in a cave drawing. In this imaginative and slightly florid scenario, Lacan's subject cannot see its own face, since it wears a mask. The face it wears is not its own, since it is a mask. The subject is therefore divided from itself. The place of the subject's articulation does not match the site of its representation (the mask). Moreover that mask of the subject's outer face does not belong to the subject. It belongs to a prior aesthetic figure in a prehistoric cave tableau, which itself was drawn by an unknown prehistoric hand. To complicate matters, this (masked) infantile subject encounters a terrifying, gigantic mantis which might consume the subject. The subject relays its own conundrum, its own anonymity to itself, through the terrifying mantis—the big Other—that confronts it. In Lacan's formulation, the subject asks of this big Other "*Que vuoi?, Que veux-tu?, What wouldst thou?*" Push the functioning, the insertion of the key, a little further and you have "*Que me veut-Il? … What does He want concerning this place of the ego?*" (Lacan, 2014, p. 6).

Crucially, the subject does not know itself and cannot recognize the place of the ego in the proliferating images reflected in the mantis' compound eye. The ego may recognize itself as split in its multiple compound mantis-like instances, but the split it recognizes in the Other's demand of it is not the same as the split between the face and the mask. The subject is both masked, multisited, fragmented, and proliferated in the moment of (mis)recognition with the mantis. The subject's look inhabits an asymmetry with the mantis' returned and fragmenting gaze. The subject's question of the Other is not only about what the Other wants. The subject's question is also about the Other's enigmatic insistence on the ego's imperilled and anxious self-placement. In Lacan's scenario, the subject does not know that it is a momentary representation (the Sorcerer's therianthropic mask) facing an abomination (the mantis) who seemingly possesses the missing object that the subject lacks. The missing object would be the "What" in the Other's demand of the subject—"What wouldst thou?" The subject wears a mask that makes of the human an animal and transacts with a mantis in an asymmetrical trans-species dialogue. The *objet a* that the mantis threatens to possess (the gaze returned to the subject's scopic drive seeking recognition—"What wouldst thou?") is the subject's loss, masked by the sorcery of the representational signifier.

The subject's acts of self-positing in language are always addressed to the demand of the Other. The Oedipus complex involves the assumption (by the

[3] This rock art was first discovered in 1912 in the Tuc d'Audaulbert Cave by Count Begoue and his three sons: Max, Jacques, and Louis (Anonymous, 1957, p. 12).

subject) of a desire that "originally is another's, and which, in its displacements, is perpetually other than 'itself'" (Mehlman in Lacan, 1972, p. 45 n. 11). Desire is displaced into an unfulfillable, and utterly neutral, impersonal medium. That neutral medium is what I would call "perpetual writing". Perpetual writing is our displacement across the signifying chain through which we fulfil a lost quest for subjective plenitude. The other point to make is that while "writing" is "impersonal" (Barthes, 1977, p. 144)—while no one owns language—the iteration of narrative directs the subject's statement toward intersubjective designs. In other words, when we speak, there is always already a structurally implicit addressee. We always speak to an elsewhere in someone else's language. The signifier is impersonal, but its trajectory is presumptively social.

I am drawn to Lacan's Möbius strip as a vehicle for thinking through the production, and analysis, of literary narrative. Literary narrative, quite obviously, relies upon a chain of signifiers placed spatially on a page. Literary narrative is, finally, the predicament of the narrator's and the reader's self-placement in a meaning-making design. In this sense, narration is a subject effect, regardless of first person, second person, or third person narration. If narration is a subject effect, it is no less "real" than the Lacanian subject's own constitutive predicaments and iterative, self-positing moments. Literary narrative, in its reliance on repetition (say, a character's name) and difference (say, the contextualizing or constellating restatement of that character's name), might be deemed "Möbian" in its meaning-making for the writing or reading subject.

I want to offer a case study from anti-Apartheid literature. My example is Bessie Head's *The Cardinals* (1995). This novella was written in South Africa, circa 1960–1962, and it was published posthumously in 1995. In the writing of *The Cardinals*, I would argue, key initial ingredients of narrative were occasioned by Head's everyday vocation as a journalist. She wrote the women's supplement, *Home Post*, of a weekly newspaper, *The Golden City Post*. Head's journalistic columns appear from approximately 31 May 1959 to 24 April 1960.[4] As these everyday journalistic ingredients from *The Golden City Post* become arranged into narrative in *The Cardinals*, they take on a violent and perverse erotic charge. I want to track several signifying chains at work in *The Cardinals* to exemplify my Lacanian theory of literary narrative modelled on the Möbius strip.

It will be helpful if I initially offer a short synopsis of *The Cardinals* to readers unfamiliar with its detail. A wealthy single mother, called Ruby, gives up her baby

[4] I have derived these dates from Head's columns signed with "Bessie", sometimes accompanied by a photograph of the author, and from Susanne M. Klausen's afterword to Juby Mayet's autobiography, *Freedom Writer* (Klausen in Mayet, 2022, pp. 160–161). However, the run of both *The Golden City Post* and the *Home Post* supplement in the Cullen Library, University of Witwatersrand, is incomplete. Within the extant supplements, authorship of individual columns by female journalists (especially Juby Mayet and Bessie Emery [later Head]) is often not directly acknowledged. On occasion, Head transcribed content instead of writing it (Klausen in Mayet, 2022, p. 198 n. 51). For these reasons, Head's individual and collaborative contributions remain historically opaque.

girl, later called "Miriam", for adoption by a woman in a South African slum[5]. An old man from the slum introduces Miriam to children's story books, and he teaches Miriam to write. Miriam is almost sexually abused as a child in the poor woman's home, but she escapes instead and flees the slum. Miriam is then renamed "Charlotte" by the Apartheid state. As a young woman, "Charlotte" seeks out and finds employment as a rookie journalist. At the newspaper, *African Beat*, an older man, called Johnny, renames Charlotte "Mouse" on account of her timidity. Johnny decides to seduce Mouse by offering to teach her how to write.

Johnny gives Mouse his short story to edit and rewrite. The story is about his own youth in loose and approximate terms—elements of Johnny are identifiable in the central character called Sammy and the (false?) memories that the rewritten story of Sammy provoke in Johnny. In Mouse's rewriting of Johnny's short story, Sammy picks up a young woman in a fish shop, takes her to the cinema, indulges in foreplay with her, and then is attacked by a gang who want him to join them. We last see him bleeding out on a pavement. Mouse's edited, rewritten story provokes in Johnny the memory of a lover, Ruby. Ruby, like Mouse's unnamed mother, puts a child up for adoption in a slum (1995, p. 52). Ruby cuts her own wrists in an act of suicide and bleeds out in Johnny's memory (provoked by Mouse's rewriting), just as Sammy has bled out in Mouse's rewritten story (of Johnny).

It becomes clear from the story about Sammy and the memories that the story provokes in Johnny that he is possibly Mouse's own father, unknown to both of them. However, because Mouse has edited and rewritten Johnny's story, we cannot guarantee this (fiction of) origin for certain.[6] Another possibility is that Mouse has written the inadvertently incestuous content into Johnny's story about Sammy. When Mouse resists Johnny's (incestuous?) sexual advances later in the novella, he becomes increasingly domestically abusive in their cohabiting arrangement. But the character of the father's abuse also reflects the kinds of violence that Apartheid inflicted on black South African citizens. Johnny's love exhibits autocratic tendencies. Johnny's idea of love contains a real or fantasized enforcement of Apartheid's worst political practices—authoritarian rule (1995, p. 89), segregation (1995, p. 21), insults (1995, p. 114), humiliation, beatings or batterings (1995, pp. 113, 15, 110), burnings (1995, p. 115), torture (1995, pp. 113, 115), killings (1995, p. 113), assassinations (1995, p. 111), killings made to look like suicides (1995, p. 111), bombings (1995, pp. 20, 115), and demands that black South Africans make way for

[5]As not all readers realize, Head takes great care not to racialize her protagonists. To have racialized them would have been to work within Apartheid's limiting logic. The positions held by Head's "Cardinals" are structural, not identitarian. Lacanian psychoanalysis, too, hinges on a structural idea of the psyche—one is either neurotic (which includes the obsessive and the hysteric), or perverse, or psychotic.

[6]As Frances Hemsley aptly puts it, "It is Mouse's creative re-envisioning of Johnny's copy—spliced through the narrative—that leads the reader to deduce Johnny's paternal relation to Mouse" and "she writes her destiny, which is incest" (2021, p. 160).

white South Africans on pavements/sidewalks.[7] Politically, Johnny opposes Apartheid. But in his amorous life, he imaginatively re-enacts it.

The advantage of the Möbius strip as a way of reading narrative in *The Cardinals* is that it allows us to trace the circuit of some innocent, parochial, and everyday signs that become psychically and hyperbolically invested in the fictional universe of *The Cardinals*. The Möbius strip allows us to track the flipping over of everyday signs into the symptoms of psychosis and incestuous perversion.[8] The basic dynamic factor in this hyperinvestment of signs is that Head equates sexuality with power.[9] For that reason, white political violence is repurposed and discharged as Johnny's domestic gender-based violence.

I draw much of my research on the signs of the everyday from Head's profession as a journalist at the *Golden City Post*. With the notable exception of Colette Guldimann (1997), the critical field has neglected Head's journalistic career as a source for her fictional career. Journalism traffics in the topical, in the everyday, in the ephemeral, and in the passing. The *Home Post* supplement offered any number of true romances, beauty columns, lonely hearts columns, fashion tips, homemaking tips, advice to teenagers, trivia quizzes, life and love advice, infant health information for new mothers, recipes, astrology columns, joke columns, and so on. Head was likely the author of some of these, some of the time. On occasion, Head merely transcribed features—and transcription is one of the most mundane, banal, and quotidian of writerly tasks. Let us look at a few of the everyday signs in play in Head's contributions to the *Home Post* and in her lived environment and relations. These everyday signs become sources of hyperbolic unconscious return in *The Cardinals*.

The hyperbolic dimension of *The Cardinals* can be seen in the epigraph from which it takes its title: "The Cardinals, in the astrological sense, are those who serve as the base or foundation for change" (Head, 1995, p. 3). The romance between Johnny and Mouse would, it is suggested, inaugurate pan-African political change—an epochal or cosmic shift.[10] The guiding idea is that both protagonists are not

[7] This petty, "informal" practice of segregation predates the formal segregation legislated for by Apartheid (1948–1993). Its prominence within racist and antiracist discourses dates to the 1930s and is historically simultaneous with the decade containing Bessie Head's own birth (1937). A correspondent with *The Star* newspaper, writing under the pseudonym "Fairplay", complained that "[natives] will not make space for a white person to pass" (20 April 1933, p. 11). The Editor answers dismissively, "[All pedestrians must use the pavements, otherwise an already high accident rate would be a good deal higher.]" By 1947, Wulf Sachs' *Black Anger* (published under its original title as *Black Hamlet*) records a traditional healer's outrage at "a native woman thrown off the pavements because she did not give way quickly enough to a European" (p. 76).

[8] In Lacan, the structures of personality are, strictly speaking, *either* neurotic *or* perverse *or* psychotic. However, the possible meaning-making effects of literary narrative allow for mutable positioning within pre-existing, complementary structures: perverse *and* psychotic. In other words, our behaviours may instance any Lacanian "clinical structure", as part of our own, proper, clinical structure's placement within reading or writing relations.

[9] Annie Gagiano argues incisively that "political force frights the intimate moments of individual encounters" (1996, p. 48).

[10] Guldimann astutely observes that "Johnny, Mouse and Ruby seem, through a careful reading of the text, to be symbolically representative of a new universe" (1997, p. 67).

merely human. They are also mythic. This idea, a different way of configuring mundane, human forms of power such as racial oppression, reframes Apartheid by diminishing its ultimate scale and the consequent degree of its application to the oppressed. Head's method is what we might term "aesthetic amplification". If one's existence is mythic and epochal, mere Apartheid becomes a trivial matter, trafficking in comparatively petty and puny oppression once measured against our stellar potentials.

But the origins for *The Cardinals*' mythic reframing of Apartheid can be found in everyday ephemera in the *Golden City Post* and in Head's lived social environment. Head's journalism for the *Home Post* supplement possibly included the astrology column, "What the Stars Say … by Kismet" (for a representative instance, see 2 August 1959e, p. 4). Head herself also featured in before and after photographs in a beauty column in which she went by the pseudonym "Isabel Starr", in "And you, too, can add to your beauty" (26 July 1959b, p. 4). The novella's title, *The Cardinals*, is not only derived from the astrology column, nor just from Head's beauty column. The title also comes from a specific road, called Cardinal Close, set just back from the beach on the Hout Bay side of Noordhoek, Cape Town. Noordhoek was, and remains, adjacent to the fishing port of Hout Bay (Johnny, in *The Cardinals* is a fisherman). Noordhoek was a holiday town that Head likely visited on a day trip[11] just prior to the forced removals of "Cape Coloured"[12] communities in the 1960s. Those removals took place to make way for white land ownership in Noordhoek.

To summarize, *The Cardinals* is an astrological term for the new black leaders representing pan-African political change sweeping the continent in the 1960s and setting an archetype for South Africa of freedom in its future. *The Cardinals* is also, conversely, a charged allusion to the cardinal sins. Lust is a cardinal sin—and incest and bestiality are two of its manifestations in Head's novella. The astrological Cardinals are implicitly at stake in pseudonym of the young journalist, Bessie Head, writing as "Isabel Starr". The astrological Cardinals are at stake in the weekly column, "What the Stars Say" by "Kismet" (itself referencing a personified form of power driving a liberated social destiny after Apartheid)—a column possibly authored or transcribed or read by Bessie Head, who may have passed by a street sign on the corner of Cardinal Close on a weekend outing to Noordhoek.

From which everyday, banal, signs and passing acquaintances might the fatherly protagonist's name, Johnny, come? In one of Head's columns, "Dear Gang", she answers a correspondent who writes that Johnny Mathis "sends me out of this world". In her response, "Bessie" admits to finding a picture of Johnny Mathis and observes that he is "mighty good-looking" (13 September 1959f, p. 3). Johnny in *The Cardinals* is also based on Head's true life romance published in the *Home Post*,

[11] Dennis Kiley, Head's *Golden City Post* editor stated that Head "used to go places like Hout Bay for a day out on a Sunday" with an old lady she befriended in District Six (Eilersen, 1996, pp. 39–40).

[12] This term was an Apartheid designation for communities of mixed-race or multiethnic heritages. But the identity "Coloured" is also proudly claimed by some South African communities in the post-Apartheid era.

"Mr Wonderful and the Mouse". In this romance, "Mr Wonderful" is a popular man, Dick, who courts a shy female narrator, Charmaine Harris. Johnny Mathis released a 1957 studio album, *Wonderful, Wonderful*, which featured a song ("Too Close for Comfort") from the musical *Mr Wonderful*. In "Wonderful, Wonderful"—the title track of the album—Johnny Mathis sings "Sometimes we walk hand in hand by the sea / And we breathe in the cool salty air". This beachside romance parallels Johnny's seaside romance with Ruby in *The Cardinals*—it is their oceanside liaison that produces baby Miriam. Johnny Mathis sending "Bessie's" correspondent "out of this world" might be termed an astrological metaphor for sexual attraction, setting in place Johnny's position as an astrological Cardinal.

Moreover, Head's advice column, "Hiya Teenagers", sits directly to the right of Head's column, "Dear Gang", in which Johnny Mathis has previously been described as "mighty good-looking". "Hiya Teenagers" features a response to a previous query about how to talk to a shy girl one fancies. Both the Mouse, "Mr Wonderful's" paramour in the true romance, and Mouse, Johnny's paramour in *The Cardinals*, might be described as shy girls. But in the spatial arrangement of the *Home Post* page, a shy girl sits directly opposite the prepossessing Johnny (Mathis) too. In these columns that neighbour each other on the page of *Home Post*, Johnny (Mathis) sits alongside a "Shy Girl" (Mouse) but does not talk to her, while Bessie Head offers love (and ultimately, seduction) advice. Johnny's personality in *The Cardinals* comes from a real life crush who Bessie Head was very taken with: the jazz musician Dollar Brand and possibly from her similarly confident fellow reporter on *Drum Magazine*, Casey Motsisi. Johnny's biography as Sammy in his short story and as a fisherman in memory is possibly drawn from a real life counterpart. Bessie Head befriended a fisherman, called Zoot (real name Amin Mohammed), in her District Six days (Eilersen, 1996, p. 52).

Where, then, do the names Miriam and Mouse in *The Cardinals* come from? On 19 July 1959d, the *Golden City Post*'s middle pages contain the *Home Post* insert. The adjacent names Miriam and Mouse are accidentally discovered alongside one another in the movement of the reading eye as it scans two headlines in *Golden City Post* and the *Home Post* insert, respectively. The reader sees on the left-hand side the partially obscured news feature "Sonny Pillay […] Wooed and Won His Miriam" (Anonymous, 19 July, 1959d, p. 10) immediately alongside the true romance "Mr Wonderful and the Mouse" on the right-hand side (Bessie Head ("Charmaine Harris"), 19 July 1959a, p. 1). Both Head's true romance story and its framing story (Sonny Pillay's marriage to Miriam Makeba) turn on acts of accomplished seduction. And both stage, as a spatial arrangement of words on a page, the movement from "Miriam" to "Mouse", the central plotline for the thrice renamed protagonist of *The Cardinals*, who moves from being "Miriam" to "Mouse", with "Charlotte" in between. As the eye moves across the page from newspaper centrepiece to supplement insert, we move from Miriam to Mouse, just as *The Cardinals* itself does. It is almost as if this accidental juxtaposition gives the surface of the newspaper as a Möbius strip, whose later metaphorical work is transacted as an incestuous symptom in *The Cardinals*, since after all, it is Johnny ("Mr Wonderful") who symbolically renames Miriam "Mouse".

Moreover, the signifier, "Mouse", has a particular relation to Apartheid. The "mouse" is a cipher for the oppressed in Bessie Head's imaginative universe. She writes in a letter that:

> In the mind of any white, whether racialist or liberal, a black man is not a whole man, with whole, horrific, satanic passions. A black man is a wee, sleekit, timorous, cowering beastie they mowed down with maxim guns a hundred years ago. A black man could not possibly be the characters in my books, so hugely vile, so hugely demonish. (Eilersen, 1996, p. 222)

A "wee, sleekit, timorous, cowering beastie" is, of course, an allusion to Robert Burns' poem "To a Mouse, On Turning Her Up in Her Nest With the Plough, November 1785" (Burns, 1785, p. 748). "Mouse" in Head's literary, and Möbian, reference is how Apartheid imagines its victims. If "horrifically impassioned" Johnny re-enacts Apartheid, then Mouse enacts those it oppresses.

Head asserts the equivalence of the races in this symptom. The black man lacks under Apartheid. But Head's own male characters (Johnny in *The Cardinals*, Maru in *Maru*, Dan in *A Question of Power*) do not lack or cower. They are overbearing, coercive, and unstoppable. Therefore, Head's protagonists are (occasionally black) men who do not lack, who embody *objet a*. They have perverse Lacanian structures for that reason—the pervert is a subject who has undergone castration and entered language but who assumes that they are the other's object, cause of the other's *jouissance* (enjoyment taken to the extreme of suffering). The pervert submits others to anxiety-causing intrusion, just as Johnny desires to seduce Mouse by making Mouse's writing speak through his own editorial framing. The counterpoint offered by *The Cardinals* is that writing, editing, and reading are two-way, intersubjective traffic. Mouse edits Johnny too. By authoring her originator (Johnny) in the story of Sammy, Mouse part-authors her gender oppression, but she submits Johnny's embodiment of Apartheid racial oppression to a perverse erotic charge.

What is the logic of this charge? Apartheid makes men mice. Johnny makes Charlotte, a woman, Mouse. Apartheid bestialized—it made people live out the degraded conditions and dehumanized dispositions of the animal. Johnny's desire is at one level readable as bestiality (the perverse sexual desire for a Mouse). Inhabiting the structures and effects of Apartheid, Johnny, who is not necessarily black, perverts it. But Johnny's unrequited encounter with a non-desiring Mouse—a subject who refuses her human harasser—also places him in the position of the Lacanian subject of anxiety, who, masked to himself, asks of an animal—in this instance, a Mouse instead of a mantis—"*What wouldst thou?*"

In his seminar on Edgar Allan Poe's "The Purloined Letter", Lacan writes that "in determining the scope of what speech repeats, it prepares the question of what symptoms repeat" (1972, p. 48). The symptoms being repeated in *The Cardinals* are unconscious father-adult daughter incest, domestic violence, and a social environment of almost universal sexual perversity. The simple question is why a very young Bessie Head—aged 22 or 23—has designed this story as symptom. Why imagine one's lover as a tyrant and as a lost father? One answer might be that *The Cardinals* follows the lead of Apartheid legislation, whose premises of power relied partly upon proscribing sexuality. Apartheid criminalized interracial love in its successive

Immorality Acts. The first Immorality Act (1927) prohibited sexual intercourse between unmarried white and black citizens. Mentally-ill divorcee Toby Amelia Emery (née Birch) transgressed this legislation when she conceived Bessie Amelia Head (née Emery) with an unknown black man.

Head knew little about her mother and nothing at all about her father. Head was conceived in an act of love or rape, in Johannesburg or in Durban, South Africa, in late September or in early October 1936. Born on 6 July 1937, Bessie Head's own person remained the only verifiable record of this lost liaison. In short, Head herself was born into a complicated Symbolic Order, in which her own embryonic origins were both unknowable and officially unlawful and in which her criminalized person remained the only body of evidence. The subsequent Immorality Amendment Act (1950) forbade all sexual intercourse between white and non-white South Africans, inhibiting the teenaged Head's own spectrum of future love choices. The Immorality Act (1957), just 2 years before Head began working as a journalist, outlawed "immoral" or "indecent" acts between white and non-white South Africans. Even non-sexual relations, therefore, became considerably imperilled. Bessie Head was in her 20s (1960–1962) when she wrote *The Cardinals*. In her journalism, Head covered some of the court cases in which interracial couples were tried for "Immorality".[13]

Unconscious incest is a curious literary response to the criminalization of cross-racial love. But for Bessie Head, any black man above a certain age—were she to desire him—might possibly have been her biological father. In this way, Apartheid's racial criminalization of Head's own origins made incest an ever-present structural risk within Head's erotic life. If we go back to our Möbius strip, and my suggestion that the signifier is presumptively social, we can see that Head's own desiring-writing is beset by a vacancy of address. Desire—and writing—in her case always risk inadvertently or randomly discovering the story of the father. Moreover, Apartheid's narrowing of desire to intraracial love choices tended toward intra-kin relationships and away from cross-racial exogamy in its own imaginative life. Apartheid's conjunction of black subjectivity with inhibited embodiment always already prefigured a challenge via disinhibition. The challenge via disinhibition is delivered in *The Cardinals*' incestuous plot, but the novella also enters into a violent erotics, due to the narrative's incapacity to separate the various attributes of the father as both loved and feared object. The violent erotics of *The Cardinals* demonstrates that freedom-seeking pleasure can never banish racial and sexual prohibition. I locate the origins of *The Cardinals*' violent erotics in Apartheid's racist

---

[13] In *The Cardinals*, one of the cases that Mouse covers as a court reporter for *African Beat* is of "a twenty year old Norwegian sailor on trial for contravening the Immorality Act" (1995, p. 60). In the Cullen Library at the University of Witwatersrand, the *Golden City Post* features three stories of sailors contravening the Immorality Act. A story on 5 April 1959a describes a Dutch "Sailor Who Thought Immorality Act Did Not Apply on Ship" (Anonymous, p. 9). On 26 April 1959b, the newspaper featured a 20 year old Dutch seaman who pleaded ignorance of an Indian lover's racial classification (Anonymous, "Didn't Know Indians Are Non-Whites", p. 6). On 3 May 1959c, three British seamen from a tanker feature in the story "Seamen Thought Jail for Immorality Act was 'A Big Joke'" (Anonymous, p. 16).

assault upon the organism of the oppressed and in its criminalization of interracial love. Apartheid's various Immorality Acts, as we have seen, retroactively criminalized Head's own mixed-race person and haunted the pleasure-seeking impulses of the oppressed and their human improvisations of the social via interracial love.

What I have been suggesting is that the Möbius strip as a circuit of signifiers and signifieds helps us to think literary production and literary narrative through the signifying chain's repetitions with a difference. Narrative, like the subject, relies upon iteration. Narrative is constituted, like signification, via repetition with a difference. The chains of repeating, but different, signs in *The Cardinals* allow us to approximate the interpretive cut that Lafont describes. The dimensions of the "inner 8" of the Möbius strip emerge not only from implicit address and the various biological or adoptive family structures within the Symbolic Order. They also emerge from Apartheid's automatic, involuntary subject production through a totalizing social structure, whose ultimate effect is to apportion white pleasure and black injury at all levels of life. In apportioning pleasure and pain—psychically indistinguishable states—the traffic of Apartheid's (excessive) *jouissance* invited unconscious response.

To sexualize power, as *The Cardinals* does, is to submit psychic life to the repeated and automatic intrusions of Apartheid's perverse environmental demand.[14] However, to sexualize power is also to inhabit constant psychic attack through the impersonal signifier's ever-present metaphoric charge. Head's early novella tries to equate racist national politics with mythical romantic partnership. But astrological epochal change must be visible in "telling" everyday signs. The unintended result is the devastation of the psyche by incessant ordinary signs that are hyperinvested and whose cosmic consequence overwhelms a sense-making subject with the epochal amplification of every banal signifier. This is not simply an effect of a monstrously racist Apartheid system. To be sure, Apartheid's criminalization of the everyday (petty Apartheid) submitted both experiential being and ordinary language to racist systems of intelligibility. Framed that way, both language and being became fraught with potential culpability in every expressive instance, in every social act. But, viewed another way, language itself always already contains its own logics of contingent inculpation.

As a socially communicative act, literary narrative becomes charged with Apartheid's perverse authoring of the oppressed's lifeworlds. Apartheid's social perversity culminates in the central love relationship in *The Cardinals* becoming (unconsciously) incestuous. Moreover, for Head as a female writer, racial violence uncomfortably expresses itself as domestic (sexual) violence. While Head cannot avoid writing in the father's language and cannot avoid the structuring regime of Apartheid as a Symbolic Order regulating exogamy, she inaugurates a proto-feminist project by shuffling the syntagmatic, sequential progression of the father's narrative. In other words, where male and white authorships of the name collude to

[14] Sisi Maqagi names Apartheid South Africa as "a society that seems to be devoid of normalcy, that is itself deviant" (2004, p. 169).

produce gender violence, female editing amounts to a scrambling of their sequential logics. The changeability of Head's own name in journalistic bylines ("Bessie", "Isabel Starr", "Kismet", "Charmaine Harris") itself introduces an editing function comparable to the renaming of Miriam (Makeba) and Mouse in ("Mr Wonderful and the Mouse") to Miriam in *The Cardinals*, to Charlotte in *The Cardinals*, to Mouse (in *The Cardinals*). In fact, as Zoë Wicomb observes, Mouse, whether as Miriam or Charlotte, repeatedly "refuses to speak or to utter her name, a self-imposed tabu" (1995, p. 11). The changeability of women's names in exogamy (Bessie Emery the unmarried journalist later becoming the married Bessie Head, for instance) mimics the editorial function in writing, in which the arrangement, substitutability, and erasure of signifiers are givens.

In one possible perspective on the Möbius strip, the Lacanian symptom is itself exercised by the subject's editorial function, foreshortening the syntagmatic, metonymic deferrals of the signifying chain to produce affectively charged and paradigmatic metaphor. To make this point, I want to demonstrate literary editing as an act of perversion in Head's true romance, "Mr Wonderful and the Mouse". *Char*maine Harris, metonymically linked to *Char*lotte in *The Cardinals*, narrates the difficulties of her shyness in a romance with the popular Dick Richards:

> Plain, unpopular Charmaine Harris, going out with the town's number one heart-throb, Dick Richards. Could any girl ask for more?
>
> Dick had brains and brawn and looks.
>
> [...]
>
> *A while ago, there had been quite a lot of speculation about a certain girl and Dick and more than once somebody hinted that a marriage was in the offing. But nothing came of it.*
>
> [...]
>
> *Dick came every day for a week. Sometimes he managed to get more than a dozen words out of me which was quite a feat.* (*Home Post*, 19 July 1959a, p. 1, italics in the original)

Dick insistently elicits speech from Mouse in a way that is similar to Johnny the editor coaxing Mouse to write in *The Cardinals* ("he managed to get more than a dozen words out of me which was quite a feat"). Further, in one possible logic of the symptom's editorial function, the renaming of the tautologous "Richard Richards" as "Dick" becomes a motivated and retroactively necessary pseudonym. The poorly named "Richard Richards" is edited to avoid redundant repetition and becomes "Dick". The more the shy and self-effacing "Mouse" retreats from the scene of language, the more the father's phallic *jouissance* ("Dick") enters the scene. To demonstrate this in Head's passage, I offer illustrative editorial deletions to the signifying chain in the story. If, as I have claimed, editing is perversely anxiogenic (anxiety-causing), I shall simply let the following edited passage speak:

> Dick [...]. Could any girl ask for more?
>
> [...]
>
> *A while ago, there had been quite a lot of speculation about a certain girl and Dick* [...] *in the offing. But nothing came of it.*
>
> [...]
>
> *Dick came every day for a week* [...] *which was quite a feat.* [*Home Post*, 19 July 1959a, p. 1, italics in the original]

My point here is not to introduce crass sexual innuendo into Head's true romance prose, but instead, to better reveal its prior presence. The signs were always there to begin with. Editing perversely—simply foreshortening the sequential signifying chain—foregrounds their intrusion, notwithstanding how discomforting and anxiety-provoking their discovered statement may be. One theory, based on the unwanted sexual attentions to which Mouse is submitted in *The Cardinals*, is that "Mr Wonderful and the Mouse" regulates sexual harassment in Head's wider environment.[15] True romance is a plot that circulates around delayed seduction. Charmaine Harris' eventual marriage to "Richard Richards" perhaps makes an honest man of "Dick" through a circuitous process of extended telling. However, in the editorial function of the symptom, signs that would ordinarily sit in contingent and *temporally deferred* relation become hyperbolically charged in their metaphoric and simultaneous unconscious equivalence. The basic steps of narration—"repetition with a difference"—are visible in "Richard Richards". But narration, once editorially foreshortened, collapses into an intrusive language of suggestion and seduction charged with the father's *jouissance* ("Dick") at every turn.eh

The paradoxical cost of Head's scrambling of the white and male authorships of the name is that the most banal conscious detail, and the most mythic levels of violence cannot be distinguished, nor managed within a coherent narrative design. The ultimate, almost inescapable result of hyperbolically charged signs, I would argue, is the devastation of the personality. In schizophrenia's speculative designs, the most ordinary of signs return to assail the psyche because the subject is submitted to the ongoing and excessive demands of the Other's *jouissance*. To summarize, the editorial foreshortening of the signifying chain's metonymic contingency converts the smallest everyday signs—in arbitrary relation—into the violent intrusions of a putatively cohesive transcendental signifier. Signification is a speculative answer to a demand whose bearing we cannot fathom. In Head's mythically charged framework of political reference, editing lays open the always potentially non-signifying subject to phallic *jouissance*'s hyperbolic return in every ordinary turn of phrase. Head's own dramaturgy of the editorial environment of *African Beat*, in which a shy Mouse is beset by constant sexual harassment, itself models perverse and violent editorial demand.[16] When Mouse rewrites Johnny's story, we observe, Sammy is set upon and bleeds out. Johnny, on the other hand, lives (for Mouse) to tell the tale.

I have tried to trace some circuits of ordinary signs (e.g. Johnny Mathis, Miriam Makeba, and Cardinal Close, Noordhoek) as they become hyperbolically invested in the process of literary authorship. To summarize in table form, we can see the movement from the ordinary to the hyperbolic for both characters:

---

[15] As Susanne M. Klausen's "Afterword" notes, both Head and the journalist who preceded her on *Home Post* experienced their first sexual encounter as rape in the years 1960 and 1961 (Mayet, 2022, p. 160).

[16] Huma Ibrahim is too quick to personalize the dynamic, calling Mouse "a young journalist struggling to function with the discoveries and contradictions of her catatonic sexual-emotional self and as an artist coming into being" (1996, p. 48).

Johnny/Sammy/Dick	Miriam/Charlotte/Mouse
Johnny Mathis, who sings song from "Mr Wonderful"	Miriam Makeba
Johnny Mathis (fancied by "Bessie" in "Dear Gang")	The "shy girl" alongside "Dear Gang" in "Hiya Teenagers"
"Dick" in "Mr Wonderful and the Mouse"	"Charmaine Harris" in "Mr Wonderful and the Mouse"
Johnny and "Sammy" in *The Cardinals*	Miriam, Charlotte and Mouse in *The Cardinals*
A fisherman like Head's friend "Zoot"	
Ebullient like Dollar Brand, Head's friend	
A journalist like Head's friend, Casey Motsisi	A journalist like Bessie Head
Father? (incest as a "cardinal sin")	Daughter? (incest as a "cardinal sin")
An astrological "cardinal sign"	An astrological "cardinal sign"

In Head's novella, the everyday amplifies into an epochal incestuous perversity—a true romance of cosmos-shaping proportions. Lacan's Möbian surface dramatizes the endless circuitry of the signifying subject. I would argue further that the signifying subject in Lacan's topological model is also equivalent to the literary writer or reader following marks on the surface of the page while dreaming of depth overleaf. Meaning-making, I have argued, is a metaphorical leap to an impossible underside or overleaf, a proleptic or analeptic moment, that neither the page, nor the Möbian loop, will ultimately yield or confirm. Instead, literary meaning-making is a symptom, comparable to the unconscious metaphorical move from the passing contingency of Miriam Makeba marrying Sonny Pillay to the construction of another Miriam—the infant subject intruded upon by unilateral paedophilic attentions in *The Cardinals*. The reader in search of meaning breaches the surface of the page or the boundaries of the book and foreshortens the signifying chain, in line with an intrusive and perverse editorial *jouissance*. This perverse *jouissance*—a potential in any meaning-making reader as I have intimated by resequencing Head's journalistic prose—is mitigated only by the sentimental assumption that literary characters are people. If our reading does violence to a book, we tell ourselves, it is always, after all, only a book.

The Cardinals' creative process is to out-narrate Apartheid using a cosmic fiction and thus establishing a different order of the legible. By contrast, the readerly process is intrusive and structurally violent. Reading—even in its most inattentive posture—restructures the metonymic relations on the page. In its intrusive violence, the literary reader's bid to interpret, by supplying an object that the page lacks, approximates perversion. The contrast between the creative process and the readerly process is sharp. The creative process is based on a narrative bid to reconstruct worldly order with formal design (replacing an unassimilable Symbolic Order with a fiction). The readerly process is based on an interpretive bid (doing violence in accordance with an implicitly assumed Symbolic Order). The hinge between the two processes is the text—a neutral object-arrangement in and of itself. What Head brings to this arrangement, and to the creative and readerly processes it inspires, is a withheld ending. Just as Johnny seems about to force Mouse's seduction without consent, the novella abruptly ends.[17]

What happens next? The meaning-making reader confronts Head's interpretive and therapeutic cut. The therapeutic cut resolves the paradox of the Möbian loop by unravelling its desiring circuitry, and with it the "inner 8" (outlining *objet a*), the cause of readerly desire. Readers, masked to their own perverse meaning-making, anticipate Mouse's impending but untold violation by her own father. This unnarrated incestuous act can only be contemplated by making a perverse forward leap in the sequence of the signifying chain. We leap forward onto an empty page at the end of *The Cardinals* and read on where no sign has ever ventured. The Mouse-like or mantis-like blankness beyond the ending makes a demand of our perverse reader. Exasperated, our reader might even puzzle "What would'st thou?" The answer never arrives, but readerly perversion persists. Our reader attributes its object to the blankness that will make its other mean, according to a familiar logic: "Walk on, little ant, if only that final sense is fated in our stars! A cosmic design once promised must surely lie in wait. Read on! Every new, unimprinted step is freighted with consequence!"

Reading on, Johnny and Mouse may meet in mutually desired incest. Reading on, Johnny and Mouse may meet in undesired rape.[18] Reading on, Johnny and Mouse may not meet. Reading on, if one may fly a kite, there are any number of remaining narrative permutations in the blue skies of the cosmos.

In the absence of an ending, all permutations are equivalent. In the absence of an ending, all permutations are simultaneously present. Head's interpretive cut, at best, allows her readers to realize, perhaps, that the only possible destination is two-faced. The destination is two-faced like the original masked subject clueless to both its inner face and outer sign encountering the demand of the Other. The destination is two-faced, like the resolved—and extended—Möbian topology. Once neared, the destination slides onward and onward once again. Once again, and again, the destination extends the signifying chain onward, with luck, into lack.

Acknowledgements The author thanks Nick Ray, Anna Madill, Paul Hammond, and Hroar Klempe who all commented insightfully on this work in draft.

[17] I disagree slightly with Jane Starfield's gendered assessment of the conclusion that "Johnny seizes the last platitudinous word about the state of the world, thereby stamping his maleness onto the blankness that has replaced Mouse's identity" (1997, p. 662). Instead, I think that Lacan's clinical structures allow us to read proactively for unfulfillable demand in Johnny's and the reader's encounters with blankness.

[18] Pucherova argues that "as the novel ends, Johnny is about to rape her" (2011, p. 115).

References

Anonymous ("Fairplay,"). (1933, April 20). Natives on the sidewalks: To the Editor of *The Star*. *The Star*, Johannesburg, Transvaal, 11.

Anonymous. (1957, August 15). Young Folks find Cave Art. *The Independent Record*, Helena, Montana, 12.

Anonymous (1959a, April 5). Sailor who thought Immorality Act did not apply on ship. *Golden City Post*, 9.

Anonymous. (1959b, April 26). Didn't know indians are non-whites. *Golden City Post*, 6.

Anonymous. (1959c, May 3). Seamen thought jail for Immorality Act was "A Big Joke." *Golden City Post*, 16.

Anonymous. (1959d, July 19). Sonny pillay tells how he wooed and won his Miriam. *Golden City Post*, 10–11.

Anonymous. (1959e, August 2). What the Stars Say ... by Kismet. *Home Post: Supplement to Golden City Post*, 4.

Anonymous (Bessie Head?). (1959f, September 13). Hiya Teenagers. *Home Post: Supplement to Golden City Post*, 3.

Barth, J. (1968). *Lost in the funhouse: Fiction for print, tape, live voice*. Doubleday.

Barthes, R. (1977). Death of the Author. *Image – Music – Text* (S. Heath, Trans.) (pp. 142–148). Fontana.

Burns, R. (1785). To a mouse, on turning her up in her nest with the Plough, November 1785. In Ferguson, Salter, & Stallworthy (Eds.), (2005). *The Norton Anthology of Poetry* (5th ed., pp. 748–749). W. W. Norton and Company.

Eilersen, G. (1996). *Bessie Head: Thunder behind her ears; he life and writing*. Heinemann.

Escher, M. C. (1963, February). *Möbius Strip II (Red Ants). 58 × 32 cm print of woodcut in red, black, and grey-green, printed from three blocks*. John D. Merriam collection. Boston Public Library. https://www.digitalcommonwealth.org/search/commonwealth:3r076s371.

Gagiano, A. (1996). Finding foundations for change in Bessie Head's *The Cardinals*. *The Journal of Commonwealth Literature, 31*, 47–60.

Guldimann, C. (1997). *Bessie Head: Re-writing the romance: journalism, fiction (and gender)*. Dissertation, Master of Arts in Literary Studies, University of Cape Town. https://open.uct.ac.za/server/api/core/bitstreams/86333436-d0a5-40fd-ba75-66c8f4e1bc19/content

Head, B. ("Charmaine Harris"). (1959a, July 19). Mr Wonderful and the mouse. *Home Post: Supplement to Golden City Post*, 1.

Head, B. ("Isabel Starr"). (1959b, July 26). And you, too, can add to your beauty. *Home Post: Supplement to Golden City Post*, 4.

Head, B. ("Bessie"). (1959c, September 13). Dear Gang. *Home Post: Supplement to Golden City Post*, 3.

Head, B. (1971). *Maru*. Gollancz.

Head, B. (1973). *A question of power*. Davis-Poynter.

Head, B. (1995). *The cardinals: With meditations and short stories*. Heinemann.

Hemsley, F. (2021). Reading heredity in racist environments: Epigenetic imaginaries in Bessie Head's *The Cardinals*. *Medical Humanities, 47*, 156–166.

Ibrahim, H. (1996). *Bessie Head: Subversive identities in exile*. University of Virginia Press.

Lacan, J. (1972). Seminar on "The Purloined Letter" (J. Mehlman, Trans.). *Yale French Studies 48*, 39–72.

Lacan, J. (2014). Anxiety: the seminar of Jacques Lacan Book X. (J-A Miller, Ed). Polity.

Lacan, J. (2006). Science and Truth. *Écrits* (B. Fink, Trans.) (pp. 726–745). W. W. Norton.

Lafont, J. (1986). *The ordinary topology of Jacques Lacan* (J. Stone, Trans.). University of Missouri, M. I. T. https://www.scribd.com/document/120878260/The-Ordinary-Topology-of-Jacques-Lacan.

Maqagi, S. (2004). Taboo, A positive transgression? A study of Bessie Head's *The Cardinals*. In H. Ibrahim (Ed.), *Emerging perspectives on Bessie Head* (pp. 167–179). Africa World Press.

Mayet, J. (2022). *Freedom writer: My life and times* (Susanne M. Klausen, afterword). Jacana Media.

Pucherova, D. (2011). A romance that failed: Bessie Head and Black Nationalism in 1960s South Africa. *Research in African Literatures, 42*(2, Summer), 105–224.

Ragland, E. (2004). *The logic of sexuation: From Aristotle to Lacan*. SUNY.

Sachs, W. (1947). *Black Hamlet*. Little, Brown and Company.

Starfield, J. (1997). The Return of Bessie Head. *Journal of Southern African Studies, 23*(4, December), 655–664.

Wicomb, Z. (1995). Reading, writing, and visual production in the New South Africa. *Journal of Commonwealth Literature, 30*(2), 1–15.

Brendon Nicholls is Director of the Leeds University Centre for African Studies (LUCAS) and Associate Professor of Postcolonial African Studies in the School of English, University of Leeds. Nicholls is the author of *Ngugi wa Thiong'o, Gender, and the Ethics of Postcolonial Reading* (Ashgate) and *Nadine Gordimer's July's People* (Routledge), with recent articles in *Cultural Critique* and *New Formations*. Nicholls was Hugh le May Fellow at Rhodes University, South Africa (2022).

Chapter 5
The Uncanny Feminine

Marcela Antelo

> *Poetry lifts the veil from the hidden beauty of the world, and makes familiar objects be as if they were not familiar.*
>
> P. B. Shelley (2004, p. 111)

Lacan delved into the realm of feminine jouissance, stripping away its veil of familiarity, a task Shelley attributed to poetry. Lacan redefined the feminine as an uncanny littoral, providing a raw insight into jouissance itself, suggesting that feminine *jouissance* is neutral and accessible to any speaking subject. However, women represent merely the surface of what we perceive as feminine jouissance. Today, this concept evokes the sensation of a body resisting symbolic representation, a notion Freud identified as uncanny.

The phenomenon of the uncanny in Freud seems to date from his approach to his female hysterical patients and their symptoms, who exhibited fantastical bodies, remarkable for their strange effects on subjectivity. The feminine appears linked to the impossibility of symbolically representing the subjects' experience of their body—so intimate and strange it cannot be shared.

More specifically, women appear in Freud's (1919, p. 237). *The Uncanny*, when he argues on the factor of repetition as a source of the "uncanny feeling," which he considers will not be easily recognizable to everyone.

The context is Freud's "random" walk, "As I was walking, one hot summer afternoon, through the deserted streets of a provincial town in Italy which was unknown

This article is an extended and modified version of: Antelo, Marcela, "Inumano litoral". In: *O feminino infamiliar: dizer o indizível* / Marcela Antelo e Iordan Gurgel (Org.). São Paulo: Escola Brasileira de Psicanálise, 2021. (pp. 146–160) ISBN 978-65-990241-1-5

M. Antelo (✉)
World Association of Psychoanalysis, Paris, France

Escola Brasileira de Psicanálise, Seção Bahia, Av. Anita Garibaldi, Bahia, Salvador, Brazil

S. H. Klempe, A. Madill (eds.), *French Psychoanalysis Revisited*, Annals of Theoretical Psychology 20, https://doi.org/10.1007/978-3-031-68534-7_5

to me." (p. 237). He comes across "a quarter of whose character I could not long remain in doubt." (p. 237). We cannot but quote it, to distill the essence of our inquiry. "Nothing but painted women were to be seen at the windows of the small houses, and I hastened to leave the narrow street at the next turning." (p. 237). Freud fails, unable to flee, going around in circles, ultimately condemned to what he terms an involuntary return to the same place, the colorful, feminine windows. Helplessness and *uncanniness* are the feelings of the *norme/mâle*. Fumbling for the light switch in a darkened room, he trips over a piece of furniture.

What is Freud fleeing? The depths of a throat, a Medusa, a devouring, female praying mantis? The easy way out is an oedipal, phallic reading, invoking the second condition and secretly familiar proximity *Dirne*-Mother, to *Dirnenhaftbarkeit*, the "status of whore" and to substantiate a rejection of femininity, a Freud who unhesitatingly leaves.

What fire do these open windows expels, and this exhibitionist quarter what does it provoke? Is it enough to point out the knot of desire and defense in the Other scene? Or is there something in these women that won't submit to castration? What opaque thing draws him back? Why does he come back again and again, making of this return an example of an *Unheimlich* experience?

In this walk, Freud illuminates the experience of what doesn't exist, what *ek-sists*. Feminine jouissance and the *Unheimlich* experience occur within the body and "*Parlêtres* in general have trouble dealing with the feminine body" (Brousse, 2016, p. 53).

In Lacan's later work, the notion of a boundary between the symbolic and the real offers a fresh perspective on Freud's famous question: "What does a woman want?" We will explore Lacan's inquiry into the feminine, posed toward the end of his life. Not in the way Freud did it, by questioning women obscure desire: "What do woman want?" but the feminine, and not the so-called women, approached as a mode of *jouissance*, a way that doesn't allow universalization, a regime which Lacan nominated as Not-All (*Pas-tout*). For Lacan, "*the* woman" does not exist for Lacan (1998, p. 80) (*La/ femme n'existe pas*); consequently, her supposed enigmatic desire does not either. This inexistence prompts a continual quest to represent, figure out the essence of her being, paint her, sculpt her, decipher, sing her, defame her, divinize or demonize her, and ultimately desire her into existence.

The Not-All implies that we can only approach women one by one, each existent, without any capital letter. Lacan introduced the table of sexuation in seminar XX (1972–1973, [1998] p. 80), where he delineated two sides and their respective logics, which do not necessarily align with traditional gender categories as he previously conceptualized in his earlier teachings (2006, p. 417), metaphorizing the law of urinary segregation in the public western life (each genre with its corresponding bathroom door). Genre is shaped by both symbolic and imaginary dimensions of existence. It is built by identifications that keep us defended toward the real.

The table delineates a dual path of *jouissance*. The phallic way is constructed by Freud, based on an exception, the father of the law, unsubjected to castration, who imposes the universal, for all humanity. Conversely, each speaking being, submitted to castration, faces the interdiction of jouissance, facing the impossibility of *jouissance*. In consequence each speaking being is prone to recovering some of the lost *jouissance* through language and all the possible discourses at his disposal, which Lacan constructs in seminar XVII (1969–1970 [2007]) to establish various social bonds. Humanity and subjectivity hinge on the availability of phallic signification or, more precisely, on language-parasitizing bodies with it. This masculine way is not an alternative to the feminine but rather one way recorded on the table alongside its supplement: supplementary *jouissance*, the feminine way of *jouissance, Another jouissance. Another jouissance* is transgender, able to be experienced by any speaking being regardless of gender identity. Here we can place something inhuman, impossible to say, to subjectify—it can only be present, not represented.

This elusiveness of the feminine, metaphorically described by Freud as the "Dark Continent," (1926, p. 212) claims for an infinite work of elucidation, driving analysts to persist in their quest rather than settling into complacency with knowledge. Between the two paths lies not a border but a shoreline, a littoral, a fluid boundary.

Searching for the Inhuman Snark

In the pursuit of the elusive and enigmatic, Freud's final reference in "Studies on Hysteria" to the myth of the Danaids—an assembly of 49 sisters condemned by Zeus to endlessly fill a leaking vessel with water—holds a peculiar fascination. However, this myth, lost in translation, was transformed into the tale of Sisyphus by Freud's English translator James Strachey in 1955, and both names curiously vanished from A. A. Brill's American translation in 1950 (1950, p. 197). The Danaids were the figure on which Freud stands to sum up the arduous task analyst of the analyst, a *Danaidenarbeit*. "The physician will not be spared the depressing feeling of being faced by a Sisyphean task" (Freud, 1955, p. 263).

Yet, no representation or historical figuration better encapsulates the inhuman quality of feminine jouissance. It's not about endless repetition or sublime exertion, akin to Sisyphus, but rather the impossible, perpetually unfulfilled endeavor embodied by the Danaids' barrel.

Understanding the significance lost with the omission of the Danaids requires delving into Rachel Bowlby's work, where she portrays them as an emblem of female labor "[...]as a spectacular illustration of female labour reduced to utter uselessness" (Bowlby, 2007. p. 79)—and uselessness, as is well-known, is for Lacan the kernel of *jouissance*.

Do we, as analysts, vainly attempt to fill the bottomless void of feminine jouissance with sense? Or are we, perhaps, mere objects adrift around it, beckoning our patients to keep saying on, failing better, as Lacan borrowed from Samuel Beckett, (1983, p.7), and ultimately concluding the experience by being cast aside dropped out?

Let's delve deeper, once again, into our second significant fundamental: the unhuman. The Danaids, a recurring motif, offer a fascinating insight—a pearl, if you will—where Rachel Bowlby describes them as "almost inhuman in the very singleness of their multi-mindedness" (Bowlby, 2007, p. 86). They are 49 but speak as one. They are a somehow bizarre entity; they embody a peculiar blend of unity and multiplicity, straddling the line between the singular and the collective—an unhuman littoral. Let's sink our feet into its soft, currently forbidden sands.

The Weight of a Prefix

Consider the weight of a prefix: "Un." Just as in Freud's concept of the *Unheimlich*, the Uncanny, and the Unhomely, this prefix signifies a negation—a proper impossibility to fully grasp the subject. It recalls the not-all we previously introduced. As Freud demonstrates on his 20-page fundamental essay, the Uncanny doesn't simply dissolve into the strange or frightening or doubtful feeling. The *Unheimlich* names what is stranger in the familiar. The inhuman, then, becomes the body's exile from humanity—an expulsion from the realm of the human, governed by the Oedipal machine and the regulation of jouissance through prohibition and castration. This prefix is a negative magnitude as Lacan borrowed from Kant (Negative magnitudes, 1763) which comes to designate the proper impossibility to tackle the subject.

The human body derives *jouissance* from the inhuman. The inhuman appears to be a name for a body's exile from the human. Let us think of humanity as the outcome of the Oedipal machine, meaning the name-of-the-father function, regulating *jouissance* on bodies, prohibition/castration, and the resulting humanization of desire and *jouissance*.

We need to recall Lacan's use of the significant "Human." Humanity is born from loss: "The human object always constitutes itself through the intermediary of a first loss," "Nothing fruitful takes place in man save through the intermediary of a loss of an object" (Lacan, 1988, p. 136). And in seminar 3: "When we say that the Oedipus complex is essential for the human being to be able to accede to a humanised structure of the real, it can't mean anything else" (Lacan, 1993, p. 198). In seminar 6:

> [...]by the fact that human beings cannot help but consider themselves to be nothing more than beings who are, in the end, missing something. Whether they are male or female, they are castrated beings. (Lacan, 2019, p. 218)

To be human, therefore, means to be perpetually wounded, eternally lacking. The inhuman in contrast, defies articulation—an unfamiliar disruption of bodily senses, an eruption without words, a mute spectacle, a burst out, but nothing to say about it.

In order to venture into the inhuman, we must view it not as a substance but as a shoreline—a littoral and not a frontier, not a border line where the inhuman meets the human, a littoral space akin to the *Unheimlich* where no clear boundary exists between the familiar and the foreign. *Unheimlich* is not the opposite of *Heim* but rather its episodic haunting, like the sea and the sand, where no decision is possible to make whether one ends or begins.

In Freud's reflection on "The Uncanny," (1919) he acknowledges an eternal infancy within each speaking body, rebelling against symbolic constructs of reality, time, and space—an inhuman anachronism that persistently resists suppression, manifesting as a perpetual trauma confirmed daily in our clinical practice. If infancy persists, if it haunts us, "nightmares" us, and catches us by surprise, the way only a real and errant drive can provoke, it proves the impossibility of fusing life and language, which constitutes our *pathos*. As the Brazilian poet Arnaldo Antunes puts it, the body is imbued with a person as stuffing; if there's an *infans* inside each body, more or less hidden and wandering, there's also a wandering inhumanity haunting the human, objects inhabiting an analyst by transference effect, as well as a persisting splitting that inhabits the body's unity.

Marie-Hélène Brousse focused on the opaque aspect of feminine jouissance (2019), articulating surprise, wandering real, and the impossibility of fusion, locating the feminine precisely at the juncture where a gravitational wave emerges—in an inhuman littoral. Analogous to physics, where a gravitational wave arises from the collision and merger of black holes, the feminine as inhuman emerges, resonating across the universe of human experience.

In the realm of aesthetics, which Freud cautiously explores, bashful and hesitant, artists reveal the exile, the extimacy of each being, the *Unheimlich* feeling, thrusting inhumanity back into the faces of all humans, as Nietzsche aptly noted. Astrophysics uses a fun, powerfully resonant name for when an object approaches a black hole: spaghettification. Objects stretching vertically within a very strong gravitational field. So intense is the stretching, the distortion, that no object can maintain its structural integrity, no matter how hard its component parts are. I thought of *spaghettified* bodies when positioned as feminine. Theses bodies, when they are far way the so-called by Lacan, *jouissance* of the idiot (1998), which has such a bad press nowadays, don't become *spaghetti* as such but do lose their shape, deformed. In the case of supermassive black holes—Brousse (2019) speaks of the feminine as a massive body—the gravitational gradient in the vicinity of the event horizon, the term for the outer edge of black holes, is far weaker, so spaghettification does not occur. Sublimation in-humanizes.

Penélope Fay (2019, p.96) suggests that the eruption of jouissance stranges to such an extent that it distorts one's own body proposing anamorphosis[1] as a means to comprehend this bodily event. One's self-image twists and transforms, starting from the image of one's own body.

Marie-Hélène Brousse's clinical insights, akin to haikus, offer a glimpse into the daily experiences she encounters: loneliness; disobedience to senses (*desobei-sens*); silence; disappearance; fading of the name, of place, of time, and of image; anonymity; concealment; shielding; letting go; forgetting oneself; not showing oneself; releasing oneself; and keeping silent (2019). Her clinical explorations of alterity are

[1]*An anamorphosis is a deformed image that appears in its true shape when viewed in some "unconventional" way*. Websters Dictionnary 1913.

journeys into the boundless frequentations of the illimited, on the surface, on the event horizon, as physics terms it.

The void of phantasmatic matter and the abundance of jouissance that intermittently inhabits the body defy psychoanalytic scrutiny. This void, as the ex-sistent of an unlocalized jouissance associated with the orifices occupied by fantasy, referred to as erogenous zones by Freud, manifests as a diffuse effect, a blurry, indecisive littoral. The subject vanishes, objects fade, and Another satisfaction erupts without finding location.

The inhumanity of this feminine from which the body obtains jouissance from, this wave, as unsayable, makes endless appearances in courtly poetry and impolite prose. We cannot cease to say the unsayable. Blanchot had already considered the invisible as that which one cannot cease to see (1982, p. 163).

The inhumanity of feminine jouissance surfaces in countless poems, in the most plaintive of tangos, among the fathers of philosophy, and above all, in our focal point of interest: Lacan.

Carlos Gardel sang "Mi noche triste" (My Sad Night) for a woman, *percanta*, between center and absence, a beautiful and inhuman creature (a poor thing?), who distorts the lover's universe, spreading her inhuman flavor to everyday objects. In the tango, the bed becomes furious, the mirror weeps, the guitar falls silent, and the lamp mourns her absence—an absurd tango that speaks of the lady's inhumanity from within.

In 1913, the poet Apollinaire, a significant influence on Lacan, remarked: "Above all, artists are men who want to become inhuman" (2010, p.11) ultimately declaring in his poem Devilfish, "This inhuman monster is I." (Apollinaire, 2010, p.40) Henry Miller seems to follow the poet, and in his *Tropic of Cancer*, he proclaims himself a traitor to the human race—two pages on the inhuman. For Anaïs Nin and Henry Miller, an exemplary symptomatic couple, the inhuman represented a parallel race to humanity: the race of artists. *Tropic of Cancer*, published in Paris in 1934, only evaded English censorship in 1960.

Anaïs Nin deserves a closer inquiry as she writes against herself, stating, "I am writing against myself, what you call my imperfections, against the woman, against my humaneness, against the continents which are giving way" (Nin, 1987, p.103). Humanly, she lacks strength; her sole source of strength arises from writing. Adorno takes up this softened inhumanity of the artist, in 1969: "art in general is loyal to humanity only through inhumanity toward it" (Adorno, 2002, p. 197).

For Albert Camus, the inhuman distilled from the bodies of men a sense of unease, particularly nausea. He contends that it is the act of putting the thickness and strangeness of the world into practice that is inherently absurd—a signifier so dear to him and with which he set a standard. In his skeptical metaphysics, at the age of 29, and 2 years from the start of World War II, Camus asserts that the inhuman determines man's greatness (1991).

Inhuman Partners

The Lacanian conception of the inhuman does not entail dehumanization; rather, Lacan embraces the inhuman as a partner. We might describe an inhuman littoral between the One who speaks under the regime of the phallus and the Other—an open space where the feminine way of jouissance is inscribed. An exemplary illustration of the inhuman can be found in "The Invention of the Partner": "Just as there are days when behind a woman's familiar face, we recognize a stranger whom we had loved months or years before, perhaps we shall even desire what suddenly leaves us so alone" (Miller, 2005).

The Lacanian inhuman does not entail dehumanization; rather, Lacan embraces the inhuman as a partner. An exemplary illustration of the inhuman can be found in "The Invention of the Partner":

> Just as there are days when behind a woman's familiar face, we recognize a stranger whom we had loved months or years before, perhaps we shall even desire what suddenly leaves us so alone. (Miller, 2005)

Lacan describes a singular partnership: the "suicidal abnegation of the vanquished party that deprives the master of his victory and leaves him to his inhuman solitude" (Ecrits, p. 263). It's worth noting the 6-year gap between "The Function and Field of Speech and Language" and Seminar VII, a classical locus of humanity in Lacan's teachings.

Lacan's renouncement of a pretended humanity, as depicted in "Italian Note," indeed positions the analyst as an inhuman partner. The notion of the inhuman partner, departing from the revered Lady of courtly love, is a creation of poetry, according to Lacan. "The creation of poetry consists in placing, according to the mode of sublimation proper to art, an object that I would call maddening, an inhuman partner" (1997, p. 150).

Courtly poetry reveals an unexpected crudeness—the Lady devoid of substance, A Dame without matter, a vacuole, a monument to emptiness with immense power, akin to a black hole that consumes anything approaching it. The Lady is basically what was later to be called, with a childish echo of the original ideology, "cruel as the tigresses of Ircania" (1997, p. 151).

An object becomes maddening and inhuman when it acquires the dignity of the Thing, the Freudian "Das Ding," beckoning from the excluded interior, from extimacy. It is the Thing that grants inhumanity. The Lady as master of man, the gentleman, the troubadour. They called her Mi Dom, my lord.

Lacan emphasizes that the Thing is not merely an object (1997, p. 112); it becomes humanized only when desire incorporates it into its circuit. When objects begin to desire, a disturbing strangeness—the *Unheimlich*—emerges. In the example from the final paragraph of "The Freudian Thing," (2006, p. 362) Lacan references another inhuman couple: Diana and Actaeon. Diana's jouissance transforms her hunting stalker into a stag and commands her dogs to devour him. According to

Ovide (1860, p. 214), she ironically challenges him to reveal having seen her unveiled, knowing the consequences. Unveiling the truth of jouissance, ignoring its color of emptiness and its power akin to a black hole, leads to the worst. This is why the unspeakable holds a place of honor in jouissance—the Other jouissance.

Lacan and the Glimpse

Miller, in the seminar class the *Being and the One*, teaches that Lacan envisions jouissance as such, *jouissance* without surname, departing from feminine jouissance. Why does Lacan glimpse it instead of seeing it clearly? This nuanced perspective may stem from the uncertain coastline, perhaps reflecting a lesson in caution learned from Actaeon's fate.

The woman with a capital letter does not exist, as we often assert. She only exists under the condition of being hidden, dreamed of, or hallucinated. Always concealed, absent, a vanished lady—the "screaming subject," as Brousse terms it, transformed into an object cause of desire, desire to know, what does the woman want? or desire to possess? It's not women but woman—the hidden, veiled, abolished, inaccessible figure—that the social bond transform into objects. *Cherchez la femme*, look for the woman, behind any affaire, behind the great man, behind any intrigue.

Brousse clinical exploration of the veil of burqas (2022, p. 50) reveals how the hidden woman occupies a place among common objects. With the veil, the hidden woman puts herself on the scene of the world and interprets and clarifies the place of an object always hidden among common objects, showing that the woman who does not exist functions as an object *a* in collective logic.

Woman has long been concealed within inhumanity since the beginning of time, and now that we live with the unleashing of women's voices, the littoral that brings them together and separates from humanity, reveals the stray, the impossible.

Lacan glimpses of *jouissance* stem from his encounters with women—those he loved, hated, analyzed, and read. He recognized two "ones," describing one as a "a true woman, in her uncompromising nature as woman *[entiereté de femme]*" (2006, p. 640). One is Madeleine, who burned 30 years' worth of letters exchanged with her love André Gide, her most precious treasure. Act that strikes him with "the ravages of 'inhuman deprivation'" (2006, p. 638). Let us remember that, for Lacan, in Gide's work, Woman exists, that is, it is with her that Gide finds partnership.

When Miller orally pronounces "The Invention of the Partenaire," (2005), he mentions the a-human as a partner of *jouissance* and the superhuman in reference to the divine, to God:

> But there is also something else than desire. There's *jouissance*. And precisely in that level that we cannot recognize ourselves. At this level there is no partner human, nor of the other sex, nor of the same.
>
> Fortunately, between *jouissance* and desire, there is love. Love allows you to believe that does it all hold together? On the one hand, the sexual partner that the desire needs; on the other, the a-human partner that jouissance demands.

Inhumanity as a littoral that is crossed by contingency, in any time, is interesting because it leads to the good clinical question:

> Is it the good clinical question that which is placed from the opening to the Other sex, to know, for example, whether or not there is a narrow door? This relation eternalizes, closes the relationship with the Other sex, or under what species does it open it?" (Miller, 2015, 2022)

The logic of the feminine prompts us to delve into the logic of difference, as articulated by several colleagues in various ways. The littoral transcends the narrow gate of One to the Other sex; it exists simultaneously, akin to Schrodinger's cat, as undecidable.

The indistinct imposes itself is undeniable:

She is so unique
Just settle for plurals
(*Woman*, Linn da Quebrada, 2017)

References

Adorno, T. W. (2002). *Aesthetic theory*. Continuum. London, 2002.
Apollinaire, G. (2010). *Aesthetic meditations on painting: The Cubist painters*. Parkstone International. New York.
Beckett, S. (1983). *Worstward Ho*. John Calder. London.
Blanchot, M. (1982). *The space of literature*. University of Nebraska Press. Nebraska.
Bowlby, R. (2007). Fifty-Fifty: Female subjectivity and the Danaids. In Bowlby (Ed.), *Freudian mythologies: Greek tragedy and modern identities*. Oxford University Press. United Kingdom.
Brousse, M.-H. (2016). *L'objet caché des femmes* (*La cause du désir*, No. 94). École de la Cause freudienne. Paris.
Brousse, M.-H. (2019). *The feminine: A mode of Jouissance*. World Association of Psychoanalysis Libretto Series. Paris.
Camus, A. (1991). *The myth of Sisyphus and Other Essays*. First Vintage International Edition. Vintage Books. New York.
Fay, P. (2019). *Démons et merveilles de la féminité*. La Cause du Désir. No. 94. École de la Cause freudienne. Paris.
Freud, S. (1919). *The uncanny* (Pelican Freud Library, v.14) London.
Freud, S. (1955). *Studies on Hysteria*. Standard Edition of the Complete Psychological Works of Sigmund Freud, Vol. II.
Lacan, J. (1988). *The Seminar of Jacques Lacan, Book 2 [1954–1955]: The ego in Freud's theory and in the technique of psychoanalysis*. Cambridge University Press.
Lacan, J. (1993). *The Seminar of Jacques Lacan, Book III [1955–1956]: The Psychoses*. Routledge.
Lacan, J. (1997). *The Seminar of Jacques Lacan, Book VII: The ethics of psychoanalysis*. Norton.
Lacan, J. (1998). *The Seminar of Jacques Lacan, Book XX: Encore, on Feminine Sexuality, the Limits of Love and Knowledge. London: W.W Norton & Company (1972–3).*
Lacan, J. (2006). *Ecrits: The first complete edition in English*. W. W. Norton & Company.
Lacan, J. (2007 [1991]) *The Seminar of Jacques Lacan*. Book XVII: 1969–1970, The Other Side of Psychoanalysis. London: W.W. Norton & Company.
Lacan, J. (2019). *The Seminar of Jacques Lacan, Book VI: Desire and its interpretation*. Polity Press.
Miller, J.-A. (2005). *L'invention du partenaire*. Audio lecture, France Culture. Available at: https://www.lacan.com/miller4.htm

Miller, J.-A. (2015). On Lacan's Gide. *Lacanian Ink*, No. 45. New York, Wooster Pres.
Miller, J.-A. (2022). Is Feminine *Jouissance* not *Jouissance* as Such? (J. Jauregui, Trans.). *Lacanian Ink*, 55/56.
Nin, A. (1987). *A literate passion: Letters of Anaïs Nin and Henry Miller, 1932–1953*. San Diego: Harcourt Brace Jovanovich, 1987.
Ovide. (1860). *The metamorphoses*. A. S. Baenes & Buke. New York.
Quebrada, L. "Mulher". (2017). Available at: https://www.vagalume.com.br/linn-daquebrada/mulher.html
Shelley, P. B. (2004). *A defence of poetry and other essays*. Project Gutenberg ebook.

Marcela Antelo is a psychoanalyst based in Salvador, Bahia, Brazil. She is an Analyste Membre de l'École (AME) of the World Association of Psychoanalysis (WAP) and the Brazilian School of Psychoanalysis Escola Brasileira de Psicanálise (EBP), former president of the Brazilian School of Psychoanalysis. With a master's degree in Philosophy from Argentina and a Ph.D. in Communication from Barcelona, her thesis focuses on "The Uncanny Strangeness in Cinema." She teaches Epistemology at the Psychoanalysis Institute of Bahia (IPB) associated to the Freudian field.

Chapter 6
The Body Beyond Castration: A Legacy of Lacan

Marcelo Veras

This text proposes the idea that, Lacan, with his most well-known phrase, "A woman does not exist," redefines a clinical approach to the feminine that diverges from the solutions proposed by Freud's Oedipus complex. Lacan's clinical perspective on the difference between the sexes, most fully articulated in his Seminar XX, is a clinic in which men and women seek their sexual position based on an alterity that never transforms into complementarity. Thus, men and women never fully complete themselves sexually in the presence of the other sex. It is a logic distinct from the one that makes men and women beings where there is a pure virile element correlated to the phallus on one planet and a pure feminine element correlated to castration on the other. We are all, regardless of biological sex, affected by what escapes the binary of phallus/castration. This way, the misconception that men are from Mars and women are from Venus is dismantled. We are all Martians in the face of an inaccessible Venus.

The Cosmetics of Bodies

I intend to reflect on the importance of Lacanian theory in thinking about the status of the human body in the twenty-first century. I will go through some contemporary examples, as the provocation of the singer Lady Gaga, and a commentary on two films that point to the post-human body. Bodies are not just dressed and made up; it is in the combination of aesthetics with the boundaries of bodily transformations made possible by various current techniques that we will consider in terms of what this new cosmetic might be. The theme of the cosmetic body opens two modes of interpretation: the body in which cosmetics, like a veil, serves as a barrier to the

M. Veras (✉)
Federal University of Bahia, Salvador, Brazil

S. H. Klempe, A. Madill (eds.), *French Psychoanalysis Revisited*, Annals of Theoretical Psychology 20, https://doi.org/10.1007/978-3-031-68534-7_6

gaze, and the body that undergoes changes—in the flesh—in the face of that gaze. In this latter sense, the body itself is cosmetics. It is entirely different to think of a body that dresses and applies makeup versus a body that transforms itself with new techniques of bodily intervention, ranging from plastic surgery to gender reassignment surgeries, from piercings and tattoos to forms of art called body modifications.

One lesson that Lacanian psychoanalysis learned from capitalism is that anything can take on the semblance of object a, in other words, of a commodity. Starting from this realization, the female body and its parts can be a gadget like any other. It is sensitive to the laws of consumption and has become a prototype condemned to be updated, just like the new products on an assembly line. The body has become a large business counter where each individual part can be bought or sold. We can establish a distinction between the body in the arts and literature, an object of contemplation, and the body in society of the absolute gaze, an object of exposure. Thus, following the logic of the media gaze that invades us through every visible pore, it is impossible to separate the cosmetic element from the gaze of the Other. Cosmetics arise from the mirror and attempt to correct the structural flaw in the constitution of narcissism that has been present since Freud in the distinction between the Ego Ideal and Ideal Ego (Freud, 1914).

It is in this gap that we will situate the Lacanian object's condition, something that is in the biological body but does not integrate into the narcissistic image. It's as if something of the body cannot be translated into the mirror stage we call the Ego. This is the object *a* (which for Lacan is always opaque in the narcissistic image) and its illusory reflection in the mirror. Here is one of the readings we can make as a Lacanian response to the question "What is a body?" In the comedy of the sexes, as we will see later, this body responds to a male fantasy, which turns parts of the body into fetish instruments for the other. With Lacan, especially when he elaborates his formulas of sexuation in the 1970s, the question of the feminine shifts from the binary concept of castration to a non-complementarity between the sexes. Thus, a woman's body conveys a *jouissance*[1]—experienced in the body—but that does not find words in the fictions of castration. After all, no woman is castrated; nothing has been taken from her by castration. It is always good to remember that castration is symbolic, a story or fabrication based on the visual observation of the anatomical difference between biological sexes and responds by attributing a sign of mutilation to the absence of the imaginary penis in the other's biological body.[2] It implies losing something that one never had.

The importance of the visible has reached unprecedented levels in the contemporary world. The gaze object has taken over all aspects of modern life. The proliferation of screens and cameras has completely blurred the line between public and private. Technology has advanced to the point where the interiority of the body was

[1] We chose to keep the French word Jouissance instead of enjoyment.

[2] It's worth checking out Freud's fun text: *Some Psychical Consequences of the Anatomical Distinction between the Sexes* (1925).

the stage for the most-watched television series in the world at the beginning of the new millennium, CSI,[3] where the victim's entrails fascinated millions of viewers. Photography, cinema, and scanning devices have been used to convey information much more quickly than texts. More than ever, we take seriously the adage that a picture is worth a thousand words. Cosmetics presuppose that it is possible to add or remove something from the image, promoting the alignment or reconciliation of one image with another without the interference of significant equivocation. In this sense, it is always a technology, an apparatus of existence to cover up not only the imaginary but also the symbolic flaw. On one hand, the specular image attempts to align a pleasurable, real substance with the imaginary; on the other hand, the *troumatisme*[4] of language obstructs this alignment. Without the symbolic, the body's relationship with the image would be purely ethological. However, when this alignment depends on the desire of the Other—on their whims—we move from ethology to aesthetics.

The clinical study of castration, a Freudian discovery, explored how the imaginary discrepancy between a and i(a) can be addressed through its expression as inhibition, symptom, or anxiety. Lacan, with the concept of object *a*, goes further and addresses the same discrepancy, no longer through castration but by exploring the relationships of extraction, separation, and approximation of the object. We will return to this point later.

In 1949, Lacan established the foundations of Ego formation in its articulation with specular identification. The function of the mirror stage is to establish a relationship between the organism and its reality. The prematurity of the infant is equated with a totalized form of the body. It is an alienating identification (the image) that initially symbolizes the Id and then, moves to the Ego. Lacan's theory of the mirror stage is then understood as the structural crossroads of subject formation (Recalcati, 2003). In summary, the fragmented body reconstitutes itself as a formal and imaginary unity, providing the real body with an ideal-type solution. From this perspective, we can think of the body and its form as a treatment.

In the globalized world, starting from the twentieth century, the massive cosmetics industry trade demonstrates that, as in all aspects of contemporary life, capitalist frenzy has elevated cosmetic practices to another level. While tradition and culture used to be determining factors, today, it is the market that dictates the rules. What we observe—especially in Brazil, a country with one of the highest rates of plastic surgeries, where the female body has become a commodity in "fashion systems" (Barthes, 1980)—is that the use of the body reveals the fragility of symbolic elaborations that can serve as a foundation.

There is a radical rupture here between thinking of cosmetics as a cultural element or as a commodity. Cosmetic products, like objects *a*, are themselves objects of drive that can lead to addiction like any other drug. We notice the change when

[3] CSI: crime scene investigations—de 2000 a 2015—is a TV series created by Anthony E. Zuiker

[4] Lacan's expression that resonates with "traumatism," in this case, the true traumatism, would not be the birth, as evoked by psychoanalyst Otto Rank, but the shock of the Other's word with the flesh. The word that makes a hole—*trou*—in the reality of the body.

cosmetics cease to be a connector between the sexes and become a mode of *jouissance* in themselves, without necessarily passing through the field of the symbolic Other. Cosmetics no longer respond to a phallic logic but attempt to capture the *jouissance* that escapes the a–a′ equation directly in the imaginary, without the twists and turns of the symbolic. Therefore, the aim is to treat the imaginary flaw with the imaginary itself.

From Castration to the Separation of the Object

It is possible to distinguish two different conceptions of the production of one's own body. The body that separates itself from its objects, where it distinguishes itself, for example, from the breast that would supposedly complete it, and the body that is produced from the cannibalism, which is the characteristic of the first Freudian identification with the father.[5] For Lacan, this operation occurs precisely through the subject's entry into language, as embodiment turns the real of the body into a body inhabited by language, or, in his words, "language eats the real" (Lacan, 2005, p. 31). However, Lacan's work in the 1970s served to emphasize that not everything in the body is marked by language: that is, the point from which an elaboration of femininity arises is not delimited by phallic punctuation.

Questions of style become increasingly important when traditions no longer guarantee a sense of belonging and recognition of a place in the Other. Finding a place in the Other is no longer a condition assured by filial relations. Nothing is more uncertain than the saying "Like father, like son." Here, we can propose our hypothesis that paternal naming, which allowed for identification with fraternity, has been replaced by an anonymous gaze. The "absolute eye," taking the title of the psychoanalyst Gérard Wajcman (Wacjman, 2010). Existence used to be guaranteed by a place in the symbolic, but today it is sustained more by a place in the visual field, the title of one of my books, *Selfie, Therefore I Exist*. In other words, from being named to being seen. This opens a new perspective for reading Freud's theory of identifications. Imaginary effects, enhanced by cosmetic technology, advance in the direction of ensuring existence itself, not existence guaranteed by group identification. Everyone has their own lifestyle.

In the past decade, singer Lady Gaga made an impact on the public and garnered significant media attention by appearing dressed in raw meat at an awards ceremony. It is precisely this new exposure of clothing and the female body that interests me. Here, there is no longer an eroticism guided by any discourse, object, or word. What is most striking is that, beyond discourse, there is a clear evocation of the raw sex appeal of this meat that covers the flesh itself.

---

[5] For psychoanalysis, it is fundamental to establish the conditions of otherness that govern the subjective experience of one's own body. This experience was described by Freud in Chapter VII of the text on Mass Psychology under the name of embodiment, *Einverleibung*.

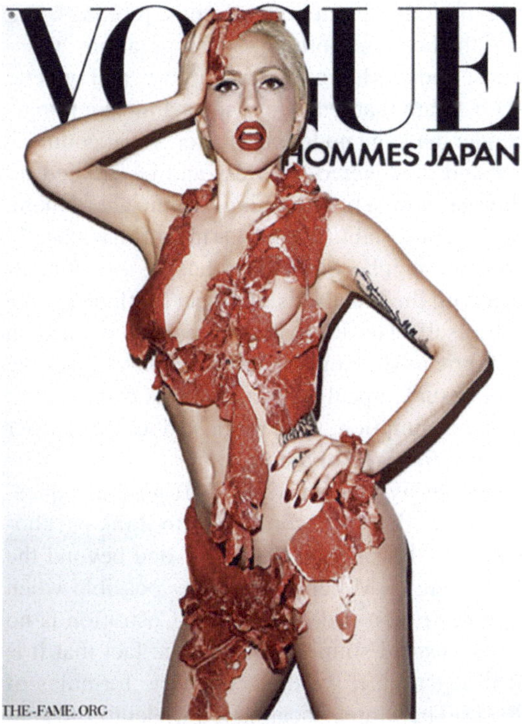

Here we realize that the cosmetic body is inscribed in a realm beyond castration. What changes with the transition from castration of the phallus to the extraction of the object *a*? If it is the phallus that gives a body to *jouissance*, then it is the phallus that establishes a dialectical, binary regime that, as a signifier of desire, promotes the transition from the narcissistic world to the social bond (Lacan, 1998). However, when object *a* gives a body to *jouissance*, without passing through the circuits of desire, we are in a nondialectical regime, without exchanges, without words. The partner, in this case, is reduced to being a dealer of objects for consumption. Singer Lady Gaga, in a nonsensical sex appeal, humorously conveyed the deposing of the classic phallic investiture whose appeal summoned desire and the symbolic field.

The reference to Mario Perniola's "Sex Appeal of the Inorganic" resonates at this point. In this book, the philosopher and aesthetics professor at the University of Rome starts from Walter Benjamin's observation about fashion to explore the intrinsic participation of the inorganic in the experience of the body as a sentient thing (Perniola, 2005). Fashion proves, through the contours of fabrics, that the body is an object-form, and its imaginary conformation depends on the inorganic elements invested in them. The mention of the inorganic is a way of highlighting the experience of the body beyond the reference to the phallus. The sex appeal of the inorganic considers the body as a "giving itself as a sentient thing and grabbing a sentient thing." From this point of view, the body is understood as clothing, that is, as an extension that we wear. The notion of a "look" summarizes the author's argument: "in the look, the experience of clothing as a body extends, prolongs, and radicalizes itself into the experience of the body as clothing: makeup, tattoos, gymnastics, hairdressing, dietetics, aerobics, bodybuilding, plastic surgery, and genetic engineering constitute the next steps on a path that leads to man as almost a thing."

In this "clothing-body," beauty, gender, and age no longer matter. What counts is "the disposition and attitude to cover and be covered, to dress and be dressed, to envelop and be enveloped by fleshy fabrics, which have nothing organic about them, which cannot be differentiated from clothing, fabrics, and garments that usually hide" (Perniola, 2005, p. 62). In this operation, it becomes clear that the loss of phallic investiture of the body is correlated with the prosthesis of object *a* offered in the market in the experience of the body itself. The logic of the market, present in everything that governs objects in the fabric of shaping the cosmetic body, raises the following question: if this nonsensical sexual appeal fuels a headless drive circuit where the body is just another object of consumption, what purpose does the partner serve beyond being a source of *jouissance* for parts of them?

Lacan's last teachings seem to be precisely conceived to confront these questions, so prevalent in the twenty-first century. In other words, how to think psychoanalysis beyond the dialectic of castration, "beyond the Oedipus," and beyond the primacy of the symbolic phallus. According to Miller, this is only possible when Lacan promotes a disjunction between castration and prohibition. Castration is no longer referenced to the phallic law and instead simply indicates the fact that it is possible to make a negation, a logical negation, if we think from the formulas of sexuation in Seminar XX (Miller, 2011). Therefore, Lacan is led to detail the anatomical separations of the object, the natural extractions of the object within the body, precisely without the intervention of an agent who would be the Other. This is what he calls, a term taken from Freud, separation. Miller draws attention to the fact that by dissociating the extraction of object *a* from castration, Lacan creates a neologism, "separtition." Not castration, but the separation of objects, the separation of organs. He speaks of "separtition" (Miller, 2005) to indicate that it is like a partition inside, which concerns the subject of the organism.

With What Body Shall I Go?

The classic question that refers to the feminine universe—"With what clothes shall I go?"—is linked to the semblance constructed by objects that, according to Brousse, "touch the female body" (Brousse, 2012). Clothing, jewelry, high heels, makeup, and nail polish are "objects that precisely make the mask itself exist, like a veil in the face of the difficulty of saying (…) these objects that group together under a category in psychoanalysis, which we call the category of the phallus." In other words, these are objects that refer to the phallic field and are related to an attempt to anchor oneself in the face of the absence of representation of what it means to be a woman.

Thus, the insufficiency of the image in responding to "Che vuoi?" and the subject's question "What am I for the Other?" can find an answer in the construction of the body image. From this perspective, body cosmetics are understood as a satisfaction linked to the body image that can help dialectize and enter the signifying game by making signs of the marks on this body. In other words, here cosmetics would help dialectize the body image, to enter the game. In another vein, modifications can take on the value of a bodily event, an entanglement with everyone's unique language.

In today's context, in the face of the decline of the ideals of the Other—I (A)—it falls to everyone to construct their own image; it is up to the ideal self, i(a), to produce their clothing, which is made with the body itself. When entering the capitalist discourse, the infinite number of fake objects that are offered as a remedy for an imaginary wound that runs much deeper. We can read this way of presenting oneself through the question: with what body shall I go? With what body do I present myself on my first Tinder date? This relates to the construction of a body designed to handle a *jouissance* that is not incorporated into the symbolic field. It is the circuit of the drive around the body itself as an object. Thus: "a new dimension emerges for the classical philosophical question of 'having' a body or 'being' a body. In the age of gadgets, we can talk about the body as something that is dressed. Dressing a body and adjusting it to the self in front of the mirror" (Veras, 2006).

Laurent, when commenting on the delusions of neuroscience in its attempt to locate the speaking being in the body, states that despite this idea, something always seems to escape. He concludes that "[...] there is no possible unified representation of the subject that psychoanalysis deals with [...] the body is always fragmented" (Laurent, 2011).

Despite the advances of the so-called society of images, for psychoanalysis, the unifying image of the body does not negate the fragmentation of the drive experience—on the border between the somatic and the mental, as Freud had already taught us (Freud, 1915). When we think about the effects of the decline of the paternal naming and the emergence of new forms of naming, which involve inscriptions often made on the surface of the body (tattoos, scarification, and piercings, for example), we conclude that in the Oedipal naming, the body is a construction that is based on an eminently symbolic function, mediating between the imaginary body and the real body, allowing for analytic interventions based on a flexible symbolic order. What would a flexible symbolic order be? It would be a symbolic order that does not have the father as the agent of castration and the establishment of the law. Therefore, the new forms of *jouissance* go beyond the symbolic order, which implies a form of jouissance that can be experienced in the body but without words to describe it.

Surgery Is the New Sex

I propose, through the analysis of two recent films, to reflect on the erotic condition of the contemporary world and glimpse future perspectives, an eroticism that no longer necessarily passes through the veil of castration. In the new film by David

Cronenberg, "Crimes of the Future," winner of the Palme d'Or at Cannes 2022, one of the characters utters the phrase: "Surgery Is the New Sex." In other words, the reality introduced by new technologies is distancing us further and further from sexuality governed by the Darwinian destiny of the sexes. With the evolution of techniques on the body, like surgical interventions and other treatments, including sex reassignment surgeries, we observe a disruption of the semblances of what were previously considered the male body and the female body. However, as we said in the beginning of the text, we learned that castration was never about the organ, which means that anatomical modifications do not provide answers about sexual relationships and the erotic condition of modern subjects.

The other film is called "Titane," directed by Julia Ducournau, which won the Palme d'Or in 2021. It is evident that the question of the post-human body unsettles the world of the arts. As psychoanalysts, it is always important to learn from the arts and not attempt to explain them.

According to the director, "Titane" is a contemporary love story of new bodies in vertiginous turmoil. What interests us in the context of our discussions is what remains of love in the film's plot. In it, the boundaries between loving and destroying, being human or being a machine and being nostalgic for the Oedipus complex or reinventing it, are profoundly modified. It tells the story of a young woman, affected since childhood by a titanium prosthesis in her skull, who becomes a serial killer starting with her parents. To evade the police, she decides to change her gender and pass herself off as the son who disappeared decades ago from a fire chief. He initially believes that she is his lost son, but the charade cannot last long because the character is pregnant from a sexual encounter… with a car. Yes, you read that correctly. Until the end of the film, it is unclear what could have been generated by the pregnancy, something human or a machine. Does the argument shock? Yes, that is one of the functions of art. But more and more, we engage in love with machines; virtual sex increasingly prevails over carnal sex. In other words, the flesh has been replaced by the image of the flesh. The new organs of pleasure allow for a suspension of castration and direct enjoyment of the object. A meeting with an analyst can reinscribe these new bodies into discourse by pointing to the absence of the sexual relationship.

It is not enough to have been biologically born as a man or a woman; the issue is more complex. The character played by Viggo Mortensen embarks on a quest for new organs within his own body. Each new organ is transformed into a work of art. Copulation is replaced by the pleasure of this new imaginary body. We are not far from the post-organic man, as described in the book by the Argentine Paula Sibília. We can think of an irony in the style of Voltaire: "God made man in his own image, and man paid him back in the same coin."

Both films show how humanity goes beyond nature and makes its destiny out of new anatomies. We are increasingly inhabited by prostheses. There is no longer a solid territory for the phallus as a metaphor for the sexual object; copulation occurs with machines, just as the future of humanity is to feed on plastic, not proteins. We are not far; in March 22, Dutch scientists detected plastic in the human blood. However, nostalgia for the old Darwinian body is futile. The intrusion of new technologies has made our bodies Lamarckian. Conceiving psychoanalysis beyond the Oedipus complex leads us to realize that everyone's *jouissance* involves opaque zones that will never be illuminated by the erection of the phallus. It is no coincidence that the issue of being transgender is so current nowadays; humanity is evolving toward the transhuman, even though, as beings anchored in the past of language, we always have one foot in phallic nostalgia.

The first step in addressing the issue of the body in Lacan is the body subjected to the father's law. Freud developed this theory in various points, for example, when he considered a difference between the Oedipus complex of boys and girls. Lacan initially formalized the Freudian Oedipus through linguistic reduction of the myth, with the Name-of-the-Father and the paternal metaphor. Through this process of symbolization, the Name-of-the-Father replaces the unknown (x) of the mother's desire and gives it meaning. The subject is thus led into a normalized relationship with desire, submitting to the symbolic Law. The effect of the metaphor is to engage the subjects in thinking, enjoying, reproducing, etc. according to the ideals traditionally associated with their gender. This formalization led him, in a second phase, to reduce the father not to a name but to a function that allows for a plurality of supports, the Name-of-the-Father, in its diversity. Lacan had, in fact, diagnosed the decline of the all-powerful father since the 1930s. There is no "The Father," but a swarm of signifiers (master signifiers) capable of naming the ways of *jouissance* of an era. This pluralization accounts for contemporary mutations and, in particular, the great diversity of sexual life: everyone invents their own way of enjoying and loving, claiming a name for scenarios that dethrone the Oedipus complex as the sole solution to desire.

Lacan had, therefore, anticipated the era of gender fluidity that goes beyond the binary of male/female. Men, women, and genders of all kinds are, above all, beings of language. Paternity and soon maternity, marriage, are all fictions. He goes on to consider a dissonance between, on the one hand, the sexual positions defined in the Other, which lend themselves to all significant shifts, and on the other hand, the surplus of *jouissance* specific to everyone, one by one, arising from great inertia. In other words, there is tension between the master signifier S1, in the perspective of discourse, which collectivizes and idealizes, and object *a*, the object of jouissance. Lacan then goes beyond this tension between S1 and a, derived from the phallus, to engage in the path of *jouissance* that resists sexual common meaning.

The "part called man" allows a subject, regardless of their biological sex, to be situated under the regime of castration, in the sense of the limit established by the function of language. The regime of lack remains on the male side of the table of sexuation. The corresponding bodily experience is one of *jouissance* limited to the phallic organ, localized, felt as outside the body. This part defines the world of sexuality where one loves and desires the other based on the fantasy: one can only mentally enjoy the body of the Other ($\$ \lozenge a$).

Being a woman does not correspond to any universal law that can be transmitted from father to son. Each woman, one by one, must therefore discover what it means to be a woman without going through paternal. Lacan postulates a properly feminine *jouissance*: a bodily, ineffable, formless, and unreasonable *jouissance*. If we say it is "improperly" feminine, it is in the sense that feminine sexuality provides its best glimpse: in imaginary terms, the Freudian dark continent, or the oceanic feeling, in logical terms, the infinite or the *pas-tout*.

This is why no name can constitute the entirety of "all women." Lacan writes this lack of a name as S(Ⱥ). Being outside of language, this feminine *jouissance* does not offer any possibility for identification; we do not recognize ourselves in it, to the point where Lacan can say that it induces more the feeling of being Another to oneself. The demand for the speech of love is the only possible way to respond to this absence in the Other.

Wouldn't this be an effort in vain, since it is impossible to speak outside of gender and outside of the body, risking being led back to silence? The path of the letter, beyond meaning, advocated by Lacan, seems much more fertile to us, as it opens a new perspective on feminization.

Advancing through Freud's dark continent goes beyond the father, but not without him. However, it is important to think that this continent is not a geographical element; it is a body with unknown lands. We are all, men, and women, condemned to coexist with this speaking part and with this enjoyment that cannot be delimited by the symbolic. Because it is what we have closest to apprehending the real, the enjoyment of Ⱥ is not a promise of enlightenment of the dark continent but a demonstration that this part is not black but opaque.

We conclude that cosmetic interventions are performed in a world where the masculine and feminine no longer exclusively revolve around the phallic law. Beyond the Oedipus complex and castration, it is around the object and the possibility of resorting to the body as a technology for locating surplus *jouissance* that the society of the gaze orients itself. It will be necessary, then, to think about the cosmetic function of the body on a case-by-case basis, making the analytical experience the foundation for the theoretical formulation of the uses of bodies in the face of the agitation of the real in contemporary times. The various reeditions of body image (plastic surgeries, excessive physical exercises to create a new shape, scarifications, among many others) demonstrate a possibility for the speaker to have a body, creating an imaginary bond in the face of the emergence of the "lawless real." According to Besset "A body is always, for a subject, something of his own. In this sense, to exist, each person depends on having a body" (Besset et al., 2010).

How can psychoanalysis respond to this frantic pursuit of an ideal body? The answer lies in the identification with the symptom, the only identification that, being an equation that takes into account the enjoyment that escapes encounters with the Other, points to the body that one is, rather than the body that one has. These can be considered acts that impact the image of the body as an attempt to set limits to excess enjoyment—nominations that occur between the imaginary and real registers, distant from the symbolic order.

References

Barthes, R. (1980). *Sistema da moda* (Tradução de Lineide do Lago Salvador Mosca). Companhia Editora Nacional/Edusp.

Besset, V., et al. (2010). Rev. Mal-Estar Subj. *Fortaleza, 10*(4), 1256.

Brousse, M. H. (2012). O que é uma mulher? *Latusa digital* ano 09, n. 49. Junho de 2012.

Freud, S. (1914) On narcissism: An introduction. In S. Freud. (1971). *Collected papers. Volume IV* (pp. 30–59). The Hoghart Press and The Institute of Psychoanalysis.

Freud, S. (1915). Instincts and their Vicissitudes. In S. Freud. (1971). *Collected papers. Volume IV* (pp. 60–83). The Hoghart Press and The Institute of Psychoanalysis.

Lacan, J. (1998). Subversão do sujeito e dialética do desejo no inconsciente freudiano. In J. Lacan (Ed.), *Escritos*. Trad. V. Ribeiro. Jorge Zahar.

Lacan, J. (2005). *Le Sinthome. Seminaire XXIII*. Editions du Seuil.

Laurent, E. (2011). A análise de crianças e a paixão familiar in *Loucuras, síntomas e fantasias na vida cotidiana* (p 43). Belo Horizonte, Scriptum Livros.

Miller, J.-A. (2005). Introdução à leitura do Seminário 10 da Angústia de Jacques Lacan. *Opção Lacaniana, 53*, 53.

Miller, J.-A. (2011). Class V of the Lacanian orientation course entitled "Lacan's work" on March 2, 2011 – unpublished.

Perniola, M. O. (2005). *Sex Appel do Inorgânico*. Studio Nobel.

Recalcati, M. (2003). *Clínica del vacío: anorexias, dependencias, psicosis*. Editorial Sintesis.

Veras, M. (2006). Dismorfofóbico. Letra Clínica, revista da Escola Brasileira de Psicanálise/seção. *Pernambuco, 1*, 97–102.

Wacjman, G. (2010). *L'oeil absolu*. Editions Denoël.

Marcelo Veras is a psychiatrist at the Federal University of Bahia, a psychoanalyst member of the World Association of Psychoanalysis, former director of the Brazilian School of Psychoanalysis, former director of the Juliano Moreira Psychiatric Hospital, and currently the coordinator of the Mental Health and Well-Being Program at the Federal University of Bahia.

Chapter 7
Pleasure of Thinking in French Psychoanalysis

Tania Zittoun

> *André Green dit non aux fausses évidences et force les aveux avec appétit, générant chez ses interlocuteurs un plaisir de penser. Cet homme de controverse et de dispute ne refuse jamais la bataille : qu'elle soit perdue ou gagnée, il est toujours prêt à dire : « Ce qu'on se sera bien amusé ! » ("André Green says no to false evidence, and forces confession with appetite, generating a pleasure of thinking in his interlocutors. Man of controversies and dispute, he never refuses a battle: whether lost or won, he is always ready to say: "We had fun, haven't we?" (My translation)).*
>
> Maurice Corcos et Alejandro Rojas-Urrégo (2006, p. 17)

Children discover the world with amazement and surprise. They stop and look at leaves and flowers; they ask questions about the origin of things; they laugh at an incongruous idea; they engage, concentrated, in a new construction; and they can be exhilarated if they found how to solve a problem. This speaks for a specific pleasure—a pleasure many of us are familiar with—the pleasure of thinking. Although such pleasure is clearly visible in children, it is rarely discussed (but see Engel, 2015; Piaget, 1992). Among "professional thinkers" (Arendt, 1978), it is mentioned at times in philosophy, in the works of Spinoza and Hannah Arendt, among others (Arendt, 1978, 2005; Billeter, 2012; de Spinoza, 1655, 1677; Zittoun, 2023); yet it is surprisingly absent from scientific psychology. Of course, now and then, it is clear that a scholar enjoys her or his work, and so their passion for research is visible to others and at times described (John-Steiner, 1985; Marrow, 1969). But, with the exception of mathematics (Debellis & Goldin, 2006), affects, and especially pleasure, are not considered to be part of the experience of thinking. Interestingly, affects and pleasure in the psyche are theorised in psychoanalysis: in that domain,

T. Zittoun (✉)
University of Neuchâtel, Neuchâtel, Switzerland
e-mail: tania.zittoun@unine.ch

S. H. Klempe, A. Madill (eds.), *French Psychoanalysis Revisited*, Annals of Theoretical Psychology 20, https://doi.org/10.1007/978-3-031-68534-7_7

authors have devoted some attention to their own pleasure of thinking—Freud, in particular, wrote enthusiastically about the movement of his own thinking (Freud, 1897; Zittoun, 2023)—or to their patients'.

In this chapter, I address the question of the pleasure of thinking via French psychoanalysis. If, for the English-speaking world, French psychoanalysis is often synonymous with Jacques Lacan's contributions and heritage, there is actually a very rich domain of study that has gone through important evolutions since the 1960s. In this chapter, after introducing Freud's views on the pleasure of thinking, I will first focus on André Green's (2002a, 2004, 2011) theoretical contribution to the domain. Having met Jacques Lacan, critical of his theory of language, he indeed proposed a complex and integrative model of the psyche, accounting for the multiple forms of affects in language and mind. Not only did he play a major role in the evolution of French psychoanalysis after Lacan but also his model enables us to conceptualise the pleasure of thinking. Second, I turn to the rare work of Sophie de Mijolla-Mellor (1992), also initially a Lacanian, author of the only psychoanalytical book specifically devoted to the pleasure of thinking, and examine her propositions. Third, I propose to complement this reading with current reflexions in developmental and sociocultural psychology, domain in which I would like to understand the pleasure of thinking (Zittoun, 2023).

Freud and the Pleasure of Thinking

Sigmund Freud (1856–1939) was a passionate researcher and scientist, who definitely knew the pleasure of thinking and who theorised the psyche in a way that became foundational for all psychoanalysis.

As Freud was trying to capture his first intuitions in his 1895 *Project for a scientific psychology* (Freud, 1950), he kept a close correspondence with his friend Wilhelm Fliess. First, building his model seems difficult: on the April 27, 1895 (Letter 23), Freud writes: "I am positively devoured by it [NB: his project], till I am overworked and have to break off. I have never experienced such a powerful preoccupation" (Freud, 1950, p. 283). On May 25, letter 24, Freud goes on: "I have devoted every free minute of the last few weeks to work like this; I have spent the night hours from eleven to two with imagining, transpositions and guesses like these; and I never stopped till I came up against some absurdity or till I had truly and seriously overworked". On June 12, Freud seems to approach a solution: "the psychological construction looks as though it would succeed, which would give me an immense pleasure. Of course nothing certain can be said as yet. To make an announcement on this now would be like sending the six-months' foetus of a girl to a ball" (Freud, 1950, p. 284). More confident, he writes on August 6 (letter 26) "after long reflection, I believe I have reached and understanding of pathological defence and (…) important psychological processes". Yet he doubts 10 days later, on August 16 (Letter 27): "No sooner that I had made my alarming announcement and called for your congratulations after climbing a secondary peak, than I met with fresh difficulties and found that I had not enough breath for the new task. (...) Anyhow, skittles and mushroom-hunting are far healthier" (Freud, 1950, p. 284). He then puts the project on hold and comes back to it a few months later. And it is on October 20 (Letter 32) that Freud writes about his joy of discovery:

> ...the barriers were suddenly raised, the veils fell away, and it was possible to see through from the details of the neurosis to the determinants of consciousness. Everything seemed to fit together, the gears were in mesh, the thing gave one the impression that it was really a machine and would soon run itself. (...) – all this fitted together and still fits together! Of course I cannot contain myself with delight. (Freud, 1950, p. 285)

In these letters to his friend, attentive to his own psychic movements, Freud writes remarkably about the affective experiences accompanying his enquiry, from a devouring preoccupation, to despair and intense pleasure when "things fit together". He uses metaphors to formulate these experiences, where thinking is like hiking or being an adventurer—risking climbing a peak exposes oneself being out of breath—and contrasts with mushroom picking; and new ideas are like a baby girl foetus—not mature enough to be sent to the ball—or a running machine. Pleasure, here, is thus connected to long time effort, endurance and risk taking and achieved when things fit together, and although one can claim authorship, the new ideas hold enough together to get an autonomous life; in addition, some part of the pleasure seems connected with sharing these results with a friend. But are these experiences of pleasure theorised in Freud's work?

It is not the place here to present fully Freud's metapsychology, and the reader is probably familiar with Freud's two topological models of the mind—the first schematising the unconscious, preconscious and conscious, later completed with a second model of the id, the superego and the ego (for an overview, Freud, 1933, 1940a, b). Here, I need to emphasise the "economic" part of Freud's theorisation, which gives us a first grasp on the forms of pleasure of thinking.

In his first *Project for a scientific psychology* (1895), Freud poses a fundamental difference between the quantity of energy passing though the organism, and its quality, which can then be experienced as pleasurable or unpleasurable. Basically, there is a "trend in psychical life towards avoiding unpleasure" (Freud, 1950, p. 312); in other words, drives and needs want to be satisfied and anger and frustrations discharged. Yet the life of our minds and in society does rarely allow for such simple and immediate solutions; therefore, we think, and thinking is a way to transform "unbound" energy in something more durable or stable, when we move from unconscious to conscious processes:

> Restraints upon motor discharge (upon action), which then became necessary, was provided by the process of *thinking,* which was developed from the presentation of ideas. Thinking was endowed which characteristics which made it possible for the mental apparatus to tolerate an increased tension of stimulus while the process of discharge was postponed. It is essentially an experimental kind of acting, accompanied by displacement of relatively small quantities of cathexis together with less expenditure (discharge) of them. For this purpose the conversion of freely displaceable cathexes into 'bound' cathexes was necessary, and this was brought by means of raising the level of the whole cathectic process. it is probable that thinking was originally unconscious, in so far as it went beyond mere ideational presentations and was directed to the relations between impressions of objects, and that it did not

> acquire further qualities, perceptible to consciousness, until it became connected to verbal residues. (Freud, 1911, p. 221)

Thinking is an alternative to other actions; it explores possibilities ("experimental") by slowing down and decomposing the affective dynamics of mind. Objects that are affectively invested can become mutually linked and synthesised in new wholes. Thinking thus "binds" affective dynamics in new and more stable constructions, which can then become conscious when associated to words. As pleasure is related to the decrease "in the quantity of excitation *in a given period of time*" (Freud, 1920, p. 20), then thinking as release of tension may be pleasurable—even though thinking itself may be for a great part unconscious (Freud, 1940b, pp. 283–284). Note, then, that some of the affective charge of thinking comes from the intensity of the drives it originates from, and from the fact that it has been slowed down and reorganised, partly unconsciously, into a stable, low-intensity construct, which requires no discharge.

Later, in his second topological model, Freud proposes that the ego has as concern self-preservation and safety and thus deals with the demands of reality especially under the double pressure of the id and the ego. Again, it is thinking that enables to find this fragile equilibrium:

> Its psychological function consists in raising the passage [of event] in the id to a higher dynamic level (perhaps by transforming freely mobile energy into bound energy, such as corresponds to the preconscious state); its constructive function consists in interpolating, between the demand made by instinct and the action that satisfies it, the activity of thought, which, after taking its bearings in the present and assessing earlier experiences, endeavours by means of experimental actions to calculate the consequences of the course of action proposed. (Freud, 1940a, p. 199)

Hence, the fact that people learn to tame their instinctual life in the name of reality "cannot be without its effect on the individual's later readiness for culture" (Freud, 1940a, p. 201); a necessary desexualisation of our drives is achieved mainly through civilisation and education via thinking, or more daydreaming in the arts. Yet "It is *science* which comes nearest to succeeding that conquest: science, too, however, offers intellectual pleasure during its work and promises practical gain in the end" (Freud, 1911, pp. 223–224). Thus, science offers intellectual pleasure, mainly to be associated to this process of binding, and satisfaction at the end, due to the awareness of such pleasure. With such explanation, Freud can himself account for his own experiences of pleasure of thinking.

In Freud's model, thus, the pleasure of thinking has two main sources. First, thinking is connected with binding "unbound energy"; it mainly occurs in the ego. It lowers the tension through more complex constructs that have a form of stability. Second, the ego reorients, under the demands of reality, some of the dynamic demands of the instinctual drives into new objects; this "desexualisation" or substitution is key for culture, and indeed, and it supports the focus of the person on all kinds of objects of interest—including thinking in science, philosophy or the arts. In addition, but without entering in detail here, some of the processes of thinking occur unconsciously, and most happen as preconscious process; thus daydreaming and free associations, closer to the logic of the dream, always remain in the background of conscious thinking and also infuse it with some of its related pleasures—something to which we will come back.

Thinking Psychoanalysis in France

The history of psychoanalysis in France has been amply written (de Mijolla, 2007, 2010, 2012a, b; Green, 2002a; Roudinesco, 1994, 2009). It is well-known that Jacques Lacan played a very important role in its development after the war and in the 1960s; his contributions are multiple and controversial. On the one hand, he did call for a welcome "return to Freud", inviting to read his texts with new eyes, also informed by developments in the philosophy and social sciences of his time. On the other hand, his own theorisation and practice of psychoanalysis generated many debates, which ended up in important reorganisations of the field. Rather than presenting Lacan's contributions here, I will directly introduce Andre Green, whose work matured in the Paris of the 1950–1970s, period during which he started to discuss Lacan's proposition; I will summarise his debate with Lacan and present his own theorisation, showing how they contribute to reflect on the pleasure of thinking.

André Green and French Psychoanalysis in the 1960s

Andre Green (1926–2012) played an important role in the "refoundation" of French psychoanalysis and its internationalisation at the beginning of the twenty-first century. Born in Cairo in 1926, schooled in a French-speaking environment, he moved alone to France in 1946 to study medicine. Admitted in psychiatry in 1953, he started working in a provincial clinic before moving to Saint-Anne in Paris. He met Jacques Lacan first in 1955 when he came to give a lecture at the Henri Ey circle—a French psychiatrist—that Green was attending (Green, 2006, p. 286). Green obtained his PhD in 1956 on schizophrenia (Pirlot & Cupa, 2012, p. 1). In the meantime, the main psychoanalytical society in France, the Société Psychanalytique de Paris (SPP), attached to the International Psychoanalytical Association (IPA), had gone through an important crisis, when in 1953 the Société Française de Psychanalyse (SFP) was created around Lacan and his circle. Green started to train as psychoanalyst after his thesis; having to choose one affiliation, he joined the SPP.

At that time, in 1956, Lacan started organising prestigious conferences at Saint-Anne, where Maurice Merleau-Ponty, Alexandre Kojève, Claude Lévi-Strauss, Alexandre Koyré, etc. presented their work. They used to go for a drink at the Flore, and Lacan invited Green to join them; Green even reports that after the conference of Lagache, he invited him to sit next to him—an indication of their mutual respect then (Green, 2006, p. 287). Green admired the man and his intelligence, and he attended Lacan's seminar between 1961 and 1968. In return, at Lacan's invitation, he gave two talks, one of the "object a" and the other on the id in 1965 and 1967 (Green, 1997, p. 24, 2006, p. 309). He also accepted a patient proposed by Lacan after a control seminar (Green, 2010a, p. 189). Green thus for some time occupied "the difficult position of the lacanian in the henhouse" of the SPP (Roudinesco, 2009, p. 989, m.t.).

Although he was durably marked by his ideas, Green always maintained a critical distance from Jacques Lacan. On the theoretical side, he reproached Lacan to disconnect his theory from his clinical work, both in his work on language and in his later more mathematising propositions (Green & Benvenuto, 2007). Notably, Green questioned some of Lacan's core theoretical assumptions—the Lacanian idea that the unconscious is structured as a language. In effect, one of the first open criticism of Green to Lacan was on his theorisation of language. In 1953, Lacan had written the *Rapport de Rome* (Lacan, 1999) where he presented his first key theoretical ideas. Green read it in 1956; in Bonneval in 1960, he discussed ideas proposed by Laplanche et Leclaire inspired by it. In 1970 Green presented a report on affect at a psychoanalytical congress in Paris (Green, 1997), a reply to Lacan; this argument will be further developed in Green's 1973 book *Le Discours vivant* (1973, 2004) (translated as (Green, 1999)). Lacan became allegedly furious when he saw this book, calling it *abject* (Pirlot, 2018, p. 1002; Urribari, 2013, p. 102). In parallel, in 1961, a group of French psychoanalysts attended the International Psychoanalytical Conference in London. There, they met the British psychoanalysts, among which Donald W. Winnicott. Green was very impressed; he realised that "what we were doing in France was a form of *analytical discourse* deprived of clinical thinking, while in England, the clinical thinking was nourished by a very strong post-Freudian stream of thought" (Urribari, 2013, p. 103, m.t). He then became more acquainted with this group and especially with Winnicott and Bion's work, notably via joint publications, visits and meetings. Thus, adds Green, "since 1961 I had Lacan on one side, and the English on the other", and thus he started "to follow an independent pathway" since 1967 (Urribari, 2013, p. 103, m.t). But before following this pathway, let us come back to the core of the controversy.

Jacques Lacan's "Rapport de Rome" in 1953 (Lacan, 1956, 1966) played an important role in French psychoanalysis and had an inaugural and programmatic function. I cannot do justice to this complex text here, but I will highlight a few points important for this discussion. Among important ideas that were formulated there are the distinction between the real, the symbolic and the imaginary and, more importantly here, a discussion on the role of language. Lacan proposed to bring back the attention of the analysis on "la parole", the speech act, taking place between the analysand and the analyst, as communicative act. Itself is made of words within a language; language is a structure organising signifiers and significants—signifiers are material, and significant are meanings, which have to be identified in the analysis. Hence, the analysis has not to bring the unconscious back to consciousness, which some reading of Fred may suggest, but rather to bring the un-thought to parole. These points, Lacan justify by drawing on Levi-Strauss's work on the structure of filiation and de Saussure's linguistics. Commentators will later say that this discussion on the parole has enabled many analysts to change their way of listening, who then started to focus on their patients' actual discourse (Safouan, 2001). On the other hand, commentators also highlight that de Saussure is never quoted rigorously by Lacan, and his ideas were rendered in an approximate way (Green, 2010b; Urribari, 2013). Note that Lacan and Levi-Strauss had collegial, at time tensed exchanges (Tardits, 2009); Levi-Strauss however did not really understand his work and did not take psychoanalysis seriously[1] (Green, 2008; Lévi-Strauss & Eribon, 2009).

The main criticism of Green to Lacan's understanding of language is that it fails to theorise the role of affects. Green agreed with Lacan on the fact that Freud himself did not really theorise language and more specifically discourse in the cure, even though he paid attention to slips of the tongue and to networks of associations. However, Green emphasises that Lacan ignored the difference made by Freud between affects and representations, and so he could not fully theorise the relation of language to unconscious dynamics and to the body (Green, 2010b). Second, Green replaced Lacan's simple signified/significant distinction by a Peircean understanding of signs and sense-making, moving from binary—dialectic—to triadic models. Such view of the sign, he read as more compatible with Freud and better able to account for the nature of language in the cure; also, it gives more room to theorise the frame. Indeed, third, Lacan is famous for the freedom he took with the practice of analysis—short and interrupted sessions, interpellations of his analysands, etc.—which caused his expulsion from the International Psychoanalytical Association. On this point, Green notices that Lacan failed to theorise the importance of the therapeutical frame itself (Green, 1984, 2004, 2010b), something he himself did drawing on his knowledge of British psychoanalysis.

Green's Theory of Language and Psyche[2]

Both in his theoretical work, as well in the work of his commentators, a triple influence can be highlighted in Green's work, after Freud of course: these of Jacques Lacan's ideas, of Winnicott, and of Bion (Green, 2002b; Pirlot, 2015; Pirlot & Cupa, 2012). In what follows, I will focus on this, leaving out his later dialogues with post-Lacanians, as he engaged his important refoundation of the field (e.g. Green, 2013).

In Green's early work, based on his critic of Lacan's theory of language and the place of affect in psychoanalysis (Green, 1973, 1999; Zittoun, 2003, 2004), Green returns to Freud's analysis of the dream work and his distinction between primary and secondary processes. In his theorisation of affect and its link to language, Green considers that language demands two forms of dynamics, connected to the fact that,

[1] About psychoanalysis, he says "I do not pay more attention to this pastime that it deserves" (my translation from "Je n'accorde pas à ce diverstissement plus d'importance qu'il n'en mérite" (Lévi-Strauss & Eribon, 2009, p. 150).

[2] This section on Green and the next one, on Sophie de Mijolla-Mellor, are adapted versions from the chapter on psychoanalysis in the *Pleasure of thinking* (Zittoun, in press).

on the one side, discourse takes place in an interpersonal relationship, and on the other, it reflects intrapsychological dynamics. Through this, two forms of bindings occur: in speech, people have to respect the logic of secondary processes (i.e. the linearity of language, causality, the rule of noncontradiction, etc.); yet primary processes (i.e. free association via formal or semantic resemblances or contiguities) are also present—they appear through associations, the selection of semantic fields, etc. To these two forms of binding, already identified by Freud, Green adds a third form of linking: as language can be more or less grounded into lived experience, ternary processes are these that anchor the language in the body, in the id. With these three processes—secondary, following logic; primary, more associative; and ternary, anchoring speech in the body, and the ways in which they are combined, Green can distinguish different modalities of discourse. Hence, in literature, classical texts respect the rule of secondarity, yet give room for primary processes, as the reader can freely associate, fantasies are evoked and undertones are felt. In contrast, in modern literature, the writing can become more deeply anchored in pure affects, in the body (as in very expressive or experimental writing), or entirely on the side of secondarity (in very elaborated and "dry" formulations, losing the anchoring in the body, as in "nouveau roman"). The process of binding primary and secondary processes to different degree, Green calls tertiary; they occur in discourses, in dreams—otherwise they could not be told—and in thinking:

> So is also the work of thinking: although it is devoted to exercise secondary processes, it remains open to primary processes which enable the irruption of creative intuition even when the most rigorous rationality is engaged. However, if these processes can be allied, they shall not upset each other. If I dream, I have to leave upper hand to primary processes. If I think or write, I need to free myself from the attacks of primary processes, so as to ensure an intellectual activity that would not be impeded by the irruption of uncontrollable quantum of affect that may break down the economics of thinking. (Green, 1973, pp. 152–153, m.t.)

Such description suggests that different forms of affects, and with them, pleasures, may come to mind: some are more connected to primary processes, more immediate; others are connected to the transformations linked to secondary processes and more controllable "quantum of affects"—and these two can enrich each other.

Later in his work, Green included other aspects of Freud's inheritance in his theorisation and especially Freud's second topological model. In his 2002 integrative work, Green proposes to consider the psyche as organised around two lines, a subjectal and an objectal one, or in words more familiar to psychologists, along an intrapsychic axis and an inter-psychological one, or as inner and interpersonal dialogues. The latter includes a self-object-other relation, by which intrapsychic dynamics can be acknowledged, supported, symbolised, etc. On the intrapsychological level, Green maintains Freud's theory of drives, the idea that psychic experiences are connected through dynamics of binding and unbinding and propositions from Freud's first and second topological model.

His and others clinical experiences bring him now to propose a theory of *gradients* (Fig. 7.1), in which psychic experiences move through different layers of experience and are more or less elaborated. His model of the component of the psyche is

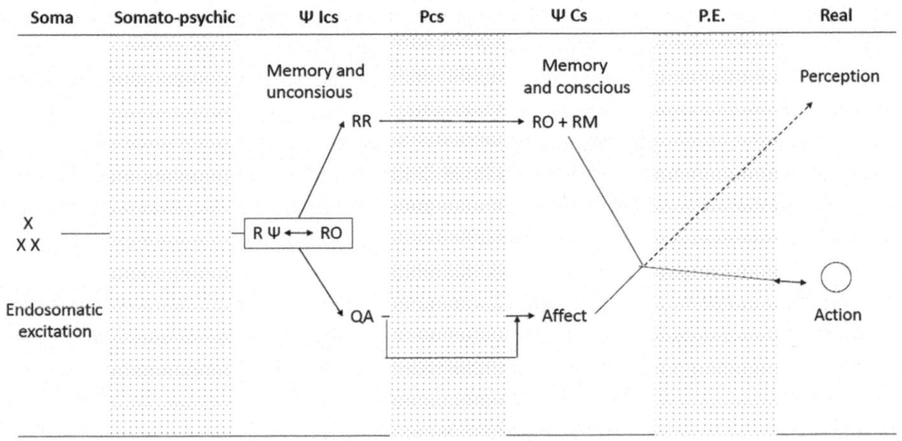

Fig. 7.1 Model of gradients adapted to English from Green (2012, p. 175)

an elaboration of Freud's model of the dream work and his later models, in the light of new findings—including the British analysts (Green, 2002b, p. 175).

The model is represented as a space, with a horizontal progression through seven zones: on the left-hand side, the soma, a somatopsychic barrier, where the psyche is close to the body and its drives, the *id*; next to the right is an unconscious zone; it is followed by a preconscious barrier and then a zone of conscious psyche, including memory and consciousness, "par-excitation" barriers and the zone of experiencing the real, involving perception on the extreme right-hand side. Green suggests that psychic phenomena can have a double origin: they can surge in the soma, as when we have excitation from with the body, or from the external world, through our perceptions. Some of our embodied experience and urges—the pulsion—remain there (we usually do not need to be aware of our organic functioning); only some drives pass through the somatopsychic barrier and enter our psyche—such as hunger, for instance. There is thus a first form of psychic inscription of the somatic motion in the psyche, which Green calls the "psychic representant of the drive"; it can then be associated to a "representation of thing", a mnesic trace of an experience of an object, which can be conscious or unconscious. This first couple has then two aspects: it contains a representant-representation that can enter preconscious experiences, as well a "quantum of affect". If these enter memory and consciousness, these are now constructing the pair representation of thing-representation of word, and affect, which can be composed in a different manner (Green, 2002b, pp. 174–175). This construct is both affective and symbolic—it binds an affect from the body, with a trace of images or experiences. It is these charged constructs that we typically find in our dreams (where hunger may make us dream of a wonderful festive meal we once had). Eventually, their two components are treated differently when they come closer to consciousness. Preconscious dynamics also act a dynamic filter; they may, or not, let some of the quantum of affect pass into consciousness, where, with some transformation, they may become affects; its more representational side may eventually become, in consciousness, a combination of a mnesic trace of words (the "representation of word") and of experience, the ("representation of object"). Hence, after various filters, the gargantuesque appetite may be turned into the idea of eating a fruit. This of course meets perceptual experience—an apple can suddenly become really attractive—and lead to an action: of eating that apple. What is interesting here is not only that ideas or experiences go through a series of transformation but also that affects do so. The diverse forms of brute drive, or more or less transformed affects, may always be active in the background, or to put it differently, at the periphery of our consciousness. I may be satisfied to eat an apple to calm my small hunger, but I still may experience my voracity in the background. In other words, I can have a heavily mediated and elaborated emotion or affect, yet it may be accompanied or supported by much more essential drives. The idea of the return of the repressed may, for instance, be translated into an unexpected brutal appetite where I eat meat savagely.

Such dynamics, I suggest, can also account for thinking. If there is, as we will see in the work of de Mijolla-Mellor, a fundamental drive to, know that drive has an embodied anchorage—it is constructed in infantile, preverbal experiences. However, the somatopsychic and the preconscious barriers will filter this pulsion to know, and this may turn it into an acceptable curiosity. This will depend on other experiences, and the sort of memories one has; it can thus, for instance, turn for someone into an interest in gardening and, for another person, into a passion for mathematics. This model thus synthesises the role of affects in thinking, for which there are two modalities: there is a first, very reduced quantity of affect needed for the inscription of traces in linking representations; second, there is a line of affects which can be discharged yet can also wake up representations, as in anxiety (Green, 2002b, p. 177). Indeed, if representations are normally linked by "concatenation", that is, an integrative form of linking, affects link through "diffusion", as in oil stains (Green, 2002b, p. 178). In addition, at the objectal level, representation and discourse are addressed to someone and are taken in dynamic of identification; therefore, one may wonder what role the other plays in the acknowledgement of these two processes. Such a model thus makes slightly more explicit the dynamic system intuitions of Freud and formalises the fact that representations have always a connection, even if it may be a distant one, to somatic experiences and affects. This, in itself, suggests that it is impossible to theorise thinking without affects, including potentially pleasure. More specifically, three main forms of pleasure may be associated to thinking: first, there is a specific form of pleasure in the building of stable liaison and systems that bind, in complex manner, reduced quantities of affect. Second, there is the affect that can be more freely experimented in case of "discharge", which then can be more freely diffused in mind. Hence, one may extend this by saying that there may be some pleasure in the activity of thinking itself, in the sense of creating links between diverse experiences, seeing consistencies, etc.; affects related to experiences are tamed, yet there is a pleasure in the binding itself—this is also probably what Green sees in the activity of reading, when he write "the object of sublimation is not the book, it is reading" (Green, 2002b, p. 64, m. t.). This is different from the third pleasure of having solved an issue at once, related to the end of tension, which can of course invade the whole mind—the Eureka, the pleasure of having found the solution of a problem of which Freud wrote himself. In addition, these take place in interpersonal relationship, which may add some intersubjective affective quality to thinking. These ideas are further explored by de Mijolla-Mellor, to which she adds an additional source of pleasure in the origin of thinking itself.

De Mijolla-Mellor: Theorising the Pleasure of Thinking with Freud

Sophie de Mijolla-Mellor (1946–) was trained as a philosopher, domain in which she graduated in 1970 in Paris, before turning to psychoanalysis. It is to be noted, then, that she belongs to the generation of French psychoanalysts just after André Green, joining the academic life in Paris during the years of the heated debates alluded to above. Sophie de Mijolla-Mellor did her thesis under the direction of Jean Laplanche, and learned her clinical work with Piera Aulagnier; she was thus trained by the group initially sympathetic to Lacan, before these scholars took distance from his work, both developing original and important contributions to international psychoanalysis (see among others Aulagnier, 2001; Laplanche & Pontalis, 1974).

In her thesis as well as in her later work, Sophie de Mijolla-Mellor (1992, 2009, 2012a) has pursued Freud's quest for the nature of thinking and its pleasure, anchored in a reflexion on sublimation. Her core question is, "what makes us think", how is it maintained, what does it bring and what are the alternatives. I here roughly summarise four elements of her analysis featuring in her book *Le plaisir de penser* (1992) ("The pleasure of thinking"[3]).

First, de Mijolla-Mellor finds an origin of the need to know in infantile desires—Freud's "scopic" instinct, that is, the need to see linked to a sexual curiosity, and a more fundamental question about one's own origin—where do I come from, how have I been desired by my mother or conceived by my parents and if it is so, how do I not risk to lose their love (if they don't need me, have other children, etc.?) Such "fantasy of the origin" is a fundamental trigger and source of curiosity: "Sexual curiosity is only one aspect of the problem, the one in which Eros dominates and that provides the investigator with some thinking pleasure not associated to the success of the research, but that accompanies the representation of its object" (de Mijolla-Mellor, 1992, p. 60)[4]. However, the most troubling issue is that even when the child wants to know and may start to explore the environment, he or she will never get a proper, definite answer. Parents don't really answer, and if they do, the

[3] At the time when I started the present enquiry, the only volume in psychology on this explicit topic—only a French philosopher edited a volume of classical text under a similar title (Comte-Sponville, 2015).

[4] For this author, here and elsewhere, my translation.

child cannot really understand what they say; this may inhibit their curiosity, or bring it to develop. The child's curiosity can thus become investigation of the world and one's own body, and the investment into questions that can only find a partial answer becomes an "investigation pulsion" (de Mijolla-Mellor, 1992, p. 63). As the child is trying to make sense of the environment and finds only partial responses to her or his questions about origins, he or she may experience a "trouble due to the discovery of ambivalence in him and the other. This provokes something which is not far from a cataclysm in the psyche by introducing a rupture in the ground of evidences on which the world of the child was laying and foremost its identificatory image" (de Mijolla-Mellor, 1992, p. 60). This supports the child's doubt, which causes the "rupture of the ground of evidence and [is] the starting point of an original thinking activity" (de Mijolla-Mellor, 1992, p. 65). But if this is the origin of thinking and its pleasures, how can it be further cultivated? According to the author, it can then become two types of searching: the "explorer", who finds himself in a unknown land and writes about the new people or environment she discovers, and the "detective", who, having a certain number of information, is looking for indices that may confirm his suspicions or may meet other facts (de Mijolla-Mellor, 1992, p. 64). These can thus become an investment into a mythical form of exploration to solve the issue, or a form of more systematic theory testing (de Mijolla-Mellor, 2012b, pp. 55–56)—there lies, according to her, the origin of the pleasure of thinking. However, this initial pleasure may also fail to develop. The author thus shows the negative of clinical cases: when parents deny the pleasure of exploring or consider the curiosity of the child as too dangerous, these can shut it down. In other words, the child's fundamental curiosity needs to be welcomed and supported: "Curiosity (…), seems natural as manifestation of interest for life, and in that respect, the tenacity of the child, intrepid explorer and indefatigable questioner, satisfies his parents, even when they complain feeling exhausted" (de Mijolla-Mellor, 1992, p. 92). Children's play—playing mother and father or the doctor—are ways to make sense of their intuitions about what they feel and see around them and thus perhaps offer "the unique mean to become conscious of a preconscious knowledge they have about the adults' sexuality and thus to dare appropriating it" (de Mijolla-Mellor, 1992, p. 94). There again, the author identifies boredom (ennui) and disinvestment of thinking as reflecting what the person perceives as forbidden thinking.

Second, the pleasures in the activity of thinking in adults demand more complex elaborations. The person searching for answers has to maintain and engage in this activity of thinking for a longer time. He or she has to abstain from the illusion of an immediate truth; delaying satisfaction thus demands a form of sublimation. In the domain of theorisation, the superego pushes forward the quest for more investigation and the need to avoid mistakes (de Mijolla-Mellor, 2012a, p. 119). Then, there is also a pleasure specific to the activity itself; de Mijolla Mellor quotes Freud (1933): "science does not only promise a practical gain at its end, it also offers intellectual pleasure while it is practised" (*New conferences 35*, p. 228, quoted in de Mijolla-Mellor, 1992, p. 133). In addition, engagement in thinking, debating or intellectual joust, is a way to experience aggressivity through thinking and the narcissistic pleasure it produces (de Mijolla-Mellor, 1992, p. 137).

Third, there is a form of pleasure in the satisfaction of finding the solution to a problem—even a momentary one—the form of illumination of "seeing", getting it, often nonconscious, which may rhythm and nourish the thinking endeavour (de Mijolla-Mellor, 2012a). Illumination, or more commonly, intuition, would thus be the realisation of a process of thinking occurring preconsciously; it is the end of a latent process (de Mijolla-Mellor, 1992, pp. 334–335). Reading through Freud and the observations of other thinkers, de Mijolla-Mellor shows that such intuitions can come as images, as aphorisms; it can make visible links that were not seen before, and it proceeds from a combination of primary and secondary processes; it can thus be a form of synthesis of very disparate material that were known or understood in very different manner. "In visionary intuition, thinking does not borrow images to be grasped by imagination through a sensible mode; it becomes itself image or schema in which primary and secondary processes are fused" (de Mijolla-Mellor, 2009, p. 351). Thus, only can an artists' or thinker's intuition at times transcend the thinking of its time.

Finally, from there, the author reflects on the intersubjective nature of thinking, which brings in a fourth form of pleasure. On the one side, there is the issue of how the thinker can convey their intuitions through language, both argumentative and more metaphorical; and on the other, she explores the very specific forms of pleasure of thinking that can occur through the psychoanalytical session. Regarding the former, she writes "The play of thinking cannot be dissociated from the act of naming and elaboration which it implies so as to remain as close as possible to the affect of the obvious briefly glimpsed, or rather to translate, that is transpose it" (de Mijolla-Mellor, 1992, p. 354). Here, the core issue is that for these two aspects, thinking needs to be able to move relatively fluidly from highly elaborated reasoning, as certain forms of secondary processes, back and forth through primary processes and images and less elaborated material, addressed to someone. I do believe that these combinations, these alliances, syntheses as well as translations, which convoke conscious and preconscious processes, have a core role in the pleasure of thinking.

In de Mijolla Mellor, we found four forms of pleasure associated to thinking—one is connected to a fundamental curiosity; a second is linked to the process of maintaining a difficult activity; the third is relational, connected to what is shared with someone else and which can be also connected to aggressivity; and the fourth is the pleasure of "getting it". Yet we have also seen that thinking itself seems, for her the main part, to be achieved beyond one's will—in great part, through preconscious processes.

Drawing on French Psychoanalysis to Think the Pleasure of Thinking

Four generations of psychoanalysts have theorised the psyche—from Freud, to the post-war authors such as Bion and Winnicott and, in France, Lacan, to French psychoanalysis including André Green and later Sophie de Mijolla-Mellor—and they have given elements to think the pleasure of thinking. Where did the French theories evolve since, and especially in what regards thinking and its pleasure? Actually, without surprise, theorisation has mainly focused on accounting for the type of difficulties their changing analysands brought to the cure, and to the obstacles in thinking they experience. The movement introduced by these authors was to move away from a focus on neurosis, to models accounting for psychosis and the so-called limit cases. On a theoretical side, this brought to many innovations: they theorised preverbal thought, the emerging conditions of symbolisation, and with it, the role of embodiment as can be manifested in psychosomatic disorders (Anzieu, 2006; Aulagnier, 2001; Golse, 2008). On the more empirical side, it lead to develop analysis so as to account for intergenerational transmission, cultural diversity, evolving gender and family dynamics, and the role of new technologies and virtuality in the psyche—which in turn required to reformulate earlier psychoanalytical propositions (e.g. Aulagnier, 2009; D'Amore, 2010; Moro, 2001; Nathan, 2007; Tisseron, 2007, 2008, 2013). However, given the strong attacks that psychoanalysis had to face—on the one hand, to the historical relevance of the domain, and on the other, against the general orientation to cognitive theories and therapies, supported by the health systems in many countries—not much space was given to new theorisations of the psyche.

Back to Sociocultural Psychology

The propositions made by the authors presented above give us the basis for theorising psyche and the pleasure of thinking. In the last part of this chapter, I wish to reimport these propositions in the theoretical field which is mine, that is, sociocultural psychology, an approach that examines human development in its environment with a specific focus on dialogical, semiotic dynamics (Grossen, 2021; Marková, 2016; Perret-Clermont, 2015; Valsiner, 2021; Zittoun, 2022a). That field, with its focus on the articulation between interpersonal and intrapersonal dynamics, its Peircean approach to the centrality of semiotic dynamics in sense-making, its developmental assumptions and, more generally, its complex system underpinning, is compatible with the new development of psychoanalysis, theorised as complex field, as, for instance, by André Green (Neuman, 2009a, b; Orgad & Neuman, 2015; Salvatore, 2018; Salvatore et al., 2021; Salvatore & Zittoun, 2011; Zittoun, 2015).

The main contribution of psychoanalysis to psychology at large is that it has extended the study of mind to include unconscious dynamics, that is, thinking processes that escape our consciousness and intention, and which have the power to create strong fields of association between disconnected part of our psyche and our experience—across time, notably based on affective and perceptual resonances with earlier experience—in our perception of the social world and others, often beyond our deliberate attention, and in the link of our psychic life to our bodies and organic experiences. Such understanding, developed notably through confrontations of theory with evidence gathered in the analytical setting (Zittoun, 2015), has shown how different forms of thinking can coexist in mind: beyond cognition and reasoning, people are engaged in conscious sense-making, as well as in daydreaming, and these three modalities of thinking may very well happen at the same time, some being more foregrounded than others in the trajectories of thinking. It also suggests that some of our thinking processes can be much more "cultivated", in the sense of culturally transformed and elaborated, than others—one may remain very intuitive in its reading of others, reacting through preconscious insights, and very systematic when approaching a specialised domain of knowledge, say, French poetry. Yet what psychoanalysis teaches us is that cultivation—the complex, culturally mediated elaboration of our semiotic capacities and understanding—is neither synonymous with consciousness, nor with distance from affects. Hence, the study of dreams shows amply that complex, socially transformed, or specialised and conceptual forms of knowledge can be pursued while sleeping (Freud, 1900, 1901; Lahire, 2018; Nathan, 2011) and even lead, at times, to real insights that will have some validity when checked in reality: knowledge can be worked through unconsciously, where primary processes and affects have the upper hand. On the other side, more mediated forms of thinking, such as in theorising, do not always need to be more distant from affects. This is a very important point: cultural psychology as well as psychoanalysis have kept an intellectual bias, by which they tend to emphasise that the elaboration of experience and affects via semiotic means, and especially language, enables to take distance from emotions and thus to achieve some "objectivity", or more reasonable thought. This kind of claims have been, and are still, of great importance when authors hope that theory, and thinking, can safeguard us from ideology or the threats of barbarism, threats that are currently resurging quicker than ever imagined. However, a thorough examination of psychoanalytical theorisation, and recent developments in many fields of psychology and social sciences, bring to question such assumptions. Indeed, not only do affects appear to be central to human experience; but even affects can be complex, highly elaborated and culturally mediated (Neuman, 2014; Salvatore, 2016; Salvatore & Zittoun, 2011; Valsiner, 2021; Zittoun, 2021). Think, for instance, of the subtly of emotional experiences that can be awaken by romantic poetry, Japanese tea ceremonies, or contemporary architecture.

Five Modalities of Pleasure

Based on these considerations, I wish now to come back to the pleasure of thinking. The reading of psychoanalysis just proposed, imported back to sociocultural psychology, can bring us to identify five modalities of the pleasure of thinking, which themselves can also be retraced developmentally (Zittoun, 2022b, c, 2024).

First, because it is grounded in a fundamental drive that can never be sully satisfied, thinking springs out of curiosity—curiosity that can then be domesticated as surprise, interested and amazement. Curiosity has in effect two undercurrents: a deep, unconscious one, that is our human lot, and that comes from the intrigue of the origins; and the second can come from the cultivation and tolerance of the unexpected, any form of gap, that, rather than being scary, may be an invitation to approach what is yet to be known and follow a fundamental need to know or to see (de Mijolla-Mellor, 1992). The first modality of pleasure is thus curiosity, spontaneous or guided, unconscious or conscious, from the infant's first surprises to the systematically cultivated surprise of the artist or the scientist.

Second, there is a pleasure related to the actual work of thinking—the process of linking, triggered by affective moments. Thinking requires indeed the binding of mnesic traces and representational and affective elements; it does involve the establishment of new relations, into progressively more complex wholes or Gestalts that have a form of temporary stability. Establishing these low-level yet stable energy configurations, which lower the state of tension while postponing emotional discharge, is per se pleasurable along the process of thinking (Green, 2002b). Again, this may be done spontaneously to contain affects, or may be systematically cultivated, as in learning-teaching activities, in research, or in any long-standing effort of pursuing an idea, building knowledge and competence, or putting in place the element that may serve for later new insights. After Piaget (Piaget, 2000), I call it a *functional* pleasure.

The third modality of pleasure is relational, or let us say, *dialogical*. Indeed, thinking is ontogenetically and intersubjectively dynamic: primary caring relations are required for the infant's capacity to symbolise experience and therefore for thinking. Along a developmental trajectory, as people think with others, these may acquire an identificatory function or shape the superego function—internal social regulation; thinking with others also is connected to shared playfulness, dynamics of recognition, approval or competition (de Mijolla-Mellor, 1992; Green, 2012). In any case, the process of thinking is fed with, or takes place, within the affective dynamics taking place within these interpersonal dynamics.

Fourth, the process of thinking demands the fluid movement of binding various psychic elements and experiences, through primary and secondary processes, with experience and affects being concatenated or freely diffusing. Thinking occurs for a great part as preconscious processes, binding unconscious and conscious elements; when this preconscious work comes to states of stability, they may be consciously experienced as intuitions, or illuminations, or the flash of having "got it". These experiences are pleasurable, and searched for, even though their result may be temporary and lead to new gaps and curiosities. In any case, given the fact that even conscious thought is anchored in deeper layer of the psychism, more and more complex and inclusive gestalts may also, even if the object of thinking may appear quite remote from self, be associated to the experience of becoming oneself more integrated (Bion, 1971; de Mijolla-Mellor, 1992; Winnicott, 1968, 1991). Hence, psychoanalysis thus accounts for the experience of *discovery*.

Finally, and fifth, we have seen that with their emphasis on unconscious dynamics, psychoanalysts are not so much interested in the conscious aspects of pleasure. However, Freud himself wrote about his pleasure of finding new models; in the epigraph at the beginning of this chapter, we read about the pleasure of Green to have a good fight; and many of the authors quoted in these pages have shared, orally or in written way, about their pleasure of cultivating curiosity, sharing thinking in dialogue working hard on ideas, or the exhilarating pleasure of getting it—and many other, professional thinkers or not, cultivate these pleasures. There is thus a fifth forms of pleasure of thinking, defined by the very specific awareness, or symbolisation, of one's own pleasure of thinking—which, drawing on the study of mathematics and philosophy (Debellis & Goldin, 2006), I would call *meta-pleasure*.

In addition, psychoanalysis calls our attention to two other transversal dimensions of the pleasure of thinking—which can all appear to different degree in any of the five modalities just singled out. First, as alluded, all these pleasures may be more or less anchored in the body, or distanced and detached from it, in all possible ways. Some people solve equations best when they are walking, or explain complex ideas when they can move their hand and their whole bodies, or nourish it with what they meet, see, smell or eat; others, at times, need absolute stillness to let ideas take shape in an abstract and conceptual way. In turn, ideas can be refreshing, enlightening or hitting hard. Second, as thinking emerges in children's first symbolisations and is importantly developed through play and imagination, a certain quality of playfulness is required in thinking. Yet again, playfulness can be more or less sought in thinking, cultivated and shared or, in contrast, reduced to the bare minimum—playfulness may be very welcome when planning a dinner with friends, yet less present when one has to justify one's expenses. In psychoanalysis, Winnicott is particularly known for his emphasis on playfulness, connected to a fundamental creativity, which can has been well identified by Green and other French psychoanalysis, and in more recent work emphasising daydream in our psychic life (Ogden, 2010).

In sum, reading French psychoanalysis from a sociocultural perspective gives good grounds to account for the fundamentally affective nature of thinking and, especially, for the pleasure of thinking.

Opening

To conclude, this short exploration of French psychoanalysis shows, I hope, that beyond the institutional conflicts that characterised the domain in the middle of the twentieth century, it has nevertheless integrated and rejuvenated the Freudian heritage and set the basis for a complex theory of thinking, notably through the integrative work of André Green but also through the curiosity and original contribution of authors such as Sophie de Mijolla-Mellor. It is my conviction that this domain, developing painfully its theoretical contribution through the complex demands of an always evolving clinically based research, can be a strong source of inspiration for today's sociocultural psychology.

In this chapter, I gave a glimpse of how that domain has enabled me to formulate and theoretically ground a formulation of the modalities of the pleasure of thinking. On this double theoretical anchorage, sociocultural psychology and psychoanalysis,

I have thus been able to follow complex trajectories of thinking, moving across time from less conscious to more conscious ones, in concrete and abstract way, at times carried alone, at time shared, and that combine all the nuances of pleasure of thinking (Zittoun, 2023). One of these trajectories is that of my own interrogation about the pleasure of thinking: it went from my initial surprise of seeing it not theorised, through the hard work of exploring the literature, to too rare moments of insights—for instance, of these five modalities—to more reflexive movements; and now, I have tried to share it with you.

References

Anzieu, D. (2006). *Psychanalyse des limites* (C. Chabert, Éd.). Dunod.

Arendt, H. (1978). *The life of the mind*. A Harvest Book. Harcourt, Inc.

Arendt, H. (2005). *Journal de pensée. Denktagebuch (1950–1973)* (U. Ludz & I. Nordmann, Éds.; S. Courtine-Denamy, Trad.; Original 2002, Vol. 1–2). Seuil.

Aulagnier, P. (2001). *The violence of interpretation: From pictogram to statement* (A. Sheridan, Trad.; Original 1975). Routledge. https://doi.org/10.4324/9780203361290

Aulagnier, P. (2009). Le droit au secret: Condition pour pouvoir penser. In *La pensée interdite: Vol. 1re éd* (pp. 15–41). Presses Universitaires de France. https://doi.org/10.3917/puf.forma.2009.01.0015

Billeter, J.-F. (2012). *Un paradigme*. Allia. https://www.editions-allia.com/fr/livre/897/le-propre-du-sujet

Bion, W. R. (1971). The Grid. In C. Mawson (Éd.), *The complete works of W. R. Bion: Vol. X* (Original 1971, p. vii). Routledge.

Comte-Sponville, A. (2015). *Le plaisir de penser. Une introduction à la philosophie. 600 textes essentiels d'Héraclite à nos jours* (1er édition). VUIBERT.

Corcos, M., & Rojas-Urrégo, A. (2006). Avant-propos: André Green ou la vérité de l'affect. In A. Green (Ed.), *Associations (presque) libres d'un psychanalyste. Entretiens avec Maurice Corcos* (pp. 13–22). Editions Albin Michel.

D'Amore, S. (Éd.). (2010). *Les nouvelles familles: Approches cliniques* (1er édition). DE BOECK SUP.

de Mijolla, A. (2007). Petite histoire d'une histoire de la psychanalyse en France. *Topique, 98*(1), 37–47. https://doi.org/10.3917/top.098.0037

de Mijolla, A. (2010). *Freud et la France: 1885–1945*. Presses Universitaires de France.

de Mijolla, A. (2012a). *La France et Freud: 1946–1953, une pénible renaissance* (1re édition). Presses Universitaires de France.

de Mijolla, A. (2012b). *La France et Freud: 1954–1964, D'une scission à l'autre* (1re édition). Presses Universitaires de France.

de Mijolla-Mellor, S. (1992). *Le plaisir de pensée*. Presses Universitaires de France.

de Mijolla-Mellor, S. (2009). *Le choix de la sublimation*. Presses Universitaires de France. https://doi.org/10.3917/puf.mijo.2009.01

de Mijolla-Mellor, S. (2012a). Dans le domaine de la pensée théoricienne. *Que sais-je?, 2e éd*, 117–122.

de Mijolla-Mellor, S. (2012b). Sublimation et pulsion de voir. *Que sais-je?, 2e éd*, 49–56.

Spinoza, B. de. (1655). *Tractatus de intellectus emendatione [et de via, qua optime in veram rerum cognitoinem dirigitur]. Traité de l'amendement de l'intellect [et de la voie par laquelle on le dirige au mieux vers la vraie connaissance des choses]*. (B. Pautrat, Trad.). Allia.

de Spinoza, B. (1677). *Oeuvres IV. Ethica. Ethique*. Presses Universitaires de France.

Debellis, V. A., & Goldin, G. A. (2006). Affect and meta-affect in mathematical problem solving: A representational perspective. *Educational Studies in Mathematics, 63*(2), 131–147.
Engel, S. (2015). *The hungry mind. The origins of curiosity in childhood.* Harvard University Press.
Freud, S. (1897). Letter 64, May 31, 1897. Extracts from the Fliess papers (1950 [1892–1899]). In J. Strachey (Éd.), *The standard edition of the complete psychological works of Sigmund Freud: Vol. 1 (1886–1899)* (p. 173-280). The Hogarth Press and the Institute of Psycho-analysis.
Freud, S. (1900). *The interpretation of dreams* (J. Strachey, Éd.; Original 1900, Vol. 4–5). Vintage.
Freud, S. (1901). On dreams (1901). In *The complete psychological works of Sigmund Freud* (New edition, Vol. 5, pp. 631–714). Vintage Classics.
Freud, S. (1911). Formulations on the two principles of mental functioning. In J. Strachey (Éd.), *The standard edition of the complete psychological works of Sigmund Freud: Vol. XII* (New Edition, pp. 213–226). Vintage.
Freud, S. (1920). Beyond the pleasure principle. In J. Strachey (Éd.), *The standard edition of the complete psychological works of Sigmund Freud: Vol. XVIII* (Original 1920, pp. 1–64). Vintage.
Freud, S. (1933). New introductory lectures on psycho-analysis. In J. Strachey (Éd.), *The standard edition of the complete psychological works of Sigmund Freud* (New Edition, Vol. 22, pp. 1–182). Vintage.
Freud, S. (1940a). An outline of psychoanalysis. In J. Strachey (Éd.), *The standard edition of the complete psychological works of Sigmund Freud: Vol. XXIII* (New Edition pp. 139–207). Vintage.
Freud, S. (1940b). Some elementary lessons in psycho-analysis. In J. Strachey (Éd.), *The standard edition of the complete psychological works of Sigmund Freud: Vol. XXIII* (New Edition, pp. 279–286). Vintage.
Freud, S. (1950). Project for a scientific psychology. In J. Strachey (Éd.), *The standard edition of the complete psychological works of Sigmund Freud: Vol. I* (New Edition pp. 281–397). Vintage.
Golse, B. (2008). Les signifiants formels comme un lointain écho du bébé que nous avons été. In *Didier Anzieu: Le Moi-peau et la psychanalyse des limites* (pp. 103–122). Érès. https://doi.org/10.3917/eres.rouss.2008.01.0103
Green, A. (1973). *Le discours vivant.* Presses universitaires de France.
Green, A. (1984). *Le langage dans la psychanalyse.* Les belles lettres.
Green, A. (1997). Le langage au sein de la théorie générale de la représentation. In M. Pinol-Douriez (Éd.), *Pulsions—Représentations—Langage* (p. 23-66). Delachaux et Niestlé.
Green, A. (1999). *The fabric of affect in the psychoanalytic discourse.* Routledge.
Green, A. (2002a). Brève histoire subjective de la psychanalyse depuis la seconde guerre mondiale. In *Idées directrices pour une psychanalyse contemporaine. Méconnaissance et reconnaissance de l'inconscient* (pp. 22–36). Presses Universitaires de France.
Green, A. (2002b). *Idées directrices pour une psychanalyse contemporaine. Méconnaissance et reconnaissance de l'inconscient.* Presses Universitaires de France.
Green, A. (2004). *Le discours vivant: La conception psychanalytique de l'affect.* Presses Universitaires de France.
Green, A. (2006). *Associations (presque) libres d'un psychanalyste. Entretiens avec Maurice Corcos.* Editions Albin Michel.
Green, A. (2008). Le rejet de la psychanalyse par Cl. Lévi-Strauss: *Texto, XIII*(4), En ligne.
Green, A. (2010a). *Illusions et désillusions du travail psychanalytique.* Odile Jacob.
Green, A. (2010b). La pensée lacanienne sur le langage. In *Illusions et désillusions du travail psychanalytique* (pp. 37–54). Odile Jacob.
Green, A. (2011). *Du signe au discours. Psychanalyse et théories du langage.* Editions Ithaque.
Green, A. (2012). *La clinique psychanalytique contemporaine.* Les Editions d'Ithaque.
Green, A. (2013). *Penser la psychanalyse. Avec Bion, Lacan, Winnicott, Laplanche, Aulagnier, Anzieu, Rosolato.* Les Editions d'Ithaque.

Green, A., & Benvenuto, S. (2007). Against Lacanism: An Interview With André Green. *European Journal of Psychoanalysis, winter-spring* (24). https://www.journal-psychoanalysis.eu/articles/for-the-love-of-lacan-4/
Grossen, M. (2021). When dialogism crosses the frontiers of psychology. In N. Muller Mirza & M. Dos Santos Mamed (Éds.), *Dialogical approaches and tensions in learning and development: At the frontiers of the mind* (p. 13-32). Springer International Publishing. https://doi.org/10.1007/978-3-030-84226-0_2
John-Steiner, V. (1985). *Notebooks of the mind: Explorations of thinking* (Revised). Oxford University Press US.
Lacan, J. (1956). Les Actes du congrès de Rome. *La psychanalyse, 1*(1).
Lacan, J. (1966). Fonction et champ de la parole et du langage en psychanalyse. In *Ecrits* (pp. 237–322). Seuil.
Lacan, J. (1999). Fonction et champ de la parole et du langage en psychanalyse. Rapport du Congrès de Rome tenu à l'Istuto di Psicologia della Università di Roma les 26 et 27 septembre 1953. In *Ecrits I* (Original 1966, pp. 235–321). Seuil.
Lahire, B. (2018). *L'Interprétation sociologique des rêves*. La Découverte.
Laplanche, J., & Pontalis, J. B. (1974). *The language of psycho-analysis* (D. Nicholson-Smith, Trad.; 1re éd.). W. W. Norton.
Lévi-Strauss, C., & Eribon, D. (2009). *De près et de loin*. Odile Jacob.
Marková, I. (2016). *The dialogical mind: Common sense and ethics*. Cambridge University Press.
Marrow, A. J. (1969). *The practical theorist. The life and work of Kurt Lewin*. Basic Books.
Moro, M.-R. (2001). *Parents en exil: Psychopathologie et migrations* (2e éd.). Presses Universitaires de France.
Nathan, T. (2007). *Nous ne sommes pas seuls au monde: Les enjeux de l'ethnopsychiatrie*. Points.
Nathan, T. (2011). *La nouvelle interprétation des rêves*. Odile Jacob.
Neuman, Y. (2009a). On love, hate and knowledge. *The International Journal of Psychoanalysis, 90*(4), 697–712. https://doi.org/10.1111/j.1745-8315.2009.00151.x
Neuman, Y. (2009b). On the alpha-function, chaotic cats, and unconscious memory. *New Ideas in Psychology, 27*(3), 305–311. https://doi.org/10.1016/j.newideapsych.2008.06.002
Neuman, Y. (2014). *Introduction to computational cultural psychology*. Cambridge University Press.
Ogden, T. H. (2010). On three forms of thinking: Magical thinking, dream thinking, and transformative thinking. *The Psychoanalytic Quarterly, 79*(2), 317–347. https://doi.org/10.1002/j.2167-4086.2010.tb00450.x
Orgad, Y., & Neuman, Y. (2015). Children's dreams. A novel interpretation. In P. J. Rosenbaum (Éd.), *Making our ideas clear: Pragmatism in psychoanalysis* (p. 275-293). Information Age Publication.
Perret-Clermont, A.-N. (2015). The architecture of social relationships and thinking spaces for growth. In C. Psaltis, A. Gillespie, & A.-N. Perret-Clermont (Éds.), *Social relations in human and societal development* (, p. 51-70) Palgrave Macmillan.
Piaget, J. (1992). *La formation du symbole chez l'enfant: Imitation, jeu et rêve, image et représentation* (8e éd, ed. originale 1945). Delachaux & Niestle.
Piaget, J. (2000). *The construction of reality in the child* (Original 1937). Routledge.
Pirlot, G. (2015). *André Green. Dialogues et cadre psychanalytiques*. Presses Universitaires de France.
Pirlot, G. (2018). The influence of Jacques Lacan's work on that of André Green. *Revue francaise de psychanalyse, 82*(4), 1001–1012.
Pirlot, G., & Cupa, D. (2012). *André Green. Les grands concepts psychanalytiques*. Presses Universitaires de France.
Roudinesco, E. (1994). *Histoire de la psychanalyse en France, tome 1: 1885–1939*. Fayard.
Roudinesco, E. (2009). *L'histoire de la psychanalyse en France—Jacques Lacan. Esquisse d'une vie, histoire d'un système de pensée* (Original 1993 & 1994). Le Livre de Poche.
Safouan, M. (2001). Le rapport de Rome, 50 ans après. *Figures de la psychanalyse, 5*(2), 7–15. https://doi.org/10.3917/fp.005.0007

Salvatore, S. (2016). *Psychology in black and white. The project of a theory driven science*. Information Age Publishing, Incorporated.
Salvatore, S. (2018). The systemic challenges facing the contemporary world. What semiotic-based psychoanalytic psychology can do and why. *International Journal of Psychoanalysis and Education, 10*(2), 5–12.
Salvatore, S., & Zittoun, T. (Éds.). (2011). *Cultural psychology and psychoanalysis: Pathways to synthesis*. Information Age Publishing.
Salvatore, S., De Luca Picione, R., Bochicchio, V., Mannino, G., Langher, V., Pergola, R. F., Velotti, P., & Venuleo, C. (2021). The affectivization of the public sphere: The contribution of psychoanalysis in understanding and counteracting the current crisis scenarios. *Subject, action, & society: Psychoanalytical studies and practices, 1*(1), 2–29. https://doi.org/10.32111/SAS.2021.1.1.2
Tardits, A. (2009). Lévi-Strauss et Lacan en 1956, une rencontre qui éloigne. *Figures de la psychanalyse, 17*(1), 27–42. https://doi.org/10.3917/fp.017.0027
Tisseron, S. (2007). *Secrets de famille mode d'emploi*. Marabout.
Tisseron, S. (2008). *Virtuel, mon amour: Penser, aimer, souffrir, à l'ère des nouvelles technologies*. Albin Michel.
Tisseron, S. (2013). The reality of the experience of fiction. In A. Kuhn (Éd.), *Little madnesses: Winnicott, transitional phenomena and cultural experience* (p. 121-134). Tauris.
Urribari, F. (2013). *Dialoguer avec André Green. La psychanalyse contemporaine, chemin faisant*. Les Editions d'Ithaque.
Valsiner, J. (2021). *General Human Psychology* (1st ed. 2021 édition). Springer Nature Switzerland AG.
Winnicott, D. W. (1968). Sum, I Am. In D. W. Winnicott. In *The Collected Works of D. W. Winnicott* (Original 1968, pp. 267–274). Oxford University Press. https://doi.org/10.1093/med:psych/9780190271404.003.0048
Winnicott, D. W. (1991). *Playing and reality* (Original 1971). Routledge.
Zittoun, T. (2003). The hidden work of symbolic resources in emotions. *Culture & Psychology, 9*(3), 313–329.
Zittoun, T. (2004). *Donner la vie, choisir un nom: Engendrements symboliques*. L'Harmattan.
Zittoun, T. (2015). Compatibility between early psychoanalysis and pragmatism. In P. J. Rosenbaum (Éd.), *Making our ideas clear: Pragmatism in Psychoanalysis* (p. 23-42). Information Age Publication.
Zittoun, T. (2021). Thinking with the rain. The trajectory of a metaphor in Vygotsky's theoretical development. *Integrative Psychological and Behavioral Science, 55*(4), 749–768. https://doi.org/10.1007/s12124-021-09646-4
Zittoun, T. (2022a). A sociocultural psychology of the life course to study human development. *Human Development, 66*(4-5), 306–324. https://doi.org/10.1159/000526435
Zittoun, T. (2022b, juin 4). *Rediscovering the emergence of the pleasure of thinking* [Paper presented in symposium « Towards an understanding of the developing child as a person: socio-cultural and semiotic perspectives », org. T. Zittoun & C. Rodriguez, disc Nancy Budwig]. 51st Annual meeting of the Jean Piaget Sociey, Philadelphia.
Zittoun, T. (2023). *The pleasure of thinking*. Cambridge University Press.
Zittoun, T. (2024). The pleasure of thinking in human development. *European Journal of Developmental Psychology*, 1–20. https://doi.org/10.1080/17405629.2024.2333949

Tania Zittoun is a professor in sociocultural psychology at the University of Neuchâtel (Switzerland). She studies learning and development in the life course; her theoretical work draws on semiotic cultural psychology, psychoanalysis and the social sciences. Her last monograph is *The pleasure of thinking* (CUP, 2023).

Chapter 8
The Constitution Issue: Arguments for a Psychology of the Subject

Sergio Salvatore

This paper moves from the idea that contemporary psychology is essentially a *psychology of objects*—an inquiry about conditions and processes that lead the cognitive agent to attribute qualities to mental objects whose existence is taken for granted. Mental objects are assumed as given and as such considered the starting point of the psychology inquiry.

The givenness of mental objects is grounded on a metaphysical assumption of the autonomous ontological status of the external reality, namely, that it consists of objects endowed with their own substance—mental contents are inner representational equivalents to self-contained entities, which have their place in the world-out-there: banknotes, screwdrivers, pens, computers, doors, soccer teams, and so forth are considered pieces of the external reality and therefore contents of our minds. They contain representations of things because there are things that can be represented. Needless to say, it is recognized that mental representations may introduce a more or less relevant degree of transformation when the external reality is mirrored in the mind, as well as that certain representations have no equivalent in reality (i.e., they are products of imagination, (Zittoun & Gillespie, 2016))—yet this does not contradict the ontological assumption of substances as the ground for mental representations.

Many philosophical and scientific arguments have highlighted the theoretical unsustainability of the autonomous ontological status of the external reality, as the metaphysical framework for scientific inquiries. Some have instead called for a processual ontology, in which the idea is to see the reality made up of dynamic distributions of energy-matter. This denies the autonomous ontological statuses of entities (e.g., Bickhard, 2009; De Luca Picione & Salvatore, 2023; Manzotti, 2010; Maturana

S. Salvatore (✉)
Department of Human and Social Sciences, Università del Salento, Lecce, Italy
e-mail: sergio.salvatore@unisalento.it

S. H. Klempe, A. Madill (eds.), *French Psychoanalysis Revisited*, Annals of Theoretical Psychology 20, https://doi.org/10.1007/978-3-031-68534-7_8

& Varela, 1980). According to this view, objects are products emerging from a relation between the observer and the reality, i.e., relationships that rather appear first and then generate what is related, instead of the opposite (Fronterotta et al., 2018).

The adoption of a processual ontology has relevant implications for psychology as a science—*it raises* the issue of the constitution of mental objects (henceforth: *constitution issue*). Indeed, if there are no substantial entities, mental objects cannot be considered as being equivalent to entities already and independently existing in reality. And this leads to the conclusion that mental objects are produced by basic mental processes that need to be modelled (Salvatore et al., 2022).

It is worth noting that the constitution issue implies an inversion of the relationship between *explanans* and *explanandum.* Indeed, the fundamental property of a mental object is that it is experienced as if it is endowed with *substantiality*, namely, with a set of invariant qualities (or just marginal variations) across time and space (Patterson, 2013). It is thanks to this sense of substantiality—working as a basic, embodied meaning attributed to elements and events of the world—that the subject experiences the mental object as a representation of the external thing. In other terms, it is the sense of substantiality that attributes the ontological status of the object rather than the opposite. Let me present an example: At this moment, I am looking at my computer on which I am typing, and I experience it as real, as an object endowed with ontological status—an entity of reality. However, this is so, not because it is so in reality but because I perceive it as persisting with a bulk of qualities that are stable enough. In sum, the experience of the object endowed with substance is not explained by the reality (*explanans*) that apparently provides its substantiality; rather, the experience of substantiality has to be explained as the output of the mental activity (*explanandum*). Leeuwenberg and van der Helm (2013) express this conclusion efficaciously (the statement refers to perception, but it can be generalized to the mental processes, see below, section "Philosophical background"): "The goal of perception is not to establish properties of given objects but to establish objects from properties of the given retinal image" (p. 1).

Recently, to highlight this inversion, I have proposed to distinguish between "meaning-making" and "sense-making." The latter is the cognitive process underpinning the constitution of the experience, whereas the former refers to the interpretation of the constituted object (Salvatore, 2019). Accordingly, the constitution issue calls for an enlargement of the psychological sphere of investigation. This implies that it is not enough to comprehend how mental objects are interpreted; we need to understand how they are constituted too. This requires modelling the basic mechanism of sense-making, which fosters the capacity of the mind: (a) to shape its objects, (b) to endow them with the quality of substantiality, and (c) to make this quality experienced by the sense-maker as inherent to the objects.

In this perspective, it must be marked that the subjective sense of substantiality forms the ground for the experience of being-in-the-world (Gallagher, 2005)—the fundamental subjective feeling of being real and alive is strictly related to the sense of substantiality of the world-out-there. This is the motive that leads to consider *constitutive* the level of psychological processes that produces such a sense: sense-making—as intended by Salvatore (2019)—is the big bang of the psychological life. This can be regarded as the basic psychic dynamics, from which the subjective universe emerges. And this forms the background for considering the inquiry of the sense-making dynamics as a project of a *psychology of the subject*.

Thus, this paper aims to address the constitution issue, as intended above. The following pages aim at outlining a model for how the mind constitutes its objects. Such a model adopts the semiotic cultural psychology framework (e.g., Salvatore, 2018; Valsiner, 2007) and integrates some ideas elaborated by Embodied Cognition and psychoanalysis. First, a brief exploration of *the issue of the constitution* of the experience is provided, encompassing some concepts from philosophy, psychoanalysis, and psychology. Then, a model of the constitution of the experience is presented, framed in the tradition of semiotic cultural psychology theory.

Philosophical Background

The constitution issue has a long history. The Kantian reversion of the relation between empirical data and categories (Kant, 1781/1998) is a fundamental reference here. One does not make the experience of space and time because such qualities are inherent properties of the world. Rather, one shapes the experience by means and in terms of such a priori categories—they are transcendental modes of organization of the experience. Thus, according to the Kantian view, the experience of time and space is the product of the constitutive work of the transcendental mind.

Brentano's view of the intentionality of psychological processes (Brentano, 1874/1995) complements this perspective. According to this view, any mental act—e.g., a perception, a feeling, a thought—cannot but be about something. This means that the object to which the mental act addresses is given to the mind regardless of its ontological status: it forms the content of the mind regardless of its quality of being a part of the world or not. This is why Meinong (Albertazzi et al., 2001) distinguished between *subsistence* and *existence* and stated that the former has primacy to the latter. Subsistence denotes the property of the object of having qualities that can be attributed to it. Existence is the most fundamental quality that can be attributed to the object (Valsiner, 2009)—e.g., one can wonder if extraterrestrials exist or not. From that descends a relevant consequence: to attribute a quality to an object implies ipso facto to assume its subsistence, that is, to make it a mental object, namely, an object of the psychological realm of signification (i.e., the realm of the object that can be predicated; for a discussion on the relation between subsistence and existence (see Eco, 2009)). In turn, this implies that the mental object does not depend on the extensional properties of the object (i.e., on the given property of the existing object), and therefore, it has to be considered as a product emerging from a mental activity.

This leads to Husserl's notion of presentification [*Vergegenwärtigung*]. There is no structural difference between phantasy and perception—the perception builds the object, as the presence of the object is a result of the phantasy. Namely, the mind operates in the same way both when the imagination makes a memory present and when the perception forms the object. Thus, the representation of the object is a matter of presentification, rather than reproduction:

> The presentification of an objective process cannot be called reproduction. The event in nature is not re-produced [...] it stands before consciousness with the character of presentification. (Hua, 1966/1991, p. 128)

Thinkers mentioned so far consider the constitution of the object in transcendental terms, namely, as an invariant mechanism operating as a structural property of the mind. The reference to Peirce enables us to conceive it differently—as the emerging product of a contingent dynamics of interpretation of reality. In this perspective, it is central to this American philosopher's view that meaning is a product of the relation between signs—rather than being held in the sign in itself. Indeed, the sign:

> (...) or *representamen*, is something which stands to somebody for something in some respect or capacity. It addresses somebody, that is, creates in the mind of that person an equivalent sign, or perhaps a more developed sign. The sign stands for something, its object. It stands for that object, not in all respects, but in reference to a sort of idea which I have sometimes called the ground of the representamen. (Peirce, 1897/1932, vol. 2, p. 228)

Thus, according to Peirce, the meaning of the sign is the interpretation provided by the following sign ("the equivalent sign"). Relevant is here to note that such an interpretation is carried out by an interpreter ("somebody," to whom the sign addresses) and consists of the specification of the aspect of the "object" (also named "dynamic object by Peirce") the previous sign stands for—what Peirce calls the "ground" of the representamen—i.e., the "respect or capacity" of the object the sign stands for. This is so because the sign does not stand for the object in all its aspects—if it were so, the sign would be identical, rather than equivalent to the object, namely, it would not *stand for* but would *be* the object. Relevant to note as well is the fact that the backward interpretation does not stop with the succeeding sign; indeed, in turn, the following sign's meaning is defined by the interpretation conveyed by the subsequent following sign, and so on, in an infinite chain of signs. One can recognize the strict connection between the two aspects highlighted above—the fact that the sign does not represent the object completely, but only in the ground set by the interpreter implies that it is always open to further interpretation, which may affirm or modify the ground (therefore the understanding) of the object. In brief, incompleteness and infiniteness of the semiosis are two faces of the same coin. This connection is evident in another well-known Peircean definition of the sign.

> Namely, a sign is something, A, which brings something, B, its interpretant sign determined or created by it, into the same sort of correspondence with something, C, its object, as that in which itself stands to C. (Peirce, 1902/1976, vol. 4, pp. 20–21)

Such a definition tells us that the mind does not mirror the object; rather, it makes it emerge continuously. This is done by setting a relation among signs that is assumed to be equivalent to the relation between each sign and the object—i.e., sign A stands for the object C as sign B stands for C—so, the A-B relation is the equivalent of C. As it stands for C, the A-B relation is the mental representation of C. And this is the same as saying that the subject has no access to the object—the experience of the object is the experience of the relation between the applied signs. In brief, the meaning does not come from the world; it emerges from inside the semiosis. Between the mental reality and the world, there is a structural, irreducible separation, which no flow of information overcomes. Rather, the mind construes within and through itself the reality by setting a dynamic relation between signs that are assumed (by the interpreter) to be equivalent to the external object and therefore standing for it.

To summarize, the Peircean semiotic theory enables us to recognize that (a) the content of the experience—i.e., the flow of signs—is in relation with other mental contents, i.e., other signs, not with the external object; (b) such a dynamic network of relations among signs is the activity of interpretation through which the mental object is built and kept active; (c) the mental object does not mirror the external object; rather it constitutes an equivalent of it: a model that maps only some quality/capacity of the external object, namely, one of the infinite grounds the external object potentially affords; and (d) the presentification of the external object in the mind consists of this a process, which makes a component of it pertinent and keeps it active (or vary) through the ongoing chain of sign (Salvatore et al., 2022).

The Constitution Issue in Psychology

The Gestalt theory has adopted the Kantian transcendental view on the constitution of the experience to model psychological functions. Most known exponents of the Gestalt movement—those associated with the School of Berlin (e.g., Wertheimer, Koffka, Köhler)—focused on the basic psychic processes based on the assumption that the mind's function of shaping the experience operates at a low level of perception in direct relation with the qualities of the sensorial field. Differently, other Gestalt theorists—the School of Graz (e.g., Meinong, Ehrenfels, Benussi) –claimed that the higher psychological functions—i.e., thoughts, desires, and volition—are involved in the construction of the Gestalt qualities. Though less popular, the reference to the School of Graz' contribution is relevant here because it leads to integrate the bottom-up view assumed by the School of Berlin—namely, the idea that the organizational principles are a function of the inherent characteristics of the external object (i.e., the qualities of the sensorial field)—with a top-down view, namely, with the recognition of the role played by the higher psychic functions. This integration is essential, as the objects we experience are far more complex than the geometric forms involved in the classical investigation of the Gestalt theoreticians of the School of Berlin.

Contemporary students of the perceptual organization are aware of that (Wagemans, 2018): they are clear about what has to be modelled is not only how the mind shapes the sensorial patterns but also how it can produce meaningful content of the experience:

> If one grants that the smallest, lowest-level visual elements are likely to be the outputs of retinal receptors and that the largest, highest level elements are the consciously experienced, meaningful environmental scenes and events that human observers use to plan and execute behaviors in their physical and social environments, then the fundamental question of perceptual organization is nothing less than this: how does the visual system manage to get from locally meaningless receptor outputs to globally meaningful scenes and events in the observer's perceived environment? (Palmer, 2015, v)

However, this stream of studies adopts a Kantian framework, thus focusing on the transcendental mechanisms involved in the cognitive elaboration of sensory patterns. As a result, this approach underestimates the fact that most (if not all) of the content of the experience are pieces of a social world. This implies that the mental operations underlining their constitution as mental objects also involve the socioculturally construed meanings provided by the social world. Take, for instance, a banknote. We do not see a piece of paper *first*, and *then* we interpret it as a banknote; instead, we make the experience of a banknote directly. The banknote is perceived as existing in the world-out-there. Now, it is evident that the banknote is not a transcendental category: it is a meaning entrenched in history, within and because of a specific cultural system of activity.

This leads to the conclusion saying that to address the constitution problem satisfyingly, the sociocultural level of sense-making has to be considered besides the perspective saying that mechanisms of the organization are transcendental.

The Embodiment of Sense-Making

The view of cognition as an embodied process has progressively gained momentum in contemporary cognitive science (e.g., Gallagher, 2005). This view is based on a core tenet saying that perception—or more generally; cognition—is strictly related to and at the service of the action (e.g., Barsalou, 2020). Making sense of the world is not an autonomous, self-contained process; rather it is part of the agent's system of regulating its relation to the world. This means that our perceptions and interpretations are not neutral pictures of reality; rather, they are patterns of bodily activation in terms of which the agent keeps itself coupled with the environment. Adopting a radical version of such a perspective, Lindblom (2015) states, "Cognition and social interaction are (sometimes) the very same process" (p. 258). From this core tenet, a relevant concept derivates. The idea is that knowledge (ideas, representations, beliefs) consists of the sensory-motor patterns in terms of which the body engages itself with the world. A reference to mirror neurons helps clarify this point: when one is exposed to an agent performing an action (e.g., grasping an object), such a scene is computed at the neurobiological level in terms of the simulation of the same form of action. In brief, to represent someone doing x consists of simulating to do x. More in general, Embodied Cognition highlights how the cognitive processes of abstract knowledge recruit grossly the same neural circuits involved in perception and control of the action (Barsalou, 2010). In brief, perception and cognition are not distinguishable, because they share the same mechanisms and are made up of the same stuff. Also the abstract forms of symbolic representation that classic cognitive science has considered ontologically different from perception and action consist of sensory-motor patterns, namely, preferences in the way the body works. In brief, any meaning is procedural; the subjective sense that all of us have that there is a structural difference between abstract and perceptual-motor representations does not reflect the ontological reality; rather, it lies in the functional characteristics of the sensory-motor patterns involved (Gallagher, 2005). As Verheggen and Baerveldt (2012) claim, we do not *have* knowledge; we *are* knowledge.

The contribution of Embodied Cognition is relevant in the economy of the discussion here proposed for two major motives. First, the ontological continuity between perception and cognition highlighted by this approach enables us to recognize the inherently interpretative nature of perception (Galetzka, 2017; Schnall, 2017). Such recognition is consistent with and supports the core idea on the grounds of the constitutive function of cognition—namely, that the meaning shapes the experience from its very basic level, already at the sensorimotor engagement with the world. Second, the fact that cognition is at the service of the action means that it is designed to provide interpretations of the relationship between agent and environment, rather than a neutral picture of the latter. This implies that the interpretation of the environment does not consist of detections of self-contained elements of the environment (i.e., objects) but of *events*—namely, courses of actions, or, more specifically, dynamic patterns of agent-environment covariations unfolding over time (Engel et al., 2015; Salvatore et al., 2022). This conclusion provides a pro argument for the idea that reality is not made up of discrete entities endowed with inherent substantiality. This is the assumption of processual ontology, which forms the grounds for recognizing the constitutive function of cognition. Moreover, the idea that the perceptual field is made up of events (rather than objects) provides a framework to model the constitution function of the mental processes—indeed, for definition, events are not inherent pieces of reality; rather, as said, they are made up of relations. The same reality can source an infinite set of events, depending on what relations are made salient—e.g., my current engagement with the environment could be experienced in the term of the event: |I am typing on my notebook|, or |I am writing a paper|, or |I am participating to my scientific community effort to understand the dynamics of sense-making|. No substantial anchorage makes one of these events preferable to the others. Since the content of my experience depends on meaning, the selection of one event over the other is a result of the salience of a given pattern of meaning. In brief, the event is not already given in reality—it has to be "extracted" from it through the process of bringing to the fore a certain network of relations and backgrounding the very many others. The constitution function of sense-making consists of that process of extraction (for the view of meaning as the extraction of relations from the field of experience, see Proulx & Inzlicht, 2012; Fronterotta et al., 2018).

Unconscious, Affects, and Subject

Most contemporary psychoanalysis consists of a *psychodynamic of contents of experience*, namely, an examination of the emotional qualities in terms of which the subject provides a lived meaning to life. To make just one example, consider the way authoritative exponents of interpersonal psychoanalysis reconceptualize the unconscious:

> In place of Freud's topographical and structural theories of mind we envision an organized totality of lived personal experience, more or less conscious and more or less contoured according to those emotional and relational experiences. Instead of a container we picture an experiential system of expectations, interpretative patterns and meanings (…). Within such a system or world, one can feel and know certain things often repetitively and with unshakable certainty. (Stolorow et al., 2001/2006, p. 675)

Thus, according to these authors, the mind (better, the unconscious mind) is not a container but a network of content ("expectations, interpretative patterns, and meanings").

Recognized that it is also true that the psychoanalytic theory has been—and still is in some cases—a *psychodynamic of the desire*, where with desire is here intended the psychic process of the constitution of the objects from the unconscious (De Luca Picione & Salvatore, 2023). Incidentally, let me add that in such a version, the psychoanalytic theory provided the most innovative and breakthrough contribution to the understanding of human affairs.

Two theoretical pathways of the psychoanalysis of the desire are worth being mentioned here.

The first is the Lacanian conception of the subject. According to the French psychoanalyst, the subject is not a given reality—rather, it is a byproduct of the language, better of the dialectics between language and reality (e.g., Lacan, 1978). The language is the Other, in the sense that the subject is immersed in it and emerges from it. As Lacan holds, the signifier belongs to the Other. The subject cannot go beyond language. This is so because there is a structural hiatus between the signifier and the signified—the signifier cannot grasp the signified—and therefore the reality; it can only refer to another signifier. Thus, the subject is *barred*—it can only fulfill the distance from the object through a signifier that, however, is unable to saturate the gap with the object. The barred subject mobilizes signifiers that at the same time relate and separate it from the object.

One can note here a similarity with the Peircean notion of infinite semiosis (see above, section "Philosophical background"). The human being is a prisoner of its most wonderful invention, what makes it human—the language. The symbolic order of the language is the semiotic glove that enables one to enter relation with the object and yet prevents having access to it.

The desire is the ongoing efforts to fulfill the hiatus between the signifier and the signified. Yet this can be done only by means of a further signifier that, however, reproduces the gap further. The subject is the exercise of such tension. The subject searches for the Object as its saturation, yet it meets only the contingent manifestation of it, the other: its signifier, that is, in Lacanian terms, its demand. Thus, the subject constitutes itself by means and in terms of the Other's signifier—as Lacan claims: the subject is always replaced by a signifier. This is the reason for which the subject is "barred": it constitutes itself only through the mediation of the Other's signifiers. This is what that the tragedy of the desire consists of—its condition of existence is also the reason for its radical incompleteness.

Lacan provides a topological representation of such tragic dynamics (Fig. 8.1). The trajectory around the torus is the chain of signifiers the subject performs in order to fill the unfillable gap (the central hole). The demand is the request of/search for the presence of the Other. Yet, the trajectory cannot fulfill the hole (Fig. 8.1a). It can only approximate it by meeting the demand of the Other (in turn striving to fulfill its hole; [Fig. 8.1b]). As Lacan stated: "from the place where the subject meets desire the first time, desire being first of all the desire of the other" (1958, p. 12): the subject searches for the Other, but it encounters the other's signifier through which the latter tries to fulfill its hole. And this is the same to say that what is desired is not what the other does to the subject, but what the other does to itself—another way to speak of the tragedy of the desire—its accomplishment corresponds to its negation.

To summarize in terms of the current discussion, Lacan helps us understand that reality is ungraspable; the subject can tend to it only, through the language in which is confined. The subject is separated (barred) from the object—therefore, the subject must mobilize signifiers to constitute it. Yet, given that this constitution is never able to fulfill the gap with reality, the subject is "condemned" to repeat it continuously. The desire consists of such asymptotical tenson, which works as the engine of the psychic life.

The second pathway is provided by a psychoanalyst who has developed the view of the unconscious as a function of signification. Melanie Klein's Object Relation Theory (Klein, 1967) is paradigmatic of that approach. According to her, affects are bodily meanings in terms of which the external reality is interpreted (Fornari, 1979). What is relevant to highlight here is that for Klein the affective meaning does not

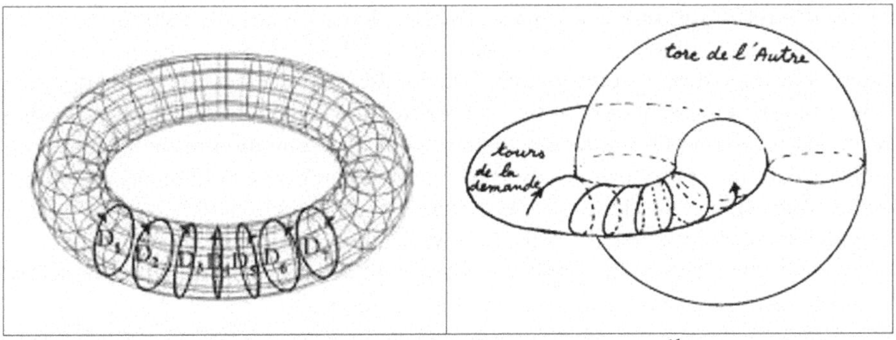

1a 1b

Fig. 8.1 The Lacan's topological representation of the desire. (Lacan, source not retraceable)

limit to connotate the external object—rather, it construes the object, constituting it as an "inner object." This is clear in the way she considers how the baby experiences the mother's absence—as the presence of the bad object. In other terms, what the baby experiences is not the absence of the same mother whose presence is enjoyed in other circumstances. Rather, the bad object is a fully opposite form of the world that takes the shape of the aversive affect. And this is the same as saying that it is not the case that there is the object before and then there is its negative connotation. Indeed, the object does not exist insofar as and thanks to the fact that it is shaped by the negative affect (Salvatore & Zittoun, 2011).

In a similar vein, it is worth referring to Matte Blanco's (1975) bi-logic theory of the unconscious. Based on the Freudian notion of the primary process, this author provides a formal model of the unconscious, intended as a mode of functioning of the mind. More particularly, according to Matte Blanco, the unconscious operates only in terms of identity—namely, it treats the terms of any relation as a relation of sameness. Thus, according to the unconscious level of working of the mind, any combination of signs makes them instances of the same class of meaning– e.g., father and son, before and after, the part and the whole, and the instance and the class: everything is the same as everything it is associated with; as a result, no time, no contradiction, and no distinction are recognized by the unconscious thought. And this is the same as saying that the unconscious works as a function of hyper-generalization and homogenization, making the subject identify itself with the whole of the experience. Needless to say, the mind should work only at the unconscious level of its functioning; no psychic life would be possible: the mind would be immersed in an indistinct totality. Yet, the unconscious is continuously antagonized by the complementary way of functioning—corresponding to the Freudian secondary process—that operates as a recursive function of extraction of relation from the indistinct class generated by the unconscious. Thus, at any moment, the encounter with the field of the experience triggers, on the one hand, the unconscious as the process of generating a homogenous whole, on which, on the other hand, the secondary process acts recursively, so to differentiate it progressively. Affects are the first forms that emerge from such a recursive secondary process of differentiation. This means that affects have to be considered the first classes of meanings whose further discretization produces more differentiated classes—till the emergence of classes of discrete objects (Salvatore & Zittoun, 2011). Thus, in conclusion, Matte Blanco's bi-logic theory of the unconscious implies that the mental content does not come from the representation of the external reality; rather, it emerges from within the mind, as the output of a recursive process of differentiation of the unconscious totality (that, in its pure form, is a sort of semiotic black hole void of any meaning). So, the Matte Blanco model suggests a reversal of the direction of the sense-making: the mind does not look like the canvas on which the painter adds colors to represent the model; rather, the mind operates as the sculptor that leaves off from the whole block of marble recursively to make the form emerge.

The APER Model

In previous collaborative works, I have outlined a model of the constitution of the experiences (i.a., Salvatore, 2016, 2018, 2019; Salvatore et al., 2022). The latest version of this model was defined as the Affective Pertinentization Model (APER model). I devote this paragraph to briefly outline this model, as it will shed light on three core questions of the constitution issue. These are: How does the mind (a) shape the object, (b) attribute a sense of substantiality, and (c) experience this sense as an inherent property of the object?

The answer to the first question is based on the Kantian view of categories as modes of organization of the experience. This finds its psychological equivalent in the Gestalt theory's principles of perceptual organization. It is worth adding that the view of categories as modes of organization of the experience is consistent with the dynamic and relational conception of the meaning provided by the Peircean semiotics (cf. section "Philosophical background"). According to his theoretical framework, the meaning is not held within the sign; rather, it consists of—and therefore emerges from—the combination of signs. As observed above, in the final analysis, meaning is provided by the following sign. Figure 8.2 compares the two conceptions of the meaning. According to the classic view, meaning consists of a set of attributes associated with a pre-given class (i.e., the meaning of an apple is provided by the set of qualities of the class of objects that share such qualities; see Fig. 8.2a). The dynamic view conceives meaning as a sort of procedure that makes pertinent certain relations among some components of the sensorimotor pattern and backgrounds the others. The object emerges from this process of filtering/extraction (see Fig. 8.2b).

Some further remarks are worth adding. First, the constitutive function of meaning is not limited to operating on a basic level of pertinentization of the perceptual forms. Rather, it also works on a higher cognitive level, in which culturally construed meanings operate. Indeed, it is at this level that social objects such as banknotes are constituted as if they were objects existing in reality and endowed

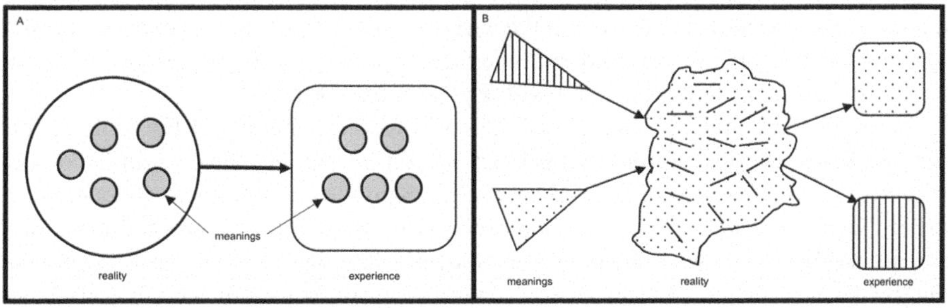

Fig. 8.2 Two ways of considering the relationship between meaning and experience (**a**) Experience is the reflection of pre-existing meanings in reality. (**b**) Meaning is the way of making some elements of reality relevant, thus shaping them, so that they emerge as contents of experience. (Adapted from Salvatore et al., 2018)

with their own ontological status. This conclusion is consistent with the Berlin school's gestalt theoreticians (cf. section "The constitution issue in psychology"), and it is supported by the Embodied Cognition's recognition of the continuity between levels of cognitive elaboration (cf. section "The embodiment of sense-making"). Based on the latter framework, one can move a step further: given that also the abstract meaning is inherently embodied (Borghi & Caruana, 2015), then it can work in constitutive terms too. Thus, it is not surprising that abstract signs such as "migrant," "nation," "soccer team", "freedom", and "love" can be experienced by the subject as objects, though void of a specific sensorimotor correspondent (for a discussion, see Salvatore et al., 2021).

Second, following the semiotic interpretation of the affect framed in the psychoanalytic theory (section "Unconscious, affects, and subject"; see Salvatore et al., 2021 too), the basic objects constituted by the mind are the affect-laden forms in terms of which the perceptual field is experienced. These forms are generalized patterns of bodily activation (e.g., pleasure/displeasure; active/calm) in terms of which the subject shapes the world. They operate from the very early stage of psychic life and consolidate themselves across the ontogenesis. In so doing, they assume the format of sensorial memories, each of which consists of the generalization of a set of similar patterns of engagement with the world (Stern, 1985). The affective meaning is continuously online and its moment-by-moment coupling with the world provides the foundational constitutive interpretation of the situation (Barrett Feldman, 2006). It is relevant here to add that a core aspect of the affective meaning is that it is inherently relational—the affective sense-making makes sense of the world in terms of an entity endowed with relational intentionality toward the subject (Salvatore & Freda, 2011). In other words, the affective meaning interprets the subject experience of reality as something animate toward her/himself. For instance, think of the anger reaction one may have when hurting the angle of the table, as if the table were an animate object wanting to hurt her/him. In brief, the affective interpretation of the world consists of the activation of a bodily memory that shapes the experiential field by the terms of a relational entity engaging with the subject in a certain way—e.g., as a feeding, destroying, pretending entity. And this is the same as saying that the basic experience the subject makes of reality is the reactivation of a relational experience construed in the early stage of life—e.g., the experience of a nice landscape as being engaged with the feeding object, or the experience of being in the city traffic as being engaged with a power, bad object.

Third, the constitutive dynamics of the sense-making operates as the sculptor (cf. section "Unconscious, affects, and subject")—it differentiates the constituted object recursively, by means of high-level signs, belonging to the linguistic and symbolic order (Valsiner, 2007). This recursive process of extraction of more and more differentiated forms leads to the constitution of discrete objects such as soccer teams and banknotes; yet, it operates however within the constraints of the basic affective meanings. As a result of that, most discrete abstract objects maintain their affective tonality, as a "trace" of the affective meaning from whose differentiation it emerges. This remark is relevant because it enables us to see that the affective meaning is however active—it does not disappear when the rule-based mode of thinking (i.e., secondary process) operates; rather the affective semiosis grounds, shapes, and constrains the mental landscape within which the meaning-making unfolds (Salvatore, 2019).

The answer to the second question—how the mind generates the sense of substantiality of its objects—moves from the observation of the fact that there happen many cases when we do not experience mental objects as endowed with substantiality but as products of imagination. Other times, objects belong to a liminal space between the sense of being substantial entities and products of the imagination. Cases like these show that the sense of substantiality is not always a given quality of the mental object. Rather, it is a contingent output of a mental process that calls for being understood both in its inner mechanism and in the condition of its variable operativity.

In a nutshell, the APER model considers the sense of substantiality the byproduct of the stability of the constituted object, therefore of the meaning shaping it. The more the meaning is stable, that is, the more the interpretative procedure it consists of is consolidated as a habit (Bourdieu, 1973/1977), the more it is taken for granted and therefore experienced as an inherent quality of the object, namely, as a *fact*. According to this view, institutions can be viewed as the most stable meanings that make the sense-maker blind to any alternative:

> Taken-for-grantedness is the degree to which institutional actors assume certain meanings to be fact-like, natural, or objective (Berger & Luckman, 1966/1967) and, thus, simply go without saying (…). (pp. 7–8)

Of note, the APER's view of the substantiality of the mental objects implies that in the final analysis, it is a function of the redundancy of the social practice, in which the sense-making underpinning the constitution of the object is embedded. This is so because, as highlighted by Peirce (cf. section "Philosophical background"), the interpretation is inherently an act—the act of producing a following sign to interpret the first one and to trigger a third one. Now, given that other sense-makers participate in the production of the following sign, the chain of signs is inherently a social action. When the social practice is stable, it works as an instituted interpretative habit that consolidates itself through the very fact of being repeated. The habit functions as a fact-like assumption, which grounds the social practice as taken-for-granted by making alternatives unthinkable (Cremaschi et al., 2021). Take the banknotes. As already observed, they do not exist in reality. They are experienced as if they did so, as if their economic value were an inherent quality of them. The interpretation of the piece of paper as a banknote is perceived as a fact by the subject. Following the APER model, this experience of substantiality is a result of a stable social practice that gives a |banknote| its meaning (i.e., the meaning of the piece of the paper as a vector of economic value). Social actors just assume the piece of paper as a banknote. They do so pre-reflectively, as a result of an interpretative routine working as an embodied assumption (viz., consisting of an irreflective meaning). Thanks to this, a domain of social practice (i.e., economic transactions) is regulated efficaciously and therefore acquires and consolidates its stability. In turn, the redundancy of the social practice so determined fosters and increases progressively the taken-for-grantedness of the embodied assumption, making it more and more a fact-like experience (for a similar view, see the concept of inter-objectivity, see Harré & Sammut, 2013).

The last consideration leads to the third question—how to explain the fact that substantiality is experienced as an inherent quality of the object. As the APER model states, this aspect is a consequence of the fact that the level of sense-making involved in the constitution of the object operates pre-reflectively, namely, at the pre-symbolic level of the perceptual elaboration of the sensations. It is worth adding that this level is not in conflict with the fact that constitutive sense-making also produces high-level, abstract meanings. As the experimental results of the Stroop effect show, there is no contradiction in the semantic interpretation of the stimulus (the meaning of the word) and the perceptual detection of the sensorial quality (the color of the lexical forms). These results rather demonstrate that the high-level meaning (i.e., involved at the level of semantic processing) is deployed already at the basic level of the perceptual elaboration of the stimulus. Moreover, the fact that the high-level meaning operates already at the basic level of the perceptual processing of the sensorial field is a matter of course once one assumes the embodied nature of the meaning, namely, the fact that also the abstract, cultural meaning is ultimately made up of the same sensory-motor patterns of perception. In sum, (a) the substantiality is experienced as inherent to the object (and therefore the latter as a fact) because the subject is unaware of the interpretative process it is the product of; (b) such unawareness is structural, due to the fact that the constitutive sense-making operates at the pre-reflective, pre-symbolic level of perception; and (c) this is possible because the abstract meaning constituting the social object is ontologically undistinguishable from the sensorimotor patterns operating at the perceptual level.

Conclusion

This chapter has focused on the constitution issue, namely, the problem of how the sense-maker constitutes the sense of substantiality of the experience, namely, the sense of the reality as something that exists autonomously out-of-there.

This issue raises once one recognizes the theoretical unsustainability of the substantial ontology, namely, of the idea that objects are self-contained entities, which exist before and independently to the observer and as such mirrored by the mind. The alternative view, the processual ontology, conceives the objects as emerging products of the sense-making relating the observer and the world.

Consequently, it becomes central to understanding by reason of what mechanism the sense-maker experiences the mental representations as if they refer to external objects endowed with inherent substantiality.

In the first part of the chapter, I have briefly outlined the long history of the constitution issue, both in its philosophical roots and in the mode the issue has been addressed in psychology. Then, I introduced some concepts from Embodied Cognition and psychoanalysis that are relevant to build a satisfying response to the issue. Finally, I proposed the APER model, as a possible view of the mechanism of sense-making underlying the constitution of the experience. This model is framed in the tradition of semiotic cultural psychology and integrates concepts from psychoanalysis and Embodied Cognition. This integration enables an extension of the classical transcendental view of the constitution issue, leading to highlighting the role played by the affective and cultural meanings, as well as by social practices in which sense-making is embedded.

The APER model conceptualizes the constitution issue in the terms of the three following tenets: (a) the sense-maker experiences the object as endowed with substantiality because she/he is unaware of the sense-making process it is the product of; (b) this is so because this process operates at the pre-reflective, pre-symbolic level, inherent to perception; (c) this is possible because, as Embodied Cognition has highlighted, the sense-meaning constituting the object is undistinguishable from the sensorimotor patterns operating at the perceptual level.

The APER model of the constitution issue, integrating transcendental and cultural mechanisms, has relevant theoretical and practical implications. From a theoretical perspective, it leads to recognizing that the cultural context is at the core of psychological life. Moreover, it shows the feasibility and utility to move toward an integrative psychological approach, able to consider both the affective and abstract, rule-based side of meaning as well as to recognize the inherent relation between meaning and social practice. From a practical standpoint, the very recognition that the substantiality of the content of the experience is an output of the mind provides psychology with the chance to empower its capacity to contribute to human progress. Indeed, one could say that contemporary societies suffer from how the sense of substantiality is distributed within the population. Many contemporary objects are interpreted in ways that make their substantiality weak: poverty, armed conflicts, and irreversible climate changes, just to mention a few examples, are experienced by many people as virtual concepts, images being void of any subjective density, namely, void of enough substantiality, and therefore they are unable to build responses at the heights of the radicality of the current crisis. At the same time, other objects seem to be characterized by, so to say, an excess of substantiality—e.g., fake news builds worlds that more and more people are keen to dwell; beliefs in some big old man foster conspiracy theories and related attitudes; meanings as nation, race, and ethnicity are lived as facts; and as such they shape and foster feelings and choices of large segments of societies and politics.

These are the kinds of challenges calling for the contribution of a psychology of the subject.

References

Albertazzi, L., Jacquette, D., & Poli, R. (2001). *The school of Alexius Meinong*. Aldershot.

Barrett Feldman, L. (2006). Solving the emotion paradox: Categorization and the experience of emotion. *Personality and Social Psychology Review, 10*, 20–46.

Barsalou, L. W. (2010). Grounded cognition: Past, present, and future. *Topics in Cognitive Science, 2*, 716–724.
Barsalou, L. W. (2020). Categories at the interface of cognition and action. In I. Fiorentini, E. Goria, & C. Mauri (Eds.), *Building categories in interaction: Linguistic resources at work*. John Benjamins.
Berger, P., & Luckman, T. (1966/1967). *The social construction of reality: A treatise in the sociology of knowledge*. Open Road.
Bickhard, M. H. (2009). Interactivism: A manifesto. *New Ideas in Psychology, 27*, 85–89.
Borghi, A. M., & Caruana, F. (2015). Embodiment theory. In J. D. Wright (Ed.), *International encyclopedia of the social & behavioral sciences* (Vol. 7, 2nd ed., pp. 420–426). Elsevier.
Bourdieu, P. (1977). *Outline of a theory of practice* (Vol. 16*)*. Cambridge University Press. (Original work in French, Droz, 1973).
Brentano, F. (1874/1995). *Psychology from an Empirical Standpoint*. Routledge.
Cremaschi, M., Fioretti, C., Mannarini, M., & Salvatore, S. (2021). *Culture and policy-making. Pluralism, performativity and semiotic capital*. Springer.
De Luca Picione, R., & Salvatore, S. (2023). Mind is movement. We need more than static representations to understand it. In J. Valsiner et al. (Eds.), *Farewell variables* (pp. 137–157). InfoAge Publishing.
Eco, U. (2009). On the ontology of fictional characters: A semiotic approach. *Σημειωτκή-Sign Systems Studies, 37*(1-2), 82–98.
Engel, A. K., Friston, K. J., & Kragic, D. (2015). Introduction: Where's the action? In A. K. Engel, K. J. Friston, & D. Kragic (Eds.), *The pragmatic turn. Toward action- oriented views in cognitive science* (pp. 1–15). MIT.
Fornari, F. (1979). I fondamenti di una teoria psicoanalitica del linguaggio [Foundations for a Psychoanalytic Theory of the Language]. Torino, IT: Boringhieri.
Fronterotta, F., Di Letizia, R., & Salvatore, S. (2018). Processual Monism: A fresh look at the mind-body problem. *Minds and Matter, 16*(2), 167–194.
Galetzka, C. (2017). The story so far: How embodied cognition advances our understanding of meaning-making. *Frontiers in Psychology, 8*, 1315.
Gallagher, S. (2005). *How the body shapes the mind*. Oxford University Press.
Harré, R., & Sammut, G. (2013). What lies between? In G. Sammut, P. Daanen, & F. M. Moghaddam (Eds.), *Understanding the self and others: Explorations in intersubjectivity and interobjectivity* (pp. 15–30). Routledge.
Hua, X. (1966/1991). Zur Phänomenologie des inneren Zeitbewusstseins (1893–1917). R. Boehm (Ed.). MartinusNijhoff; On the phenomenology of the consciousness of internal time (1893–1917) (J. Brough, Trans.). Kluwer Academic Publishers, 1991.
Kant, I. (1781/1998). *Critique of pure reason*. Cambridge University Press.
Klein, M. (1967). Contribution to psychoanalysis, 1921–1945. New York: Mac Graw-Hil.
Lacan, J. (1958). *The Seminar of Jaques Lacan. Book VI. Desire and its Interpretation (1958–1959).* Translated by Cormac Gallagher from unedited French typescripts. Retrieved from http://www.lacaninireland.com/web/wp-content/uploads/2010/06/THE-SEMINAR-OF-JACQUES-LACAN-VI.pdf
Lacan, J. (1978). *The four fundamental concepts of psychoanalysis*. Norton & Co, Inc.
Leeuwenberg, E., & Van der Helm, P. A. (2013). *Structural information theory: The simplicity of visual form*. Cambridge University Press.
Lindblom, J. (2015). *Embodied social cognition* (Vol. 26). Springer.
Manzotti, R. (2010). There are no images (to Be Seen) or the fallacy of the intermediate entity. *APA Newsletter on Philosophy and Computers, 9*, 59–66.
Maturana, M. R., & Varela, J. F. (1980). *Autopoiesis and cognition. The realization of the living*. Reidel Publishing Co.
Palmer, S. E. (2015). Foreword. In J. Wagemans (Ed.), *The Oxford handbook of perceptual organization* (pp. V–IX). Oxford University Press.

Patterson, J. (2013). Three forms of meaning and the management of complexity. In K. D. Markman, T. Proulx, & M. J. Lindberg (Eds.), *The psychology of meaning* (pp. 17–48). American Psychological Association.

Peirce, C. S. (1932). On Sign. In C. Hartshorne & P. Weiss (Eds.), *Collected Papers of Charles Sanders Peirce (Volume II)*. Harvard University Press. (Original version: 1987).

Peirce, C. S. (1976). *The new elements of mathematics* by Charles S. Peirce. C. Eisele (Ed.). Mouton Publishers. (Original version: 1902).

Proulx, T., & Inzlicht, M. (2012). The five "A" s of meaning maintenance: Finding meaning in the theories of sense-making. *Psychological Inquiry, 23*(4), 317–335.

Salvatore, S. (2016). *Psychology in black and white. The project of a theory-driven science*. InfoAge Publishing. 978-1-68123-117-4.

Salvatore, S. (2018). Cultural psychology as the science of sensemaking: A semiotic-cultural framework for psychology. In A. Rosa & J. Valsiner (Eds.), *The Cambridge handbook of socio-cultural psychology* (2nd ed., pp. 35–48). Cambridge University Press.

Salvatore, S. (2019). Beyond the meaning given. The meaning as explanandum. *Integrative Psychological and Behavioural Science, 53*, 632–643. https://doi.org/10.1007/s12124-019-9472-z

Salvatore, S., & Freda, M. F. (2011). Affect unconscious and sensemaking. A psychodynamic semiotic and dialogic model. *New Ideas in Psychology, 29*, 119–135.

Salvatore S. & Zittoun T. (2011). Outlines of a psychoanalytically informed cultural psychology. In S. Salvatore & T. Zittoun (Eds). Cultural Psychology and Psychoanalysis in Dialogue. Issues for Constructive Theoretical and Methodological Synergies (pp. 3-46). Charlotte (NC, USA): Information Age Publication

Salvatore, S., Fini, V., Mannarini, T., Veltri, G. A., Avdi, E., Battaglia, F., Castro-Tejerina, J., Ciavolino, E., Cremaschi, M., Kadianaki, I., Kharlamov, A. N., Krasteva, A., Kullasepp, K., Matsopoulos, A., Meschiari, C., Mossi, P., Psinas, P., Redd, R., Rochira, A., Santarpia, A., Sammut, G., Valsiner, J., & Valmorbida, A. (2018) Symbolic universes between present and future of Europe. First results of the map of European societies' cultural milieu. *PLoS ONE, 13*(1), e0189885. https://doi.org/10.1371/journal.pone.0189885

Salvatore, S., Palmieri A., Cordella, B., & Iuso, S. (2021, online first). The decay of signs' semiotic value. A cultural psychology interpretation of the contemporary social scenario. *Culture & Psychology*, *27*(4), 539–561. https://doi.org/10.1177/1354067X211027276

Salvatore, S., De Luca Picione, R., Cozzolino, M., Bochicchio, V., & Palmieri, A. (2022). The role of affective sensemaking in the constitution of experience. The Affective Pertinentization Model (APER). *Integrative Psychological and Behavioral Science, 56*(1), 114–132. https://doi.org/10.1007/s12124-020-09590-9

Schnall, S. (2017). Social and contextual constraints on embodied perception. *Perspectives on Psychological Science, 12*(2), 325–340.

Stern, D. N. (1985). *The interpersonal world of the infant*. Basic Books.

Stolorow, R. D., Orange, D. M., & Atwood, G. E. (2006). World horizons. A post- Cartesian alternative to the Freudian unconscious. In A. Cooper (Ed.), Contemporary psychoanalysis in America. leading analists present their work (pp. 671–689). Washington DC: American Psychoatric Publishing, Inc. [First published 2001: *Contemporary Psychoanalysis, 37*(1), 43–61].

Valsiner, J. (2007). *Culture in minds and societies. Foundations of cultural psychology*. Sage.

Valsiner, J. (2009). Between fiction and reality: Transforming the semiotic object. *Σημειωτκή-Sign Systems Studies, 37*(1–2), 99–113.

Verheggen, T., & Baerveldt, C. B. (2012). Mixed up perspectives: Reply to Chryssides et al and Daanen and their critique of enactive cultural psychology. *Culture & Psychology, 18*(2), 272–284.

Wagemans, J. (2018). Perceptual organization. In J. T. Wixed (Ed.), *Stevens' handbook of experimental psychology and cognitive neuroscience* (Vol. 2. Sensation, Perception, & Attention, pp. 803–872) Wiley.

Zittoun, T., & Gillespie, A. (2016). *Imagination in human and cultural development*. Routledge.

Sergio Salvatore is a professor of Dynamic Psychology at the Department of Human and Social Sciences, Università del Salento (Lecce, Italy). His scientific interests regard the psychodynamic and semiotic theorization of psychological and social phenomena and the methodology of analysis of sociocultural and mental processes as field dynamics. He also takes an interest in the theory and the analysis of psychological intervention in sociopolitical, community, scholastic, organizational, as well as clinical fields. On these issues, he has designed and managed various scientific projects and published more than 320 works—among volumes, chapters, and articles.

Chapter 9
Rene Lew and Psychoanalysis as an Impredicative Science

Osvaldo Cariola

***

Freud's clinical practice consistently shows that psychoanalysis involves a materiality originating from a very specific function. A function he initially labelled "psychological"—to distinguish it from physiology pure and simple—but which later, as he realised that the unconscious is not a coincidence but a constitutive effect of saying, was given the name libido. Freud's main endeavour was to study this function. And to this end, he set himself the task of developing a theoretical schematism to account for it. Freud's "metapsychology" is a project that could not be completed because its framework was too limited (psychoanalysis as the basic science of psychology, etc.).

Jacques Lacan gradually realised that understanding the Freudian libido requires contemplating die *Repräsentanz*, as seen in Freud's exploration of the drive and his discussion of the *Vorstellungsrepräsentanz* of the drive (Lacan, 1966). In his effort to conceptualise this connection, Lacan proposes to study it in terms of what the signifier relation tells us about the formation of meaning. This is partly because Freud's *Vorstellungsrepräsentanz* seems to correspond to what linguists understand by the term "signifier". But also, because Lacan believes that the signifier relation is the key to understanding the "symbolic order" underlying the unconscious and thus the Freudian "psychic apparatus".

In this motion, Lacan abandons not only the idea that a simple psychological function (memory, perception, consciousness, or other) should be the basis of psychoanalysis. He also stops talking about a "psychic apparatus", preferring instead to focus on the study of the unconscious subject as an effect of the interplay of signifiers. In this regard, the subject's position is critical. One must view this not as a physiological or psychological matter but purely as a logical one. Psychoanalysis

O. Cariola (✉)
Psychoanalyst, Copenhagen, Denmark

S. H. Klempe, A. Madill (eds.), *French Psychoanalysis Revisited*, Annals of Theoretical Psychology 20, https://doi.org/10.1007/978-3-031-68534-7_9

must now clarify this. It is in this context that the question of the elaboration of an "organon for psychoanalysis" becomes relevant, as the organon project is historically linked to the formalisation of logical relationships. We know the term today from Diogenes Laertius, who in the third century refers to the discussions in antiquity regarding the perception of the place of logic in philosophy. This is resumed in the late eighteenth century with Frege's proposal for a *Begriffsschrift*, whose predicate logic subsumes the classical Aristotelian syllogism. What we are now concerned with is explicitating the logic that Freud discovered in and with the unconscious. As we will see, the organon that psychoanalysis needs concerns the topology of the subject.

Paradoxically, however, the same resources that made Lacan's decisive contribution to psychoanalysis possible (linguistics, set theory, cybernetics, structuralism, etc.) prevent him from achieving his goals. Just as Freud saw the positivism of his time as a turning point and an obstruction, Lacan similarly had to struggle with his time's dominant logical positivist ideology. He was aware of this and tried to deal with it but could not escape the question of the "foundations" with which the entire twentieth century was encumbered and which still today invoke the right to define the criteria of what is to be understood by rationality.

Such is the context within which René Lew inscribes his contribution to psychoanalysis.

René Lew in Psychoanalysis

For the past 40 years, René Lew has been developing an organon for psychoanalysis. The basic idea behind such a conceptual system and such schematism is to account for a peculiar aspect of the function of speech that the Freudian experience brings forth, which Lacan called "saying" (*le dire*).

From the outset, however, this project has been under great pressure. Psychoanalysis has gradually learned to get along with caution concerning any notion of a causal origin, which is why it is constantly at odds with the so-called theories of science, which are exactly searching for "foundations" and, on this basis, believe they can disqualify psychoanalysis in terms of rationality. So, René Lew's proposed organon must show at least two things: first, that the "ground without foundation" (*fondements d'infondé*) on which psychoanalysis is based is completely logical, and, second, that it is easy to understand what is right for the signifier relation based on this. Hence, there is no need for another "return" but rather an unfolding of Lacan's intuitions.

We can summarise Lew's relationship to Lacan's work with these two questions:

1. Are we able to go beyond the point reached by Lacan in following his intuitions just mentioned? Furthermore, in this regard, can we overcome the sometimes essentialist aspects of his vocabulary?

2. What aspects of the schematism Lacan produced in his endeavour to account for analytical practice need to be highlighted? Not least here the use of the concept of "function" needs our attention. Particularly regarding what indeed is to be understood by the term "function of speech" in this context.

***

This text pretends to be a brief introduction to the perspectives that, from Lew's point of view, are necessary for the existence and development of psychoanalysis. Since René Lew's work is quite unknown to the public, I will begin with a brief presentation of the man and his work.

The Man

René Lew was born in Paris in 1946, immediately after the war. His parents were Jewish refugees from Eastern Europe; his mother had official status as such, and his father was stateless despite having been a French prisoner of war in Germany. During the Shoah, his parents' families disappeared. Without realising it, Lew himself was stateless until the age of 16. It was not until he obtained French nationality that his paternal surname was officially recognised.

In 1969, he began studying psychiatry, and in 1971, he started his own analysis. He participated then in the activities of the *École freudienne de Paris* without being a member (the minutes of the school's congresses bear witness to his three interventions just before its dissolution in 1981). He participated in the constitutive forum of the *École de la cause freudienne* with a presentation on "Metonymy and the Institution as Metaphor".[1]

Although trained as a psychiatrist, he has always worked as a psychoanalyst, both in private practice and in the institutions he has been associated with, including as a hospital doctor. He works with children, adolescents, and adults. Lew was the director of a medical-psychological-educational centre in Ivry-sur-Seine for 35 years, and he continued his practice at the Esquirol Hospital in Saint-Maurice (formerly Charenton) for 47 years. He currently works at a medical and educational centre for young people with autism. He is interested in philosophy, logic, and mathematics; in physics, biology, and legal sciences; in history, literature, and art; etc., all based on the questions raised by psychoanalysis.

Since 1981, he has initiated several seminars. In 1982, he founded the publication *Cahiers de lectures freudiennes* and the *Association de la Lysimaque*, both of which continue their activities to this day, publishing books and organising

[1] Integrated in *Situation de la psychanalyse au tournant du XXIème siècle*, Lysimaque, 2022a, pp. 105–155. References to the texts by René Lew from now shall be made according to the books he has started publishing since 2015, with the indexation used in this article, cf. the Bibliography. In the present case it will be notated as (2022a, p. 105).

conferences and seminars. In 1994, together with some colleagues, he founded the association *Dimensions de la Psychanalyse*, which promotes various activities in collaboration with other associations, both French and foreign. He has written numerous articles and regularly participates in colloquia and research conferences each year. In 2014, he began publishing his works, which to date count 16 volumes (and he has at least 20 more in preparation).

Lew's work capacity is illustrious. Over the past 50 years of his working life, he has initiated numerous study programmes dealing, in parallel or in coordination, with topics of interest to psychoanalysis: clinical, epistemological, political, logical, etc. It is this peculiarity that enables him to address the various aspects of the psychoanalytic field in an original and innovative way that few others can do.

General Framework

As just indicated, René Lew's work covers the full range of issues that psychoanalysis encompasses. The work programme deals with the various topics involved, in parallel. He summarised his efforts with the following points:

1. Topology is essential for conceiving the Freudian clinic.
2. The coherence of psychoanalysis originates in Freud's texts.
3. As a practice, it relates to the non-spherical logic that characterises the unconscious.
4. Topology is not merely a "frame" or an "illustration". Discourse is topological ab ovo.
5. Therefore, theory in psychoanalysis is much more than the "tool" it is often reduced to. Theory is an integral part of the analytical act.
6. Formalising the knot, which organises analytic practice (Freud called it a *Knotenpunkt*) gives access to the structure that the knot in question is an expression of.
7. This structure is interesting because it must be understood on the background of the temporal function organising the dynamics of the unconscious. In this sense, the economy of the subject is linked to a temporal structure.

Summarising Description

Time and Psychosis

The 1970s are the period in which René Lew wrote his medical thesis (in 1976 with a text on Freud's *Verneinung*), completed his personal analysis, and began his psychiatric training. At that time, he was primarily interested in two topics (besides the question of negation, which basically vectorises all his studies from then on): the question of time and the question of psychosis, themes that have nourished Lew's reflection ever since.

Time, insofar as it is constitutive of subjectivity. And, in a certain sense, time coming to a standstill causes psychosis. Psychosis reveals time's inner logic.

We currently have two books from this period at our disposal: *Le temps de l'inconscient*, published in 2019, and *Temps et psychose*, published in *2020.*

Intension and Extension

The problem of intension and extension emerges very early as central elements in the Lewian elaboration.

These terms have a long history. They were already familiar with the medieval logical tradition, implicitly or explicitly formulated in any reflection that pretends to account for the relationship between phenomena and structure. This is also true in the case of psychoanalysis, where the connection between the *latent* and the *manifest* is fundamental.

Lacan knew very well that the relationship between intension (note the "s" because the term does not refer to any intentionality) and extension—or, more precisely, the relationship between definition in intension and definition in extension—is crucial (see, e.g. *Autres écrits*, 2001, p. 250). Intension and extension are concepts that logicians have used from the beginning of logic thinking, under different terms, to distinguish between what we today refer to as "the structure" and "the phenomenon". In psychoanalysis, they are retained to emphasise the primacy of the unconscious. Fundamentally, this is what distinguishes Husserl from Freud. Whereas the former strives for an intentionality (with a *t*) sustaining the philosophy of consciousness, Freud insists on the overdetermination and its intensional (with an *s*, i.e. in this context, unconscious) presumptions. However, Lacan settled for simply applying them without further clarification. René Lew revisits the issue and makes the terms function as a fundamental pair of concepts in psychoanalytic epistemology.

René Lew repeatedly returns to Gottlob Frege's work, attempting to clarify the criteria for integrating this issue into psychoanalysis.

The Functionality of Joining the Real, the Symbolic, and the Imaginary

According to Frege, the sentence (*Gedanke*[2]) and the world (*Umwelt*, "concrete" or "imagination") are not the same thing. This creates a logical difference (and, by extension, a relation) of a functional nature (in this case, mathematical) between *Sinn* and *Bedeutung*.

[2] *Gedanke* is the word for thought in German, but thought being considered as a proposition, we can point out that thinking is going on in a sentence.

intension		**extension**
	Gedanke ⟷ Umwelt	
Sinn		*Bedeutung*

Lew, on his side, proposes to conceptualise the internal and global relations established between the registers according to a similar but principally extended schema:

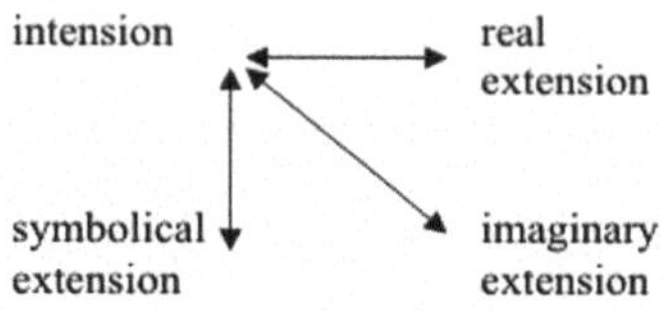

This should clarify the dynamics of the subjective structure from a new perspective (also emphasising how crucial the question of the mutual passage between the intension and the extensions, indicated by the arrows, is).

The Rhetoric of the Unconscious

The 1980s paved the way for a reformulation of these problems by studying systematically the linguistic tropes that the unconscious makes use of (particularly those relating to metonymy, metaphor, and synecdoche).

René Lew emphasises the importance of metonymy for subjective organisation (a question not obvious following traditional Lacanism, where the metaphor is given priority—"metaphor of the Father's name", "metaphor of the subject", etc.), which brings him to reformulate the problems of foreclosure (*forclusion/Verwerfung*). Metonymy is the basis of unconscious logic.

Lew's preoccupation with the grammatical form known as "Irrealis" (*Irrealis-mood*, in English; *conditionnalité irréelle*, in French) already emphasised the importance of the hypothetical within the subjective device. This theme constitutes, without doubt, one of the main axes of the Lewian conceptualisation.

Revision of the Concepts of Psychoanalysis

He initiated an extensive project in the mid-1990s aimed at reformulating (and thereby reactivating) psychoanalytic concepts. It's a considerable task that, in many ways, is still going on.

At the beginning of it (i.e. in the first 5 years, from 1995 to 2000), Freud's terminology was revised (starting precisely with the concept of *Repräsentanz* and going on from his new reading of Lacan's translation of this word). However, Lew gradually incorporated new topics into the discussion, clarifying both Freud's and Lacan's ideas (and thus the specificity of psychoanalysis).

All these elaborations gather around a core, accounting for how the *unconscious*, *language*, and *the making of meaning* are in fact interwoven. Or, to put it in a different and even more precise way, it was a matter for Lew to prove the strange fact that such matters, which are indeed essential in the definition of the human as such, relate to one and the same (temporal) structure.

Oedipus and Modal Logic

Studying Lacan's proposals[3] on the Oedipus complex, as transmitted by Freud in modal logical terms, enables this work. As a consequence thereof,

... the Oedipal theme ...

... the Oedipal theme ...

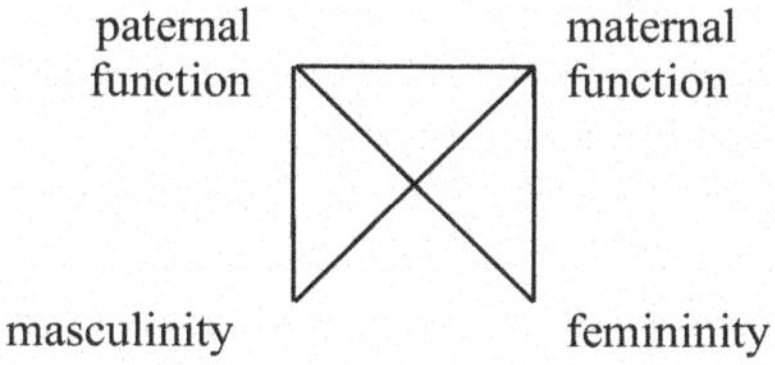

... presented here in terms of modal logic (ontic in this case) ...

... presented here in terms of modal logic (ontic in this case) ...

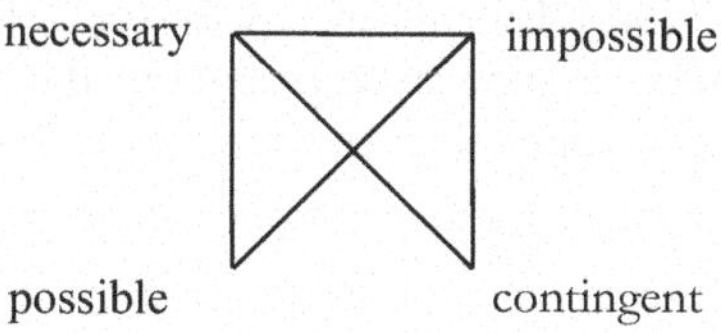

... in line with psychoanalytic schematism's basic structure:

[3] Cf, e.g. the conversation Lacan had in the seminar about the psychoanalyst's knowledge (*Le savoir du psychanalyste*), June 1, 1971.

... in line with psychoanalytic schematism's basic structure:

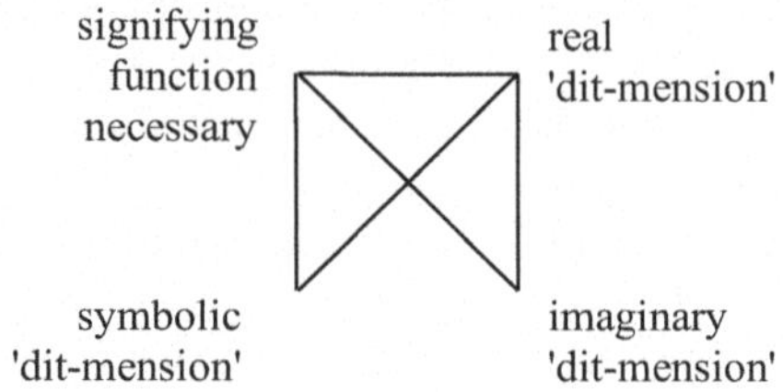

Negations as a Complex System

This is an important point in the development of René Lew's thinking and theoretical elaboration. From now on, he says that the unconscious (and by extension, language and the making of meaning) is the creation of "a structure of emptiness" (*structure de vide* or *structure d'évidement*[4]), which unfolds—and this is very important—through a complicated system of negations, the function that belongs to the significant order.[5]

If Freud says he found an "apparatus" for the so-called psychic, then this apparatus can only be a "logical apparatus", which means it is a one-of-a-kind structure that calls for a rethinking of the rules of *negation*, *identification*, and *the excluded third party* that classical and modern logic use.

The 1995–1996 seminar, *Théorie de la représentance*, marked a significant milestone, while the 1995 text *Freud ou l'Autre rationalité*[6] played a crucial role in defining the direction of the project Lew has been working on ever since.

Let us in this connection observe a methodological feature of Lew's reading of Freud and Lacan, in his endeavour to prove the appropriate rationality of psychoanalysis. Two texts serve as anchoring points for René Lew in the task he has undertaken. One is Freud's *Aphasia Studies* (from 1892), which introduces the question of how reticular networks participate in linguistic acts. The other is Lacan's *L'étourdit* (from 1972), which in its own way seeks to go beyond the distinction between statement and utterance by introducing the problem of the relationship between *le dit* and *le dire* (between "the said" and "the saying"). We can now see

[4]Cf., e.g. Du symbolique au réel, a conference held by Lew at the *Institut Universitaire de Recherches Scientifiques de Rabat, Marocco*, October 26, 1995. Planned publication in a book whit the title "Constructions in psychoanalysis".

[5]Cf. *Les négations freudiennes*, 2017b, and *Récursivité des negations. Les negations lacaniennes* (in press).

[6]First published in *Psychanalyse et réforme de l'entendement*, nos 20–21 of the *Cahiers de lectures freudiennes*, Paris 1997. It is also planned to incorporate a coming book. If you ask me How to enter Lew's world? I would answer: *Freud ou l'Autre rationalité*. Another entrance could go by the text already mentioned: *Du symbolique au reel*.

how René Lew is re-reading Freud and Lacan's entire oeuvre along the lines of these two highlights.

Because of this, Lew says that psychoanalysis should be based on the "hypothetical foundations" (*les fondements hypothétiques*, or *fondement de non-fondement*), which he likes to call the "non-predicative foundation".[7] And it is this "hypothetical foundation" (a foundation that only the hypothesis can transmit) that in turn supports the enormous project he has set up for himself, namely, to elaborate an *organon* for psychoanalysis. Lacan's *L'étourdit* significantly influences Lew's thinking, serving as a crucial anchor that orients all his work.

Psychoanalysis and the Structure of the Real

Consequently, and not surprisingly, this imposes the priority task of clarifying how to understand the structure of the real with which psychoanalysis is concerned. This question has been a stumbling block since Lacan, due to certain prejudices on his part regarding nominalism, which led him at times to adopt unnecessary realist positions. Based on what Lew calls the *Théorie de l'écart*, he proposes to revisit this whole issue. He mainly reflects on the formal implications of what Freud referred to as *Entstellung*—a term with no real conceptual status in Freud that René Lew, via Lacan, shows how crucial it is to the functioning of the unconscious.

Strictly speaking, the (now) concept refers to transformation through continuous deformation. It relates less to a "distortion", which is the usual translation of the term *Entstellung*, and more to a topological transformation. We therefore must deal with a logical matter, since topology has something to say in psychoanalysis only insofar as it gives access to the logical foundation (*de non-fondement*), of the subject's structure. As a result, for Lew, the problem lies in giving *Entstellung* its logical value.

From this point of departure, the "subject" becomes nothing more than "the real that emerges in and with language", as Lacan puts it (*Autres écrits*, 476). In this sense, and above all, the "subject" is the language's exchange structure. And, as Lacan himself specifies it in the next line, this has nothing to do with a "good form", i.e. a gestalt.

This is the structure René Lew tries to account for. Not just for "theoretical" interest, but for very concrete practical reasons, the so-called psychopathology is a matter of unfavourable subjective positions being the result of blockages or disturbances in such an exchange structure.

[7] This position is summarised by Lew in the following sentence: "*J'oppose [...] un fondement en termes de non-fondement à une fondation predicative des choses*", in *Une psychanalyse hors camp (6)*, a text from November 28, 2019.

The Unconscious and the Real

However, simply saying that "the unconscious is structured like a language" does not provide a sufficient explanation for this.

The unconscious is the foundational hypothesis of psychoanalysis. It is the name of the surprise we get when confronted with the "psychopathology of everyday life". But what is special about psychoanalysis is that it does not ignore the sexual anchoring on which these "psychopathologies"[8] are based. Sexuality concerns knowledge in general, especially when it relates to the unconscious. The knowledge that the unconscious carries within it shapes and influences the human being. Therefore, one cannot be a psychoanalyst for purely legal reasons (based on "authorisation", "revelation", or something else). The individual psychoanalyst must know how his or her own economy of love and pleasure is organised.

On the Emergence of Significance

One theme recurs in all these years of work, namely, what René Lew calls *engendrement d'existence* (say "creation of existence"—if we translate it by emergence, we miss the point about generating—it's about the occurrence of the logical existence). It resumes the Freudian logical work about *Die Verneinung* on the relationship between existence and attribution judgments.

Lew's reflections go way back to the question of "existential" as a modal structure (see, e.g. the text *L'orientation psychotique* from September 1991, where he reflects on the problems of the ways out of psychosis).[9]

Understanding this necessitates considering the interconnectedness of at least two issues:

1. That the signifier function organises itself through retrogradation (*nachträglich*, as Freud said) within a temporal structure that encompasses a network of at least two presuppositions
2. That the subject's logical existence depends on such presuppositions

Ad I) A signifier (as "one" signifier) does not exist in itself and for itself but only because of a hypothesis (at least the assumption that the signifier in question

[8] Meaning what Freud called "the unconscious formations"—dreams, slips of the tongue, jokes, etc. but also the symptoms originating in the unconscious, as well as the character and the personality. Sigmund Freud, (1901) *Zur Psychopathologie des Alltagslebens. Gesammelte Werke IV*. Freud's German terms and concepts are the key to understand what psychoanalysis is about, and both Lacan and Lew have read Freud in his language, using the German terms in their texts, e.g. *Verneinung* is not the same as negation, denial, nor denegation.

[9] About psychosis and its clinical and logic aspects, see also *Positions subjectives données comme psychotiques*, 2017a.

"follows" the signifier that precedes it), which, again, precisely requires assuming that such a condition is actually given, that is, "exists".

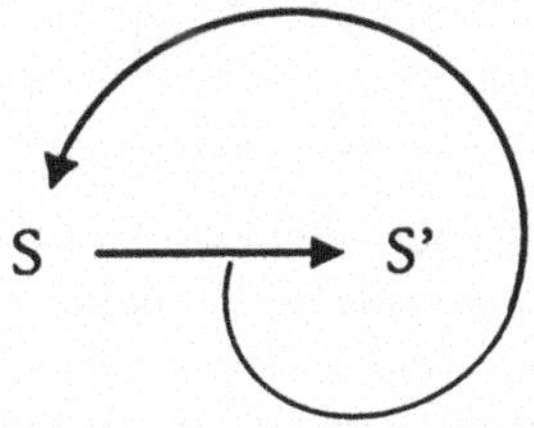

Once we assume the existence of the first signifier, we can say that the second derives from the first at a later time …

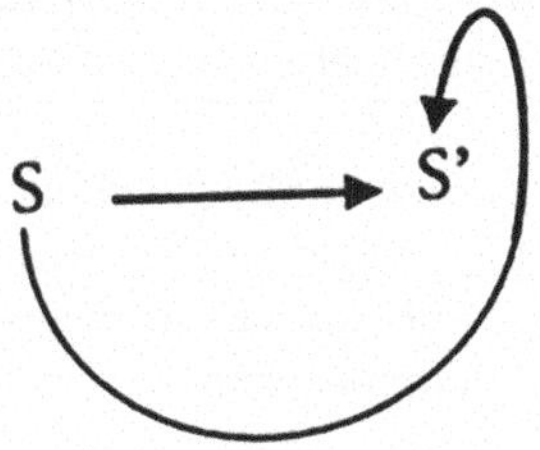

… the temporal pulsation of existence then requires at least a Moebian reversion.

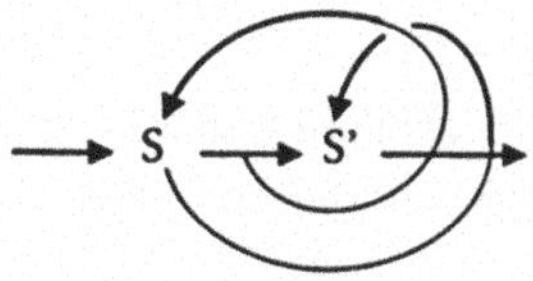

Ad II) Thus, the existence of the signifier has no ontological foundation. An unreal condition (or "Irrealis", as the grammarians call it) must constantly renew and reactivate itself.

Such an existence arises when one signifier takes over another, displacing it in the process. Every signifier is dependent on another's displacement. Therefore, it is difficult to imagine what the signifier relation consists of, and the same difficulty also hits the subject of the unconscious, being only the effect of the production of such a hypothetical dialectic working on "itself".

Explorers can uncover the secrets of this vast area. However, we can outline its contours as follows:

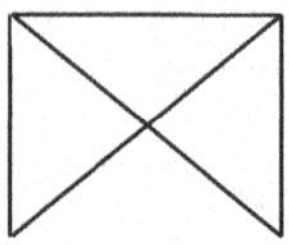

It constitutes, so to speak, the very clockwork of the subjective structure, whose dynamics determine the economic side of the matter.

What is at stake, now expressed in Freudian terms, is the comprehension of how the libido (i.e. the phallic function, with Lacan and Lew) acts ab ovo and constructs "the psychic apparatus" through a signifier interaction. Such *Wechselwirkung*, to use the German term, organises, in turn, the structure of the unconscious through a dialectical interplay of negations. But when we say it this way, we are in fact creating problems. Especially because it evocates an underlying phylogenetic idea of searching for "a beginning", complicating the Freudian reflection in an unnecessary way.

The interplay of negations discovered by psychoanalysis (this point can only be implied here, yet it is intimately linked to the structure of the hypothesis) is so important because, in principle, it liberates us from any ontologising of the "origin". This is exactly what I will try to demonstrate.[10]

Every Structure (Including the Subjective Structure), per Definition, Is Functional

According to René Lew, only by accepting that every structure is functional (i.e. an interplay of interactive relations) can we get closer to answering the question we have just asked.

Conceiving the structure as a functional entity is decisive for how we define the subject. From this perspective, the subject is conceived as the way in which the concerned structure acts upon itself. This assumption is indeed thought-provoking and radicalises Lacan's conception of it. Given this preamble, the subject's coming into being proceeds between the signifier function as such (S_1, the significance in intension) and its transcriptions (in extension). For exactly that reason (because it acts on itself), the structure is presented as basically a quadratic, according to Lacan's categories of the symbolic, the imaginary, and the real.

[10] Cf. here *Les négations freudiennes*, 2017b. In process of writing, *Récursivité des négations, Les negations lacaniennes*. It is evident that all Freud's attempts to thematise these problematics by his German prefix *Ur-* participate to this investigation.

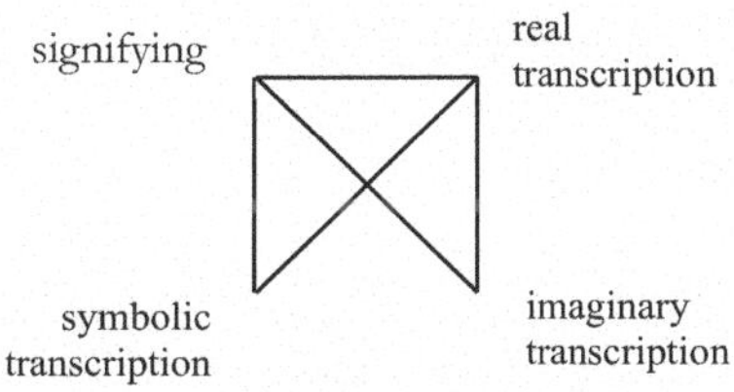

This also makes it possible, as already said, to understand the structural context for how psychoanalysis conceptualises the issue of the signifier:

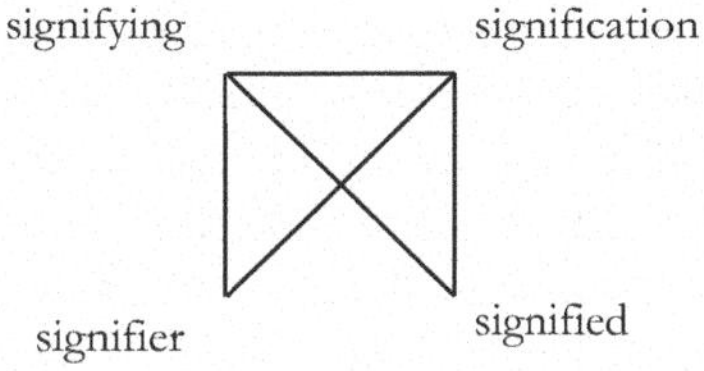

This line-up also clarifies how the unconscious hypothesis contributes to understanding the dimension of meaning.

The Subject

There is a "circulation" of the unconscious subject, or more specifically: the subject of the unconscious is in tune with the dynamics of the structure and depends on it.

Therefore will any retention (Freud called it *stasis*) cause symptoms, which can then take on a pathological form when it turns into regular fixation (Freud then talks about *Fixierung*).

This has at least two significant implications for future conceptualisation.

On the one hand, the "existence of the subject" is logical and doesn't need any kind of beginning. The "object *a*"—created simultaneously with the emergence of the signifier operations—subsequently influences the forms of enjoyment by which the subject will be defined.

On the other hand, it is now evident that essentially, the "construction"[11] work of psychoanalysis is not a "reconstruction" (of a "happy", "sad", "traumatic", etc. past), as the doxa commonly understands it (after all, psychoanalysis emerges precisely when Freud abandons the cathartic ideology) but a new elaboration (a production). This construction can only be a new one.

[11] Cf. S. Freud, *Konstruktionen in der Analyse*, from 1937

The Nominalism of Psychoanalysis

Lacan with Hintikka

Such questions are behind Lew's project "Revision of the Concepts of Psychoanalysis" shaping it as a cross-reading of (a) Freud's clinical practice, (b) Lacan's concepts, and (c) the latest developments in logic.

René Lew could now rethink the classical logical criteria of *negation*, *identification*, and *the excluded third* (issues that both Freud and Lacan had already addressed in their own ways), but most of all, what gave him a better understanding of the problem was a renewed focus on the issues raised by nominalism.

Study of Nelson Goodman's work drew already his attention in the 1990s; but discovering and studying the work of the Finnish logician Jakko Hintikka (from 2004 onwards) gave the interrogations of René Lew about the relationship of psychoanalysis to logical and philosophical questions a new impetus.

This occupation culminated in a colloquium—held on November 21 and 22, 2011 at the Finnish Institute in Paris and attended by Professor Hintikka himself—where logicians, philosophers, mathematicians, and psychoanalysts discussed the new logic resulting from Hintikka's reevaluation of the classical tradition of analytical philosophy.

These changes occur in two main directions: first, reevaluating the semantic game that establishes the truth of the proposition (revising the classical referential definition), and, second, addressing the informational independence maintained by any interpretation.

It is evident why the psychoanalyst is interested in these thoughts. At the time, Lacan was working in the same direction. Lacan's assertion challenges the prevailing empiricism of his era and leads to fundamental concepts such as *the time-based nature of discourse* and *the unconscious as the discourse of the Other*.

Of course, the fact that a logician sets out to systematically reconnect these two linguistic figures (semantics and interpretation) impacts, necessarily and profoundly, how we conceptualise the Freudian field.

Nominalism Is Not Simply a Matter of Naming

Here is where the question of nominalism arises. The essential thing in this regard (and which we need to understand) is the following: at stake in the problem of nominalism is not so much naming (as is commonly thought) but presumption.

In fact, "nomination", as nomenclature, does not escape the surrounding referential realism, i.e. the belief that reality is there, "in front of us", and that it is only a matter of labelling it with the right words. This "nominalism" is entirely imaginary; it is a nominalism of contents.

The real nominalism, if I may say so, the one engaging logic (and thus also psychoanalysis), is a nominalism of syntax, a nominalism in which the hypothetical nature of every assumption is decisive.

Hence, again

Jakko Hintikka's logic reflections have brought this about, and Lew cannot simply let it pass, because it goes directly to the very heart of the psychoanalytic act. Now we can distinguish between a nominalism based on the signified, *le signifié*, and a nominalism that follows the signifier, *le signifiant*, and this distinction seems crucial.

The Signifier and the Hypothetical

Hintikka's work is important in this context because it confirms and formalises some of René Lew's key intuitions. The hypothetical is a critical function because it brings the signifier's *recursivity* into play. René Lew had already been working on this affair for some time, but from 2011 onwards, he succeeded in fully justifying it.

The hypothetical ensures a (presumed) anchoring to something that is not actually given in advance.

As a result, the hypothetical involves two simultaneous and intertwining movements: an anticipatory and a retroactive movement. The antecedent depends on the hypothesis of its existence, which in turn assumes that the claimed existence has already done its work, making it dependent on the consequence, which then calls the hypothesis into existence to sustain itself.

Thus, in the hypothetical work, two movements of *Nachträglichkeit* (après-coup, *afterwardsness*) are active. One is retroactive, going from the consequence to the antecedent, and the other, proactive, going from the antecedent to the consequence.

The Moebian way articulates both movements.

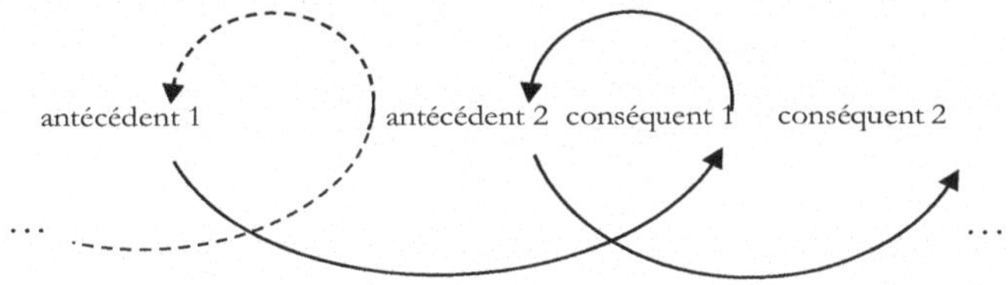

In other words, anticipation generates retroaction, and retroaction generates progression (the Moebian character of the structure, which is shown here in open form, ensures that such a chiasmus occurs). It is simple to see how this issue is intimately entangled in Freudian inquiries when it is done in this manner.

The Drive as Example

What we are examining here can be applied quite explicitly to what Freud called "the drive" (*Trieb*), although he did not go any further with it in these terms. The exploratory and anticipatory connections established by the drive, between the body and the signifier (which is why Freud defined the drive as "representation of the somatic in the psychic") are of this nature. Lacan, on his side, makes them work in the opposite direction. For him, it is no longer a question of "the somatic" and "the psychic" but of the impact of the saying (*le dire*) on the body. Between Freud and Lacan, we can notice that the drive takes on a Moebian organisation.

Hence, *recursivity* (which is René Lew's contribution and which we shall finally look at in the following section) takes place in the body; indeed, it produces the body as something else than a mere organism, i.e. the signifier infiltrating the body. Or we might as well say the signifier can only be efficient, by involving the body (having just made it) as an invariable anchoring.

Towards an Impredicative Approach in Science

A new elaboration of psychoanalysis that is still unfolding today is now on René Lew's working table. I shall limit myself in this summary to pointing out one singular aspect of a problem encompassing the entire Freudian field (clinical, ethical, political, philosophical, scientific, etc.).

The concept we just mentioned, namely, *recursivity*, introduced by Lew into psychoanalysis to account for the dialectics of signification, is the turning point. René Lew goes further than Lacan and summarises (and, in a way, concludes—or at least resumes in new terms) that psychoanalysis is basically Freudian. He does this by talking about the main problems of psychoanalysis, which are *overdetermination*, *repetition*, and *the death drive*. These are all things that Freud identified with the prefix "Ur-," which he used to talk about an unfathomable cause (*Urverdrängung*, *Urnarzissmus*, *Urgeschichte*, etc.).

Recursivity

One can understand the term in two ways. Firstly, as "calculation" (as used in mathematics), and, secondly, as "procedure" (which emphasises the process of the procedure, regardless of the object that may be involved in it). The latter meaning is what piques René Lew's interest.

In logical terms, then, the *recursive definition* of a function can be based either on the function itself (in *intension*) or on the object corresponding to that function (i.e. in Frege's terms, as an *extensional* transcription of that function).

René Lew uses the term "recursivity" when referring to a function that operates according to a Moebian rather than a "circular"[12] referentiality. Especially in the case of an open Moebius strip (whose edge allows for a spiral path), which, by not simply repeating the same "thing" iteratively, allows for a progression from the starting point, therefore systematically moving away from any return to an alleged origin.

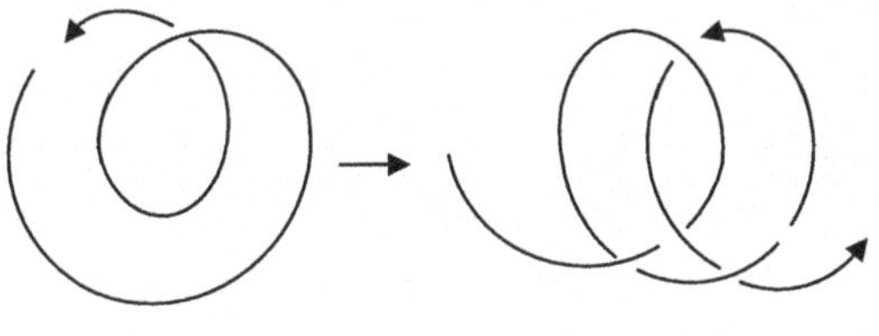

Moebian recursivity. Open Moebian recursivity

In the latter case, this shift (*décalage* as Lew calls it in French, *Verschiebung* in Freud's terminology) implies a distance, or at least a deviation, and then appears as a transcription of the antecedent into the consequence. This does not happen without a (shifted) return of the consequence to the antecedent to institute the latter.

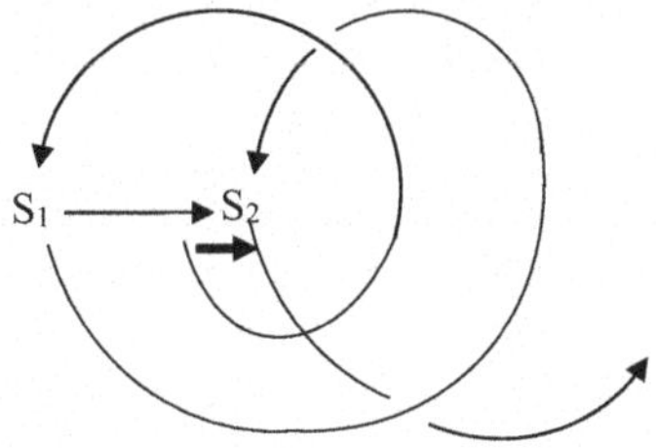

[12] Circularity is also explicitly rejected by Lacan, e.g. when he talks about alienation, cf. *Lacan* (1964) pp. 188–189.

According to this schematism, *a hypothesis causes the antecedent to happen.* Counterbalancing the consequence to the original vacant guarantees its existence by attributing it to something (*Etwas*, in German).

Predicativity

Thus, we are dealing with a difference in continuity between what is not yet there but seeks to emerge and the consequences of this original absence (vacancy), which only later comes into being. This introduces a separation between before and after, a difference that, at the same time, functions as a passage (which Lacan tried to understand in the last years of his teaching when he dealt with *littorality*). Essentially, the consequence achieves its consistency by integrating the original absence/vacancy into itself.

Thereby, both the relationship and the difference between the *intensional* and the *extensional* are certified.

The logical relation between a function and its corresponding object

$$\text{function} \rightarrow \text{object},$$

presented as intensional and extensional definitions

$$\text{intension} \rightarrow \text{extension},$$

then provides, in the psychoanalytic field, a quaternary structure (as is probably true of any structure) when the registers of the real, the symbolic, and the imaginary are considered.

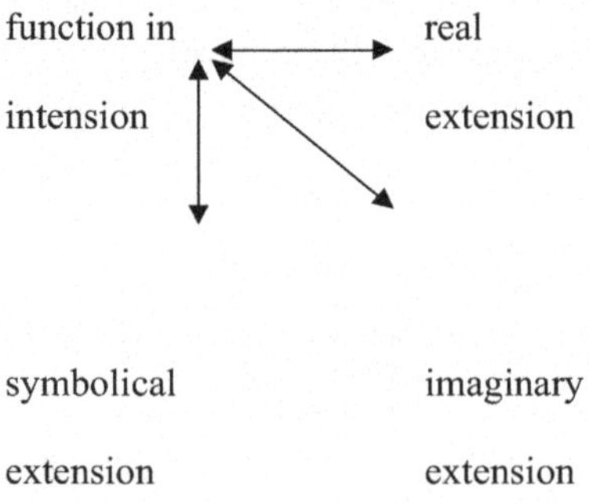

René Lew typically translates this as

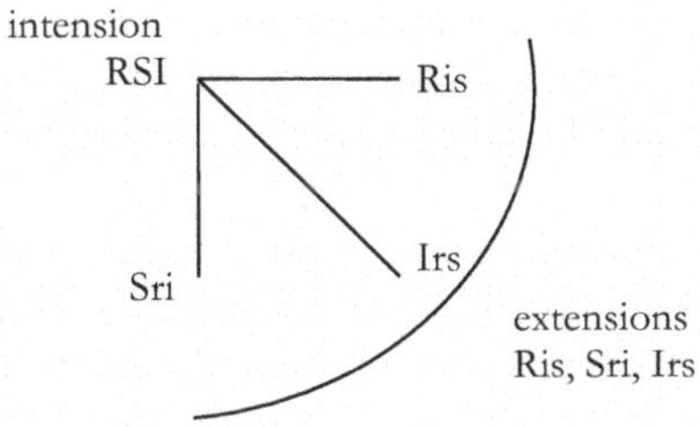

The essential feature of such an operation is the constant Moebian reversibility between extension and intension and vice versa (a movement called "constructive" when it goes from intension to the extensions and "deconstructive" when it goes from the extensions to the intension).

construction deconstruction

Such a Moebian movement is essential; it is even decisive for the work (and thus production—in this case, positions for the subject) that the structure in question will be able to perform.

From this point, we can now say the following: *While recursivity can be considered the peculiar operation of intensionality and is characterised by a persistent production of presumptions*[13] *and conjectures, signifier-involution completes its work at an extensional point, which then achieves the rank of an object.*

This "object" (which can be an artefact, an image, or a word, depending on the context and the extensionality) thereby acquires a predicative value, finding its place among the things-in-the-world. In this sense, we may say that *to the intensional recursivity corresponds an extensional object*, which (in turn and at best) must return to the intension by following the structure's involutivity movement. The predicative is part of a dialectic.

Impredicativity

However, we have a problem here. Additionally, it is serious.

Because if we settle for the following formulation, it may lead to undesirable outcomes:

recursively hypothetic in intension	→	**predicativity** objectual in extension,

[13] Presumption about the signifier, presumption about the subject, etc., presumption about Lacan's knowledge, etc. all of them endlessly intertwined.

Postulating that there should be a simple interaction without further ado between recursivity and predicativity (let's say, between the unconscious and the conscious), we are not leaving the realm of realism (classical or not) that the nineteenth century instilled in us, situating the soul (or the thinking) opposite to the world (or creation). In other words, it leaves us with a schema—setting the tone for any so-called epistemology—which psychoanalysis is designed to undermine.

We must reintroduce the problem of impredicativity (or, more correctly, of impredicative definitions) into scientific consideration. Admittedly, in this case, from a somewhat unexpected angle, since it is precisely the hypothesis of the unconscious that reintroduces it, but nevertheless, we may consider it sure enough. Lacan touched on this when he said that psychoanalysis reintroduces the question of truth into scientific reflection. The problem is without doubt epistemologically interesting[14] because it concerns not only the foundations of mathematics but also the status of logic and formalisation in general. The question of impredicativity concerns all disciplines dealing with reticular and complex systems in general (biology, quantum mechanics, etc.). From a psychoanalytic point of view, it is the very possibility of a rational definition of the signifier that is at stake.

Historically, and if we follow B. Russell's definition—*a function is said to be 'predicative' if it defines a class; otherwise, it is non-predicative*—impredicative refers to any "self-referential" definition, i.e. any definition of an object that is either quantified by the set to which it belongs or cases where the set-in question is defined with reference to itself. This alleged "auto-referentiality" made H. Poincaré speak of a *cercle vicieux*, rejecting its logical validity. What was at stake then (and still is today) is the validity of set theory, which, as the basis of mathematics, cannot itself remain without a foundation.

This question is highly relevant to psychoanalysis, but we shall leave it here. Let us just remark that Lew is pointing out how Lacan's definition of the psychoanalytic signifier, strictly speaking, is impredicative, since the statement: *a signifier represents a subject for another signifier*, indicates a crucial place for *definiendum* in the *definition* itself. This matter, however, points out that in this case we are in no way dealing with something that can be characterised as "autoreferential".

The reason therefore is that a signifier is characterised precisely by the fact that it cannot—since it inscribes itself within the framework of a recursive, i.e. Moebian, function—represent itself. Freud's *Nachträglichkeit* is indeed more than just feedback; we are in fact not dealing with a self-referential procedure. That is the question for psychoanalysts to elucidate.

The problem is, of course, much broader than what we can cover here; it requires detailed developments. Here, however, it is important to emphasise that the

[14] This problematic is indeed relevant for most of the branches of science (having been explored by N. Bohr in physical science, E. Benveniste in linguistics, A. Grothendieck in mathematics, J.-Y. Gerard in logics, to mention just a few), and it makes it possible to affirm some of the most important Freudian intuitions. For details and documentation of the classical discussions about this issue, see Gerhard Heinzmann *Entre intuition et analyse: Poincaré et le concept de prédicativité*, Paris, 1985. This author has also published a collection of texts about the same problem in *Poincaré, Zermelo et Peano, Textes de la discussion (1906–1912) sur le fondements des mathématiques: des antinomies à la prédicativité*, Paris, 1986.

preceding accounts allow us to distinguish between two kinds of objects (being of crucial importance for psychoanalytic considerations in this regard). Some strictly *predicative objects* show up in a purely ontological form, which makes them seem like dogmatic claims that are separate from the recursive dialectic. *Impredicative objects*, nourished by the displacement inherent in recursivity, are types of objects that we must recognise as not ontologically grounded. Within this framework, Lacan inscribed the challenging distinction between the "object of desire" (*objet du désir*) and the "object that causes desire" (objet cause du désir). Categories such as *a*, S, and S_2 are evidently impredicative objects and must be conceived as such. It is on the study of such questions that the future of psychoanalysis depends.

Standard Logics and 'Abnormal' Logics

A fundamental discussion underlies these considerations regarding the status of standard logics and, most importantly, the logics that must be considered when accounting for the position of the subject. This means situating the impredicative aspect of the problem we are considering.

The discussion of the so-called vicious circle or logical paradoxes refers not so much to the impredicative (Moebian, non-spherical and non-orientable space) destroying the predicative (spherical and orientable), as the logical positivism claims, but to the fact that the spherical is not sustained in any other way than by the elimination of the non-orientable.

In his insistence that propositional (i.e. extensional, and predicative) logic is the only valid logic, the American logician W.V.O. Quine makes this point very clear. He labels other kinds of logic as "deviant" because he believes they follow the so called vicious circle principle. This includes logics that study *modality*, *temporality*, *indicators of subjectivity*, *intuitionistic logic*, and so on.

René Lew claims the opposite. It is predicative logic that involves a "vicious circle" when it refuses to deal with the unpredictabilities that are the object of intensional logics (in the plural). As it is, Lew cannot do otherwise, since it is precisely these logics that sustain the existence of psychoanalysis as a rational practice. All these "evil" logics, with their heterogeneity, are necessary to define the unconscious. A heterogeneity organised differently from the canonical logic of consciousness belongs to the propositional approach.

Only such heterogeneous logics allow access to the unconscious because they make it possible for the analyst to situate the words of the analysand's and thus listen to the other saying (*le dire*) that sustains and determines the produced discursive text.

***

René Lew's contribution to the continuation and progress of psychoanalysis as a discourse and practice is invaluable.

Scholars will recognise his work as a genuine contribution to Freud's endeavours as they adopt his terminology and approach to psychoanalysis in the coming decades. At least for now, we can already recognise the *difference between predicative and impredicative psychoanalysis.* Whereas the former relies on the classic distinction between method, technique, and theory (for "investigation", "treatment", and "teaching", respectively), the impredicative approach emphasises the relationships differently.

In Lew's words, psychoanalysis is *at once science, social practice, therapeutic art, and, above all, a poetic questioning of the subject […] in the world it [the subject] constructs.*[15]

A continuation and further explanation of what I have only summarised here could easily be based on this definition.[16]

To Date, Texts from René Lew's Site

(2015) *Politique du corps et de l'écriture.*
(2017a) *Positions subjectives données comme psychotiques,*
(2017b) *Lesen négations freudiennes,*
(2018a) *Variantes et invariants de la psychanalyse,*
(2018b) *Imprédicativité de l'acte psychanalytique,*
(2019a) *Le temps de l'inconscient,*
(2019b) *La civilisation contre la culture,*
(2020a) *Poésie et psychanalyse,*
(2020b) *Temps et psychose,*
(2020c) *Émergence des fonctions subjectives en symptômes,*
(2021a) *Hölderlin, la littoralité et la structure poétique du discours,*
(2021b) *Politique de la lettre en période d'épidémie,*
(2022a) *Situation de la psychanalyse au tournant du XXIème siècle,*
(2022b) *Le hors point de vue de Freud à Lacan,*
(2022c) *L'économie littérale de la jouissance,*
(2023a) *Pulsion de mort et pulsion de destruction.*

Forthcoming Texts (Excerpts)

- *Constructions des réels.*
- *De l'indiscernable en psychanalyse*
- *Dérive et dérivations*
- *Épistémologie de la psychanalyse.*
- *Équivocités et glissements signifiants.*
- *Récursivité et imprédicativité en psychanalyse.*
- *Féminité et psychose*
- *L'Acropole freudienne*

---

[15] In *La civilisation contre la culture*, (2019b), p. 655, "à la fois science, pratique sociale, art thérapeutique et surtout mise en question poétique du sujet […], dans le monde qu'il se construit"

[16] Many thanks to Lis Haugaard for her work on the translation from the Danish version. Any errors and omissions are of my responsibility.

- *La passe en réseau.*
- *Le sujet de la psychanalyse.*
- *Les états littoraux*
- *Les pathologies littorales*
- *La passe hétérogène.*
- *Le schématisme borro-projectif en psychanalyse.*
- *Nomination en psychanalyse*
- *Positions du sujet en psychanalyse. Le complexe d'Œdipe.*
- *Récursivité des négations. Les négations lacaniennes.*
- *Rhétorique et topologie.*
- *Théorie de l'autisme*
- *Théorie du signifiant en psychanalyse*
- *Théorie fonctionnelle des psychoses*
- *Vademecum de psychanalyse à l'usage des psychiatres*

[…]

References

Frege, G. (1879). Begriffsschrift, a formula language, modeled upon that of Arithmetic, for pure thought. In J. van Heijenoort (Ed.), *From Frege to Gödel: A source book in mathematical logic, 1879–1931* (pp. 5–82). Harvard University Press, 1967.

Freud, S. (1891). *Zur Auffassung der Aphasien*. Fischer, 1992.

Freud, S. (1901). *Zur Psychopathologie des Alltagslebens*. Gesammelte Werke IV, Ideenbrücke Verlag.

Freud, S. (1937). *Konstruktionen in der Analyse*. Gesammelte Werke XVI, Ideenbrücke Verlag.

Heinzmann, G. (1985). *Entre intuition et analyse: Poincaré et le concept de prédicativité*. Blanchard.

Heinzmann, G. (1986). *Poincaré, Zermelo et Peano, Textes de la discussion (1906–1912) sur le fondements des mathématiques: des antinomies à la prédicativité*. Blanchard.

Lacan, J. (1964). *Les quatre concepts fondamentaux de la psychanalyse*. Seuil, 1973.

Lacan, J. (1966). *Écrits*. Seuil.

Lacan, J. (1971–1972). *Le savoir du psychanalyste*. (Unpublished).

Lacan, J. (2001). *Autres écrits*. Seuil.

Lew, R. (1991). L'orientation psychotique (Unpublished).

Lew, R. (2017a). *Positions subjectives données comme psychotiques*. Lysimaque.

Lew, R. (2017b). *Les négations freudiennes*. Lysimaque.

Lew, R. (2018). *Imprédicativité de l'acte psychanalytique*. Lysimaque.

Lew, R. (2019a). *Le temps de l'inconscient*. Lysimaque.

Lew, R. (2019b). *La civilisation contre la culture*. Lysimaque.

Lew, R. (2020). *Temps et psychose*. Lysimaque.

Lew, R. (2022a). *Situation de la psychanalyse au tournant du XXIème siècle*. Lysimaque.

Lew, R. (2022b). *Le hors point de vue de Freud à Lacan*. Lysimaque.

Osvaldo Cariola has worked as a psychoanalyst in Copenhagen since the 1990s. Together with some others, he is the initiator of Freuds Agorá (freudsagora.dk) and an active participant in the work community "La Lysimaque" in Paris (lysimaque.fr).

Chapter 10
Dream Processes, Sound, and Cognition

Sven Hroar Klempe

When Freud wrote his seminal book *Psychopathology of Everyday Life* (1901/1990), he took a great step in normalizing apparent abnormal behaviour. The point of departure was *The Interpretation of Dreams* (1899/2010), in which some careful changes in his research position can be traced. Most likely, he partly searched for standardized aspects of dreams in the beginning, whereas he ended up regarding the dream as a private result of the dream work provided by the primary processes. The privacy of dream processing is explicitly expressed in *Jokes and its Relation to the Unconscious* (1905/1989), which even more highlighted a close connection between the primary processes, dreams, and normal acts in awaken states.

This close connection between the unconscious and normality is brought to a higher level by Lacan, who in publications from the late 1950s explicitly revised the Saussurian thesis of the arbitrary sign as a device for understanding the unconscious. He had had contact with Roman Jakobson as well, and this mixture of the two linguists' theories initiated a broad understanding of the use of language but also for a more intimate connection between the normal use of language, thinking in general, and the unconscious.

In this chapter, therefore, I will pursue further to what extent a psychoanalytic understanding of dream processes may explain normal cognition by starting with an anonymous painting analysed from a psychoanalytic perspective. Bringing in other psychological perspectives from the early twentieth century will successively broaden this. Some aspects of early experimental psychology, the Gestalt pioneers, Vygotsky, and others may provide examples of alternative scholars dealing with thinking, speech, and imagination in a manner that may challenge the stereotyped understanding of cognition today. The point of departure for this discussion,

S. H. Klempe (✉)
Department of Psychology, Norwegian University of Science and Technology (NTNU), Trondheim, Norway
e-mail: hroar.klempe@ntnu.no

S. H. Klempe, A. Madill (eds.), *French Psychoanalysis Revisited*, Annals of Theoretical Psychology 20, https://doi.org/10.1007/978-3-031-68534-7_10

however, is an amateur painting from 1948, in which the painter aimed at reproducing a dream about a concert in a symphony hall.

A Painting

The painter is a 24-year-old student, who had different artistic activities as his hobbies. Although he sketched several paintings, this was probably the only painting he completed. He died in 2005. The painter was a creative person, as he also played piano and transverse flute, and for a long time worked as a photographer for living. His grandfather was a cousin of one of the more important painters in Norwegian fin de siècle realism, Gustav Wentzel (1859–1927).

A Dream—amateur painting 1948

There are several reasons for introducing this painting in this context. It expresses a dream the painter himself allegedly had. When he retold the content of the dream, he focused on the experience of having seen a symphony orchestra from above. More interestingly, however, the whole painting demonstrates in an efficient way the two most fundamental dream processes Freud pointed at in the *Interpretation of Dreams*, specifically condensation and replacement. In addition, to see the symphony orchestra from above, some diffuse colourful figures are presumably producing some sounding aspects of the music performed. This illustrates very well why

Jacques Lacan relabelled 'condensation' as 'metaphor'. In many languages, we express the quality of sound in terms of different shades of colour, as if colours can describe the experienced character of the sound. Such descriptions unite in fact quite incomparable entities, which may very well count as a definition of a metaphor in general. Lacan renamed 'replacement' as 'metonym', which in this painting is best illustrated with the green pillar that covers the painting from the bottom to the top. This easily produces an association to a classic concert hall as pars pro toto. Pillars are often parts of a classical building, either inside, outside, or both.

Another important aspect of this painting is the portrayal of sound. There are very few examples that demonstrate the presence of sound in dreams. In this painting, sound forms the most central part, as it depicts a symphony orchestra playing. This activity is even strengthened by the abstract figures in movements, which appears as strange in both colour and shape. These figures dominate the whole painting as they form the principal focus. The different bright colours imply energies that apparently explode and unfold in different directions. They are not just musicians playing different instruments, but they most likely depict the actual tone quality of the instrument they are playing. This is expressed in colours. Since the instruments are hardly definable, they appear as if they are the sound itself. If so, and by means of the different colours, the painting expresses the polyphonic structure of the music in the sense that different sounds are apparently being produced at the same time. The dynamic movement of music, which may contradict a still painting, is captured by the seemingly heavy moving figures tied together in a line. The line includes also a noticeable heavy square. In addition, the polyphonic structure in the music is presented as figures in different colours, and the musical movement appears from the background, depicted as a gradual change from dark brown to very bright colours.

Sound in Dreams

Quite recently there have been found close connections in brain activity when perceiving in dreams and awaken states (Aru et al., 2020). This means that there are neurological connections between received and self-produced sensory impression. This principle is very much in line with both a Freudian and a Lacanian perspective on dreams, namely, that imaginations in dreams and awake states are closely related. If this is the case, the painting referred to here may broaden our perspectives on imaginations in dreams, as it includes some sounding impressions. Freud never referred to music, which he partly regretted, yet also admitted that he disliked. Although the French philosopher Jean François Lyotard (1972) confirmed Freud's aversions to music, Lyotard also underlined that this concerned only music as a topic. Sound as a phenomenon is highly present in Freud's writings. Lyotard's project in the early seventies was primarily to turn the Freudian libido into a general dispositional system of bodily embedded life energy (Lyotard, 1974), in which enjoyment comprises agony as well as joy (Lyotard, 1991). During his authorship, he very often refers to music as the best example of this combination in terms of harmonic tension and release (Leipert, 2012). In Lyotard's article on music from 1972, he underlines how Freud focused on the aspects of sound in his analysis of hysteria. The link between hysteria and sound is that they both avoid being grasped and understood in terms of simple words. They are both ineffable, as they are entrenched in the sensational system embedded in the body.

Moreover, in Freud's analysis of the structure of a joke, the American psychiatrist Daniel Sabbeth (1990) found that the joke has much in common with music. This is especially true for the first example Freud presents in the *Jokes and Their Relation to the Unconscious* (1905/1989), the neologism 'famillionairely' from Heines Reisebilder. After having met the rich Baron Rothschild, the poor lottery agent and corn remover Hirsch-Hyacinth felt that this neologism was appropriate: 'And, as true as God shall grant me all good things, Doctor, I sat beside Salomon Rothschild and he treated me quite as his equal – quite famillionairely' (Sabbeth, 1990, p. 49). Freud mentioned this example to demonstrate how the dream process of condensation may be prominent in jokes as well. Sabbeth (1990) brings this a step further, with regard to condensation and replacement, stating: This multiple use of sound materials is a facet of the joke technique that is also important in music (p. 51). The point is that 'familiar' and 'millionaire' share some sounding aspects, sufficient to blend the two terms into 'famillionairely', and in musical polyphony the melodic lines are also partially coincident and different.

The blending structure, in which two different sequences of sounds are compressed into one, is highly prevalent and demonstrable in the polyphonic structure of music. The distinction, however, is that in music the series of pitches and sounds are still distinguishable as different voices or instruments articulated at the same time. This is the polyphonic and contrapuntal structure, which is fundamental in music. Coincident articulation in music stands in deep contrast to a well-formed use of language, as the latter can be characterized by mutual exclusion of its elements (Martinet, 1964). This is also why the use of 'famillionairely' appears as a joke; it is an unexpected and not well-formed use of language but still understandable.

We can now return to the painting above. If this painting is enjoyable, it might very well be because of its expressive structures, comparable to that of jokes and music. The painting is characterized by unexpected displacements and condensations in the sense that the orchestra is placed upside down on the top, it depicts a concert hall in terms of a pillar, the sound is presented with strange figures in different tones of colours, and the whole thing appears as a cacophony in colours and motives, which in total may give an allusion of extreme polyphony. Dreams, therefore, are not limited to visual and verbal factors. In the same way as this painting includes music, dreams may very well also include other sense qualities, such as sound, taste, and smell, although these tend to be transient and, as such, harder to recall. We remember what we saw in our dreams, less so what we experienced in other sense modalities, but this is different from those not existing in dreams. Thus, dreams may play with the whole register of aesthetic impressions, but they are presented in line with an internal way of organizing these impressions, and this organization is apparently detached from the outer world.

Language and Reality

Detachment from the outer world is apparently valid for the use of language in dreams as well. If we manage to recall what has been said in dreams, they appear as malapropos without clear connections to the dream content or anything else. This points towards the fact that verbal statements in dreams are incomparable with a rational use of language. Although Freud admitted connections between the unconscious' use of language and that of the everyday, his own use reveals language as an unambiguous and rational tool. This is demonstrated in a couple of famous anecdotes about how he practiced psychoanalysis. One is when the composer Gustav Mahler consulted him in 1910 and another when the young American psychologist Gordon Allport visited him in Vienna 10 years later.

The life of the composer Gustav Mahler, who died in 1911, was turbulent and difficult. He summarized his identity problems by referring to his background as a German-speaking Jew in Bohemia which contributed to a sense of un-belonging in multiple respects. He married the 19-year-old younger composer Alma Schindler in 1902 but, as an authoritarian character, did not allow her to practice as a composer. Alma had problems with this, and the conflict was a severe burden for their marriage. Their eldest daughter died of diphtheria at the age of 5 in 1907, and at the same time, it was ascertained that Gustav's heart was weak. His relationship with Alma suffered and he decided to seek Freud's help. This analysis was 25 years later reported in a letter to Theodor Reik, in which Freud wrote: 'In highly interesting expeditions through [Mahler's] life history, we discovered his personal conditions for love, his Holy Mary complex (mother fixation)' (In Mitchell, 1975, p. 73). According to Mitchell (1975), Mahler did not fully accept that he suffered of a mother complex, but his relationship to Alma improved after this meeting.

Another situation in which Freud ascertained a specific and unambiguous understanding of a person was when the young American student Gordon Allport happened to meet Freud in Vienna in 1920. Allport was just 22 years old, and in retrospect he regarded this meeting as seminal for him. He had arranged a meeting while he was visiting Vienna (https://www.youtube.com/watch?v=bxtY7YP1cpA). When he met Freud in his office, Freud welcomed him in a friendly manner but sat silent on his chair waiting for Allport to start talking. Allport was not prepared, and he did not find a better story to tell than his experience on a tram on his way to this meeting. He had seen an upper-class 4-year-old boy together with his mother demonstrating an obvious symptom of dirt phobia. The boy rejected to sit on any chair, as they all were too dirty for him. Allport thought it could be of interest to discuss phobias in such an early age with Freud. However, surprisingly for Allport, Freud turned the story completely upside down by posing the question: 'And was that little boy you?' According to Allport, Freud mistook his motivations for visiting him, and for Allport this event was a source to later focus on manifest motives instead, which he thought psychoanalysis underestimated.

Allport was highly influenced by psychoanalysis, but this experience made him sceptical to end up with too categorical statements. His trait theory implies, for example, that personality is a composite entity. However, it is a question if Allport misunderstood the role of conclusions Freud drew. Freud's report from the analysis of Gustav Mahler refers to 'expeditions through [Mahler's] life history', which most likely included mutual use of free associations by as well the analyser as the analysed. This mutuality of the use of free associations between the analyser and the analysed was crucial from the very beginning in practicing psychoanalysis. Thus, the truth is not only managed by the analyser but even as well by the analysed. However, both conclusions in the cases above give the impression of the analyser as the only one that can ascertain a clear diagnosis. There is no doubt that much psychoanalytic practice in the wake of Freud was performed as if this was the case. This also happened in France, and this was most likely one of the reasons why Jacques Lacan published the article *Au-delà du 'Principe de réalité'* in 1936. It paraphrased one of the metapsychological texts of Freud, "Beyond the Pleasure principle", but in this article of Lacan, he wanted to go beyond the principle of reality as well.

Lacan Goes Beyond the Reality Principle

This article from 1936 is ground-breaking as it discusses the question about truth in psychology. His point is quite simply that the concept of truth in psychology contradicts how it is normally conceived in science. That is, the truth is fundamentally relative, as psychology as a science is constituted by associations around objects and not by objects per se (Lacan, 1966, p. 73f). This statement is at the core of psychoanalysis, as the truth in this context is primarily a result of free associations in a collaborative setting with both the analyser and the analysed. This process must be free from systematic thinking and in this sense aims at considering elements that appear associatively. A systematic approach will rather count as a prejudice, narrowing the associations and functioning as a defence against unconscious conflicts. The key sentence in this is: 'Ainsi aux phénomène psychiques n'est reconnu aucune réalité propre' (Lacan, 1966, p. 78). 'Hence, the psychic phenomena do not recognize a proper reality'. Thus, the true psychological reality is as much a hallucination as a common sense. Ontology, therefore, is a stranger to psychology, and belongs rather to philosophy (Klempe, 2016).

Hence, Lacan's catch phrase 'beyond the reality principle' may very well be understood on three different levels. First, when it paraphrases one of Freud's metapsychological texts, this underlines the fact that even Freud made progress and revised his theoretical thinking during his intellectual lifespan. This contradicted some psychoanalytic practices, which could be quite dogmatic and closed sometimes, as could be the case for a common understanding of the reality principle. According to Lacan, even the reality principle should be regarded as a relative entity. Hence the second level is related to the phenomenological movement, which took off in the 1930ies, and not least in France, where Edmund Husserl gave his famous "Paris Lectures". At the same time, Husserl also published his famous

Vienna lecture about the crisis in Western sciences (Husserl, 1935/1970). In the latter lecture, Husserl attacked naturalism, which is also at the core of this article of Lacan. The third level of going 'beyond the reality principle' concerns that 'reality' and 'truth' in a Lacanian psychoanalysis have to be treated differently from a philosophical perspective. Although Lacan may have been inspired by Husserl's philosophical writings, Lacanianism is not phenomenology.

There are, however, more links that must be noted in this context. Lacan is not the only one to focus on relativity. The experimental psychologist Carl Stumpf had already in the second volume of his *Tonpsychologie* (1890) discovered that all types of perception are fundamentally relative. His focus on the relative in perceived consonance and dissonance in music exposed this. At the same time, Christian von Ehrenfels (1890/1988) defined the melody as an entity which did not depend on its elements but solely on the relationship *between* the elements. The latter became the ground-breaking basis for the Gestalt psychologists Köhler, Koffka, and Wertheimer, who were all students of Stumpf. Moreover, Edmund Husserl was also a student of Stumpf, to whom he dedicated the first volume of *Logical Investigation* (Husserl, 1900/2001). This is also the thesis in which Husserl makes a sharp distinction between psychology and his own philosophical project. This distinction forms also one important aspect of the background for why Lacan aimed to go beyond the reality principle.

Saussure and Language

Although Lacan primarily seems to be an independent successor to Freud, he is inspired by more than just Freud and phenomenology. He is catching up intellectual streams that were at stake in Europe during the first half of the twentieth century. One of Lacan's main sources is also the Swiss linguist Ferdinand de Saussure, and his posthumous compilation of lectures was published in 1916 (de Saussure, 2011). There is a big discussion about Lacan's understanding of Saussure's thesis on the arbitrary sign. Some will say he misunderstood it by contrasting the signifier (the sign itself/signifiant) and the signified (the reference/meaning/signifié) so fundamentally. However, there is no doubt that one of the most crucial aspects of Saussure's contribution to linguistic is that he opened up for a radical understanding of this distinction. This was not a new discovery, and the existence of different languages demonstrates that a word is not in some way caused by its referent. Nevertheless, the assumption has been that the meaning of a word is a result of the term itself; that it is sufficient to know a word to understand it. Saussure breaks with this by defining the signifier and the signified as distinct orders related like the two sides of a piece of paper. Lacan goes further by stating that the two orders are from the very beginning separated by a barrier resistant to signification (Lacan, 1966,

p. 497).[1] In the wake of this assertion, an urgent question is raised: From where does meaning then come? The Lacanian answer is that meaning is created from neither the word nor the reference per se. Instead, meaning arises in the *space* between each signifier. That is, the opposition between signifiers is the crucial factor, as they fill up with meaning the apparently empty space that exists between them. It might sound strange, but this phenomenon is highly comparable with Ehrenfels' discovery in 1890 regarding the understanding of melody. That is, it cannot be the tones per se that produce a melody because these can be replaced, such as when a melody is transposed into a new key. Instead, it is the sequence of intervals, i.e. the apparent empty spaces between the sounding tones that provide a melody. In the same manner, we can use different words and even different languages, but it is the relationship between the words, i.e. the way the words stand in opposition to each other, which provides the meaning of a sentence.

Lacan was also highly influenced by the linguist Roman Jakobson who emphasizes the importance of phonetics (Brandt et al., 1973). For Jakobson, the elements that constitute the order of the signifiers are the phonemes. These do not convey meaning of themselves but provide the differences. In other words, meaning is produced within the apparent empty spaces that exist between the different sounds. Again, it is not the sound of a phoneme that produces meaning but the established oppositions—or what we can call the ineffable space—between them. In line with this, Lacan notes the existence of phrase openings like 'I would have never…[Jamais je ne…], Nevertheless…[Toujors est-il…], Maybe anyway…[Pout-être encore…]' (Lacan, 1966, p. 502). Such openings are sometimes articulated without the ongoing implied content, yet they are not meaningless and may, for example, act to invite the interlocutor to complete it themselves in one of many ways. The first interlocutor may then go on to complete the same opening with another meaningful point. There are, in other words, many layers in a discourse present at the same time. Hence, Lacan utilizes the concept of polyphony drawing parallels between discourse and a musical score, which he underlines is especially true when it comes to poetry (Lacan, 1966, p. 503).[2]

Metaphor and Metonymy

The polyphonic aspect is in fact afforded by a much more fundamental feature of language than normally admitted. It is entrenched in the distinction Saussure (2011) made between the syntagmatic and the associative relation. The former refers to the

---

[1] 'La thématique de cette science est dès lors en effet suspendue à la position promordiale du signifiant et du signifié, comme d'ordres distincts et séparés initialement par un barrière résistante à la signification' (Lacan, 1966, p. 497).

[2] 'Mais il suffit d'écouter la poésie, ce qui sans doute était le cas de F. De Saussure, por que s'y fasse entendre une polyphonie et qui tout discours se avère s'aligner sur les plusieurs portées d'une partition' (Lacan, 1966, p. 503).

actual use of language, in which 'words acquire relations based on the linear nature of language because they are chained together' (p. 123). This forms the horizontal relation in language. In contrast, the associative type forms the vertical relation in language, as each one of the words articulated at the same time will 'unconsciously call to mind a host of other words' (p. 123). These terms have a sort of presence 'in absentia'; they are activated in the mind of the speaker along with the actual discourse. They can be word classes, different grammatical forms of the same word, but also other words that draw to mind the articulated term which is *in praesentia*, as Saussure called it. Whereas the syntagmatic chain represents a *mutual exclusion* (Martinet, 1964) between the words, as just one word can be articulated at the same time, the associative relations form a *mutual inclusion* of words.

The Danish linguist Louis Hjelmslev renamed Saussure's 'associative relation' the more widespread label 'paradigmatic'. While both index the vertical axis of language, there are reasons to remember the original term. 'Paradigm' can narrow the repertoire of relations to grammatical word classes and forms, whereas 'associative' includes psychological functions. When the linguist Roman Jakobson in the 1920ies launched the term 'phonology', he brought linguistics into a broader sphere. By this he defined the sound aspects of speech as the core of the human production of language (Jakobson & Halle, 1956/1980). Moreover, he saw the different, and sometimes contradictory, aspects of elements in language, like vowels versus consonants and other contrasts, collaborate and merge into a whole. These contrasts constitute what we call language which is for certain the case when it comes to the horizontal and vertical dimensions of language. To depict this, he introduced the two classical contrasting tropes in rhetoric: metaphor and metonymy (Jakobson, 1971): 'The two opposite tropes metaphor and metonymy, present the most condensed expression of two basic modes of relation: the internal relation of similarity (and contrast) underlies the metaphor; the external relation of contiguity (and remoteness) determines the metonymy' (p. 41). These two tropes form a double axis in which metonymies form the vertical axis and metaphors the horizontal. They are both so prominent in language as to dominate everyday use.

Aphasia, Psychosis, and Normality

Metaphor and metonymy form the background for Jakobson's interest in patients with aphasic impairments. There are many different versions of aphasia, but one group contains those who 'have difficulty in arranging code units according to their similarity' (Jakobson, 1971, p. 44): that is, a problem regarding metaphor. In such a case, the patient struggles to find synonyms or heteronyms and turns to contiguous, i.e. metonymic, relations instead. One example is, rather than referring to beer in terms of 'a pint' or 'pilsner', to use terms such as 'the pub', 'the pals', 'the bar', or other metonymical relations. This is just a simple example, and just one version of aphasia, but demonstrates core aspects of these as linguistic impairments handling the fundamental axes of language: i.e. metaphors and metonymies, and how the two axes may replace each other.

Such considerations seem to lie behind core aspects of Lacan's understanding of the psychosis (Lacan, 1966, pp. 531–583), although there are different ways to interpret Lacan's complicated analysis. One important premise is that Lacan understands psychosis in terms of a breakdown of the father metaphor—'l'échec de la metaphore paternelle' (Lacan, 1966, p. 575). Lacan derives this from the Freudian term 'Verwerfung', which he translates into French with 'forclusion' (p. 558)—foreclosure or refusal in English. This is not only a question about foreclosing one's father but rather the One-Father, which is the absolute and the univocal other, or big Other with a capital. Psychosis, therefore, is not only a breakdown of the father metaphor but a dissolution of connections between signifier and signified. Although not stated explicitly, a natural conclusion, which brings Lacan close to Jakobson, is that the breakdown of the father metaphor is replaced by father metonymies, i.e. peripheral or even non-existent associations and vague contiguous connections between the signifier and the signified.

A revisit to the amateur painting mentioned earlier can illustrate this. The coloured figures in the painting may have a metaphorical connection to music, as we can talk about a colourful orchestration when the sound of the music is impressive and overwhelming. The figures themselves also have a metonymic connection to music, as the musicians form a kind of *pars pro toto* for a concert. However, a figure per se should be detached from music as the signification of it. Although the figure in the front, apparently a conductor, can be directly associated with music, the other figures have diffuse shapes and can be associated with the Lacanian term 'corps morcelé'—'fragmented bodies'. The term refers to the early childhood and ambivalences in the child's identity. Hence, when this appears in a mature life, it is related to regressions. However, a comparable identity crisis might appear in musical peak experiences, as many refer to these as turning points in their lives when it comes to self-identity (Gabrielson, 2011). In other words, the strange figures in the painting demonstrate partly an aphasic replacement, as the metaphorical presentation of music by means of colours is combined with an axis of metonymies. Moreover, this replacement turns also into a psychotic dissolution of connections between the signifier (figures) and the signified (music) and vice versa, as the term 'figure' never signifies music and 'music' does not signify a human. Since the figures are fragmented bodies as well, this painting exemplifies also how a regression easily can be turned into a normative impression of a peak experience in music.

The focus on the signifier, i.e. the sound of the word instead of its content—the signified—marks one of the great differences between Freud and Lacan's conception of psychoanalysis. Especially in the beginning, Freud referred to the 'concept' as the core of hysteria. In an early paper (Freud, 1893/1971), he stated 'that the lesion in hysterical paralyses consists of nothing but the inaccessibility of the *concept* of the organ or function to the associations of the conscious ego; that this purely functional change (the *concept* itself being intact) is caused by the fixation of that *concept* in subconscious association with the memory of the trauma; and that this *concept* cannot become free or accessible as long as the affective value of the psychic trauma has not been eliminated by an adequate motor reaction or a conscious psychic process' (p. 58, italics added). Although Freud may have gradually changed his early position, he focused still on the concept of 'this boy' in the meeting he had with Gordon Allport in 1920.

Thus, in his understanding of the psychoanalytic process, Lacan changed the focus from the signified to the *signifier*. This highlights an alternative perspective on the role of the word representation in psychoanalysis. It is not necessarily the content of a concept that represents the cause of either neurosis or psychosis but rather the word sound on which must be focused. This is obvious with the neurotic character, which normally invests an enormous energy on metaphorical rephrasings to establish a defence strategy. This mechanism is not so easy to detect in a psychosis, as the signifier and the signified are almost completely detached from each other, as the metonymic relationship between terms may appear enigmatic, if not impossible to grasp.

What creates the experienced distinction between sounds or words does not just depend on the sounds themselves but on the affective loading one invests in a sound. For both the neurotic and the psychotic, this loading process is apparently a private and individual thing, likewise the extent of the affective investment. However, the process of producing distinctions by means of affective loading is also a universal human mechanism. Already Wilhelm Wundt implied this when he stated in his introductory book on psychology that, in general, '*series of sensational qualities are bounded at their extremes by maximal differences; series of affective qualities are bounded by maximal opposites*' (Wundt, 1902, p. 37, original italics). This quotation appears in a context, in which Wundt separates psychology from physics and physiology by emphasizing that the two latter sciences focus on outer reality, whereas psychology is about the human *experiences* of that reality. In an introduction to Wundt's *The Language of Gestures*, Arthur L. Blumenthal comments that Wundt's 'lectures on the psychology of language were the most heavily attended in the world, and those who heard him included de Saussure' (Blumenthal, 1973, pp. 12–13). Saussure's aim, though, was to avoid psychologism in linguistics, and the term 'opposition' does not have to be psychological but can highlight relativity as an embedded part of the linguistic system. On the other hand, when Lacan combined Saussure with psychoanalysis, the term 'opposition' is re-psychologized in line with Wundt.

Whereas linguists studies language itself, psychologists are interested in how language is used and internalized, the two perspectives complementing each other. Commensurate with this, language and all the systems humans use for communication, like music, logic, or gestures can be regarded from the perspective of their internal organization *or* from their psychological function. Likewise, the psychological perspective can be divided into a focus on normal or deviant behaviour. This is what Freud and Lacan do by focusing on neurosis and psychosis and what Jakobson does by considering disorders like aphasia, that is, deviations which illuminate the process of normal functioning.

Vygotsky, Thinking, and Speech

According to Jakobson, the two figurative tropes metaphor and metonymy are not restricted to rhetoric but form the two fundamental associative axes of similarity (metaphor) and contiguity (metonymy). Hence, they are related to a more fundamental cognitive capacity which goes beyond language. However, the use of language reflects and builds upon this capacity of sorting elements in terms of similarity and contiguity. Language is not just one well-formed system of words but contains several forms of speech in which the childish egocentric talk forms one of the more important arenas for investigating cognitive capacities. Jakobson follows up Vygotsky on this in a short article entitled *Anthony's Contribution to Linguistic Theory* (Jakobson, 1971, pp. 31–35). In this article he discusses a 2-year-old boy's monologues while the boy falls asleep, partly dreaming at the same time. Again, he finds a connection between apparent rational and irrational uses of language.

The small boy, Anthony, formulates several meaningless syntagmatic series of words while he falls asleep: 'There's a hat... There's another... There's that...There's hat...There another hat...That's a hat...' (Jakobson, 1971, p. 33). Graphically, Jakobson presents these phrases above each other to demonstrate that they represent the vertical and associative axis in language. 'Thus in the pre-sleep speech, lexical, morphological, and phonemic sets appear to be projected from the paradigmatic axis into the syntagmatic one' (p. 33). As similar phrases can be heard articulated by any small child, they form a salient trait of the childish egocentric talk. Since the boy partly sleeps, the example also indicates a close connection between the childish egocentric talk and how language is disposed and structured in dreams.

Jakobson's aim with this example is to highlight the 'intermediate link between the overt and the inner speech' (Jakobson, 1971, p. 31). This is exactly what Vygotsky disclosed. Yet he did more, as he detected that the childish process of acquiring language followed exactly the order Jakobson indicates. The egocentric speech, Vygotsky says, is a form of speech that provides 'the transition from external to inner speech' (Vygotsky, 1987, p. 75). This implies that the development of speech starts with a rudimentary exchange and imitation of sounds with carers. Consequently, verbal communication starts as a fundamental social act. These exchanges of sounds turn gradually into meaningful egocentric speech, like the one Anthony exemplifies above. Thus, egocentric speech is still social and cannot be characterized as autistic. On the contrary, even Anthony is still aware of his mother's presence, to whom his speech is addressed. Thus, the projection of the paradigmatic axis into the syntagmatic one is not a deviational use of language but highly normal and salient trait of egocentric speech.

Yet, by following Vygotsky further, the importance of egocentric speech does not stop there. Inner speech has a very special role in the human mind in that it 'is thinking in pure meanings' (Vygotsky, 1987, p. 280). Thus, thinking is an activity that may include words, concepts, and language in general but at the same time may go far beyond language. This is why Vygotsky says, 'in inner speech the word dies away, and gives birth to thought' (Vygotsky, 1987, p. 280). In other places he also uses the term 'evaporates' (p. 257), which underlines how thinking can be completely different from grammatically well-formed uses of language. Vygotsky thusly concludes, 'thoughts flow and movements does not correspond directly with the unfolding of speech', and continues: 'The units of thought and speech do not coincide' (p. 280). Inner speech, therefore, is thinking, which in structure has more in common with the childish egocentric speech compared to a mature grammatically correct use of language. Thinking as an activity is therefore only partially comparable with an actual and well-formed use of language and, consequently, are to be regarded as very different types of activities.

Conclusions

If we now go back to the painting that was presented initially, it was specified that this is about a dream the painter himself allegedly had experienced. It depicts also very well the most important Freudian dream processes of condensation and displacement. By means of these visualizations, the painting appears irrational and detached from the everyday reality one might experience in a waken state. However, Freud considered that dream processes are traceable in waking states, for example, in slips of the tongue and in jokes, although still recognizably irrational behaviours depending on context in which they appear. From a Lacanian perspective, however, this border between rational and irrational behaviour is even more subverted. This is done by separating the content of the use of language from its sound by referring to the Saussurian linguistic thesis of the arbitrary sign. Moreover, by building on Roman Jakobson's principles of phonology, he manages to isolate the signifier, which is exactly the sound of the sign. Jakobson's understanding of language in terms of the two axes metaphor (similarity and contrast) and metonymy (contiguity and remoteness), demonstrated by means of different types of aphasia, is also a crucial argument for a very close connection between apparent normal and abnormal uses of language. The crucial argument for this, however, is given by Vygotsky, who made a principal distinction between thinking and language. As the well-formed language evaporates in thinking, cognition must be analysed as an activity of the mind that goes far beyond and is principally independent of language.

In line with this, the painting is probably not just about a dream. It is, rather, a demonstration of actual human cognition, in which aesthetical impressions of figures, colours, sounds, smells, and tastes form the processes of uniting and discerning, which are the basis for all human-based systems, no matter if it is language, logic, music, dishes, or odours.

References

Aru, J., Siclari, F., Phillips, W., & Storm, J. F. (2020). Apical drive – A cellular mechanism of dreaming? *Neuroscience and Biobehavioral Reviews, 119*(2020), 440–455.
Blumenthal, A. L. (1973). Introduction. In W. Wundt (Ed.), *The language of gestures* (pp. 11–19). Mouton.
Brandt, P. A. A., Buchwald, M., Kragh, B., Olsen, O. A., & Pedersen, J. M. (1973). *Jacques Lacan. Det ubevidste Sprog. Psykoanalytiske skrifter*. Rhodos.
de Saussure, F. (2011). *Course in general linguistics* (W. Baskin, Trans.). Columbia University Press.
Freud, S. (1893/1971). Some points in a comparative study of organic and hysterical paralyses. In S. Freud (Ed.), *Collected Papers. Volume 1* (J. Riviere, Trans.) (pp. 42–58). The Hogarth Press and the Institute of Psycho-Analysis.
Freud, S. (1899/2010). *The interpretation of dreams*. Basic Books.
Freud, S. (1901/1990). *Psychopathology of everyday life*. W.W. Norton & Company.
Freud, S. (1905/1989). *Jokes and its relation to the unconscious*. W.W. Norton & Company.
Gabrielson, A. (2011). *Strong experiences with music. Music is much more than just music*. Oxford University Press.
Husserl, E. (1900/2001). *Logical Investigations, Volume 1*. Routledge.
Husserl, E. (1935/1970). The Vienna Lecture (Philosophy and the Crisis of European Humanity). In E. Husserl (Ed.), *The crisis of European sciences and transcendental phenomenology* (pp. 269–299). Northwestern University Press.
Jakobson, R. (1971). *Studies on child language and Aphasia*. Mouton.
Jakobson, R., & Halle, M. (1956/1980). *Fundamentals of Language*. Mouton Publishers.
Klempe, S. H. (2016). A philosophical vs. A psychologocal perspective on borders. *Integrative Psychological & Behavioral Sciences, 50*(1), 77–90.
Lacan, J. (1966). *Écrits*. Éditions de Seuil.
Leipert, T. (2012). Destination Unknown: Jean-François Lyotard and Orienting Musical Affect. *Contemporary Musical Review. 31*(5-6), 425–438.
Lyotard, J.-F.(1972, Novembre). Plusieurs silences, *Psychoanalyse musique, Musique an jeu*. No.9, 64–77
Lyotard, J.-F. (1974). *Économie libidinale*. Les Éditions de minuit.
Lyotard, J.-F. (1991). *The inhuman. Reflections on time* (G. Bennington & R. Bowlby, Trans.). Polity Press.
Martinet, A. (1964). *Elements of general linguistics*. Faber & Faber.
Mitchell, D. (1975). *Gustav Mahler. The Wunderhorn years*. Faber and Faber Ltd.
Sabbeth, D. (1990). Freud's Theory of Jokes and the linear-analytic approach to music. A few points in common. In S. Feder, R. L. Karmel, & G. H. Pollock (Eds.), *Psychoanalytic explorations in music* (pp. 49–59). International Universities Press.
Stumpf, C. (1890). *Tonpsychologie. Zweiter Band*. Verlag von S. Hirzel.
von Ehrenfels, C. (1890/1988). On Gestalt Qualities. In B. Smith (Ed.), *Foundations of Gestalt Theory* (pp. 82–117), Philosophia Verlag.
Vygotsky, L. S. (1987). Thinking and speech. In R. W. Rieber & A. S. Carton (Eds.), *The collected works of L.S. Vygotsky, Vol. 1. Problems of general psychology* (pp. 39–285). Plenum.
Wundt, W. (1902). *Outlines of psychology, 2nd Engl. Ed.* (C. H. Judd, Trans.). Wilhelm Engelmann.

Sven Hroar Klempe (Mag.art., Dr.art.) is a Professor in Psychology at the Department of Psychology, Norwegian University of Science and Technology (NTNU), Trondheim, Norway. His background includes the following: Professor in Musicology, Assoc. Prof. in Media Studies, teacher, and journalist. His research is cross-disciplinary with an emphasis on the history of psychology, culture and psychology, theory of science, communication, and music psychology.

Index

S. H. Klempe, A. Madill (eds.), *French Psychoanalysis Revisited*, Annals of Theoretical Psychology 20, https://doi.org/10.1007/978-3-031-68534-7

SPRINGER NATURE

GPSR Compliance

The European Union's (EU) General Product Safety Regulation (GPSR) is a set of rules that requires consumer products to be safe and our obligations to ensure this.

If you have any concerns about our products, you can contact us on ProductSafety@springernature.com

In case Publisher is established outside the EU, the EU authorized representative is:

Springer Nature Customer Service Center GmbH
Europaplatz 3
69115 Heidelberg, Germany

The manufacturer's authorised representative in the EU is Springer Nature Customer Service Centre GmbH, Europaplatz 3, 69115 Heidelberg, Germany. If you have any concerns regarding our products, please contact ProductSafety@springernature.com

Printed and bound by CPI Group (UK) Ltd, Croydon, CR0 4YY
30/09/2026
02225607-0019